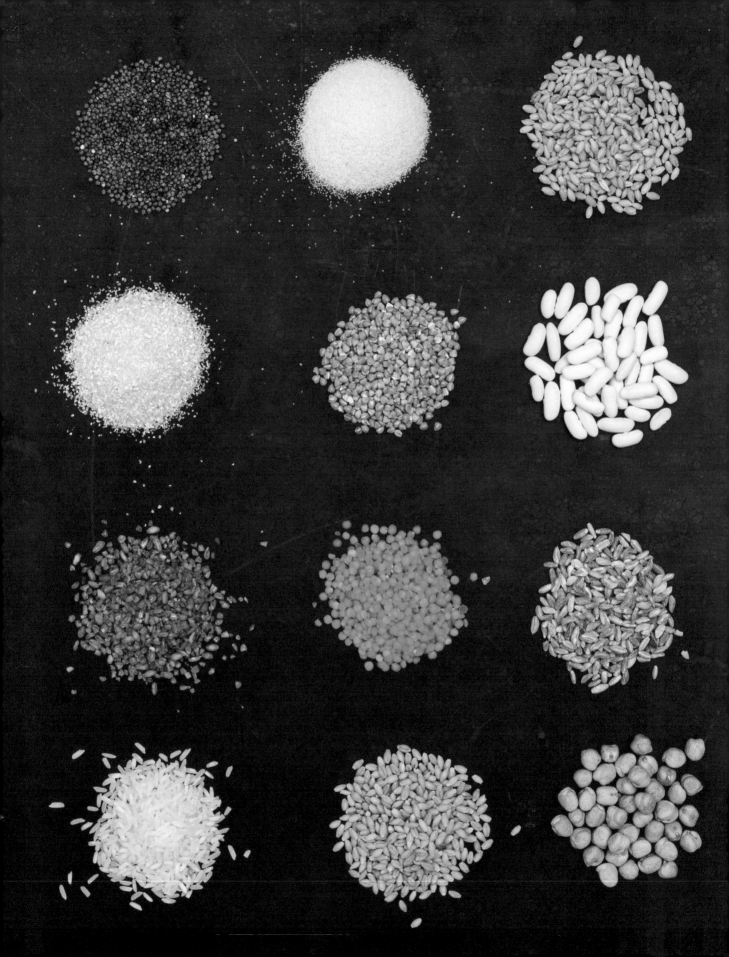

The Seasonal Jewish Kitchen

A FRESH TAKE ON TRADITION

The Seasonal Jewish Kitchen

A FRESH TAKE ON TRADITION

Amelia Saltsman

Foreword by Deborah Madison
Photography by Staci Valentine

STERLING EPICURE
New York

STERLING EPICURE
New York

An Imprint of Sterling Publishing
1166 Avenue of the Americas
New York, NY 10036

Text © 2015 by Amelia Saltsman
Foreword © by Deborah Madison
All photographs © by Staci Valentine except for the following:
© Alison Ashton: 29 (plums), 200, 247 (chickpeas); © David Karp: 60;
© Amelia Saltsman: 123 (green garlic and legumes); © Ralph Saltsman: 7, 239

ISBN 978-1-4549-1436-5

Distributed in Canada by Sterling Publishing
c/o Canadian Manda Group, 664 Annette Street
Toronto, Ontario, Canada M6S 2C8
Distributed in the United Kingdom by GMC Distribution Services
Castle Place, 166 High Street, Lewes, East Sussex, England BN7 1XU
Distributed in Australia by Capricorn Link (Australia) Pty. Ltd.
P.O. Box 704, Windsor, NSW 2756, Australia

For information about custom editions, special sales, and premium
and corporate purchases, please contact Sterling Special Sales at 800-805-5489
or specialsales@sterlingpublishing.com.

Manufactured in Canada

2 4 6 8 10 9 7 5 3 1

www.sterlingpublishing.com

Designed by Christine Heun and Barbara Balch

For my family

Contents

FOREWORD

I've known Amelia Saltsman for many years, but it wasn't until we both attended a writers' conference in the 1990s that I learned that she was of Iraqi Jewish heritage. The discovery was a window into the unusual food histories and perspectives that we all carry.

At the time, Amelia was deeply involved in her local farmers' market, and some years later, she published her first book, *The Santa Monica Farmers' Market Cookbook*, a collection of utterly appealing recipes and engaging stories about the culture of farming. I have enjoyed cooking from this book enormously. *The Seasonal Jewish Kitchen*, her second book, is different from the first yet similar, for Amelia is a scholar and a cook, and, as a cook, she is devoted to food that is grown by people she knows. Both roles come forcefully into play in this new book.

The Seasonal Jewish Kitchen offers a fascinating and thoughtful framework for exploration in which Amelia casts a light on such fundamental questions as, what is Jewish food? She also shows why six seasons of Jewish—or of any—cookery, rather than the usual four, make sense in terms of both the Jewish lunar calendar and the natural growing cycles of any year.

The book's diverse and interesting recipes stem from Amelia's complex personal heritage; she is the daughter of an Ashkenazic Romanian mother and a Sephardic Iraqi father, both of whom were raised in Israel. From earliest childhood, Amelia was not only intimately familiar with the seasonings and flavors of the Ashkenazic and Sephardic kitchens, but also with those of California, where the Mediterranean climate and foods parallel those of Israel. She is a true representative of the Jewish Diaspora.

Although Amelia's food experience as a Californian leans more toward a Mediterranean palate than an eastern European one, schmaltz and *gribenes* are hardly neglected. In fact, Amelia makes you want to prepare them as soon as you possibly can and use them in all the different ways she suggests.

The recipe that opens the first chapter of the book does so with a bang: it is Tunisian Lemon Rind Salad. This is Jewish food? Who knew? It is light and spice infused—yet also warming for winter—robust and, somehow, contemporary. And the recipes just get better. A rustic chopped liver (duck *or* chicken) has the refreshing accompaniment of a parsley and celery salad. Instead of the red borscht and sour cream I knew as a kid, how about a golden borscht with buttermilk and ginger? There's an intriguing smoky *harissa*, a farro soup with chickpeas and escarole (sounding modern as well as ancient), and a variety of latkes (the parsnip variation served with roasted apples and pears immediately caught my eye). I was thrilled to find a rose geranium syrup, one of my favorite uses of that herb, for a cake, and a sorbet made from cactus pear, a fruit local to the deserts near my home in New Mexico. I am also drawn to amaranth greens with olive oil and lemon because I grow amaranth and because I love such simple dishes. Amelia's salad of carrots, dates, and preserved kumquats brings me immediately into this fresh new world of Jewish food. Actually, there isn't a recipe that isn't appealing, and there's not one that I don't want to make. California, Romania, Israel, and other parts of the Jewish world, which are very much a part of Amelia's world, all play a role in *The Seasonal Jewish Kitchen*. It's never one cuisine versus another, and the possibilities are many indeed.

I also appreciate that the recipes, whether from Amelia's Romanian grandmother, Syrian friends, or shaped by new ways of eating in America, are tied to the seasons of the year *and* to the Jewish holidays that occur during those times, from Rosh Hashanah to Purim to Hanukah and beyond. One thing that sets some foods apart is that they are associated with particular occasions. Obviously, you can eat sweet potatoes or pecan pie any time, not just on Thanksgiving, but there's something special about enjoying celebratory foods in their proper moment.

The use of the word *seasonal* in the title not only reflects its everyday meaning but also amplifies the passage of time within the context of life's celebrations. Of course, these ideas do overlap. I make my grandmother's raisin squares only around the holidays because that's when they arrived in a carefully packed box sent from Hartford to California when I was a child. I truly savor their goodness then, despite knowing that I could make them at any other time of the year. I like that they're a winter holiday food, and I like *The Seasonal Jewish Kitchen* in the same way, even though I am tempted to just plunge in and cook my way through all the recipes—now!

Another compelling observation in these pages is how traditional foodways, so often based on the necessity of thrift, have become our contemporary foodways here in the United States. Sour greens like sorrel, both wild and cultivated, have been rediscovered, as have organ meats, rendered animal fats, and the foods typically cooked in the fats. Freekeh, green wheat that's harvested then scorched, is enjoyed for its smoky flavor, and still made today, much as it was in ancient times, by a few intrepid farmers, such as Anthony Boutard in Oregon. Ancient farro has returned, too. Flavorful chickens and better meats, raised like they used to be, are in markets once again. All of these foods are relevant to both traditional Jewish dishes and today's new way of cooking. Jewish or not, we've begun to discover—or rediscover—these foods, and we have a new appreciation of their value in our lives.

At the same time, foods that are relatively recent arrivals to North American kitchens, such as quinoa, green garlic, and radicchio, can easily find their place in this fresh approach to traditional cooking. We eat quinoa, so why not include it in a Jewish recipe? This openness to new foods expands the world of Jewish cookery.

Jewish culture is tied to food, for better or worse. I think of my mother. She was not at all attracted to the heavy Russian Jewish foods of her mother's house, and she often expressed her dislike of the meats her mother cooked and the ponderous foods she grew up with. That she drifted away from her Jewish roots for many years might possibly have had something to do with that. When she returned to Judaism later in life, those foods had long disappeared for her. My mother too had migrated to California when she was young, where food was so different, so fresh, so alive. I can't help but wonder if it might have made a difference for her if she had had Amelia's book as a culinary guide to the Jewish year. I believe that the dishes in *The Seasonal Jewish Kitchen*, with their exciting seasonings drawn from recipes that are both rooted in history and expressive of today's foods and tastes, would have made her very happy. This book is smart, appealing, and truly a blessing.

Deborah Madison
Galisteo, New Mexico, January 2015

INTRODUCTION

Inspiration for this book arrived in a pan of tzimmes—roasted carrot and sweet potato tzimmes, to be precise, caramelized from its time in the oven and infused with fresh orange. I was preparing a family Seder, and as I cooked, I shared the experience via social media. The tzimmes recipe aired on KCRW's *Good Food* show and quickly generated thousands of views on the radio station's blog. My own blog on leek and green garlic matzah brei went viral within minutes of being shared. So did a snapshot of homemade gefilte fish simmering on my stove. In the instant that tradition and technology collided, it dawned on me that many cooks are seeking the kind of Jewish cooking I do: modern, seasonal, ingredient-driven, lighter and brighter, relaxed rather than formal, and reflective of the many flavors of the Jewish Diaspora. I took the moment as a sign that a new generation of cooks was looking for a fresh approach to Jewish food.

The idea had actually been simmering for quite a while. I just hadn't connected the dots. I am not religious, yet I have long believed that how I shop for food and cook it are opportunities for mindfulness. The occasion offers a moment to give thanks to hardworking farmers, marvel at the wonders of the natural world, and consider how the simple act of procuring food for my family can have far-reaching benefits for others. In short, it's an opportunity for communion with something bigger than myself.

The pan of tzimmes (Yiddish for "big fuss") raised a tumult of questions. What is my family food heritage and how does it inform my contemporary cooking and values? What is Jewish food anyway, and how does it fit into the bigger picture? Do you have to keep kosher to eat Jewish? (That would disqualify a lot of people.) Can a person observe Jewish dietary laws without having to resort to imitation food substitutions? Do you have to be Jewish to know Jewish food? And so began my journey of exploration.

A MELTING-POT LIFE

Jewish food crosses many cultures and borders. Ashkenazic (eastern European), Sephardic (Mediterranean), the Middle Eastern melting pot of modern Israel, the Jewish American Diaspora—I am all of the above.

I am the daughter of a Romanian mother and an Iraqi father who met in the Israeli army and immigrated as students to Los Angeles, where I was born and raised. My culinary upbringing has been equally eclectic. One grandmother used parsley, the other, cilantro. One cooked potatoes, the other, rice. On family visits to Israel when I was a child, I watched my Romanian grandma (*saftik*) stretch translucent dough over the kitchen table for a delicate apple strudel, and my grandpa (*sabik*) pour *mamaliga*—polenta with cheese—onto a board and cut it with a string.

My blue-eyed Iraqi grandmother (*safta*) served long-cooked beans (*loubia*) over rice and fashioned miniature meat-filled semolina dumplings (*kubbe*) with breathtaking dexterity. I ate steak hot off the grill in the avocado orchard of my farming family's moshav (collective farm), and long before the resurgence of farmers' markets in the United States, I accompanied city-dwelling aunts to the souk (Middle Eastern marketplace). But mostly, isolated from our extended family and traditions, my parents, sister, and I re-created the foods of memory and explored the flavors of my parents' adopted, and my native, homeland.

This book encompasses the food story of my family, the Romanian Haimers and the Iraqi Ben-Aziz clan (Abdulaziz in Iraq), both of whom relocated to the British Mandate of Palestine in the early 1930s. But our tale is emblematic of those of countless other families: Gordian knots of migrations, unions, and regional influences that create myriad unique personal culinary histories.

The Seasonal Jewish Kitchen reflects these varied stories through the diverse flavors of a global cuisine, dishes for today inspired by the cooking of the Middle East, North Africa, Italy, Spain, eastern Europe, California, and more. It features Old World ingredients like buckwheat, pickled herring, organ meats, and rendered fats that are not only enjoying a renaissance in mainstream cooking but are also traditional Jewish foods. For example, when used with a light hand and made from quality poultry, *gribenes* (crispy bits of chicken or duck skin and fried onions), a.k.a. Jewish cracklings, add a perfect finishing touch to many of today's casual, yet sophisticated, recipes.

SIX SEASONS OF JEWISH COOKING

The Jewish cooking calendar is a great template for today's eating habits. Even if you don't know the names of all the holidays, a year's worth of Jewish food bears a striking resemblance to any market-driven cook's seasonal road map. When you divide the year into six two-month microseasons, you can readily see how the foods in each mesh meaningfully with the holidays that occur during that time. With one click of the lens, all snaps into focus. In January or February, you can turn to a warming bowl of Roasted Roots and Their Greens with Wheat Berries and Horseradish Cream spiked with dried fruits, which happens to include the traditional foods of Tu b'Shvat, the New Year of Trees. Symbolized by the flowering almond tree, the holiday is celebrated during this two-month period with vegetarian meals that feature grains, vegetables, and dried and fresh fruits.

Similarly, milk, which is especially plentiful in May and June after spring calving and tastes of young grass, is the starring ingredient of Shavuot, the holiday that commemorates the spring harvest and the giving of the Torah. Cheese and Honey Filo Pie, A Pashtida: Baked Pasta with Spinach, Ricotta, and Brown Butter, and Cheese Blintz Soufflé pay homage to "a land flowing with milk and honey" (Exodus 3:8) and remind us that to every food there is a season, even milk.

When I divided the book into these six seasons, chapter themes instantly revealed themselves: dairy for May and June, storage crops and preserved foods in the depths of winter. In March and April, lush herbs and green shoots are at the heart of the Passover observance and perfect for updating classics like matzah brei and *kigelach* (mini-kugels), and for turning an ordinary Seder plate into an exciting taste sensation. The harvests of late summer and early fall yield the sweet and spicy flavors of the autumn holidays: quince and butternut squash in a lamb stew seasoned with *ras el hanout*, fresh Concord grapes as a flavoring agent, pomegranates paired with orange in a refreshing gelée, and fresh prunes (a.k.a. Italian or French plums) in a meringue-topped plum torte.

This doesn't mean you can only make a chapter's recipes in its two-month window or that there are only milk and cheese dishes in the May and June chapter. A crop's appearance in the market varies by region and microclimate. Where it makes seasonal sense, I encourage you to use recipes across chapters to create menus. I've also included recipes based on pantry ingredients—so-called evergreen recipes—that live in particular chapters because they suit the time of the year or are the perfect canvas to show off seasonal accompaniments. By all means, enjoy Kitchri: Red Lentils and Rice with Golden Garlic Puree, Carob Molasses Ice Cream, or Cozonac: A Simple Sweet Yeast Cake any time of the year.

CONNECTING THE DOTS

The Seasonal Jewish Kitchen is filled with delicious connections that enrich the Jewish experience but that you may have forgotten or never known. (These associations also make me think about broader overlaps, such as the ancient commonalities between Shavuot and Pentecost, or Passover, Easter, and Nowruz, the Iranian New Year.) Although this is not a holiday cookbook, its stories, sidebars, and headnotes give Jewish context to seasons-based cooking and link the interest in current food issues with past traditions. As you will see, one cannot be more biblical than today's field-gleaning projects to feed the hungry, which echo the commandments in Leviticus, Deuteronomy, and the Book of Ruth.

Today, when we talk about the importance of knowing where our food comes from, we're usually referring to matters of food safety and justice, sustainability, and support for small local farms. But the concept can take us farther back, putting food's ancient past into modern context. The twists and turns of my own food history have driven my search for deeper connections in food that give substance to a melting-pot life. For me, this wellspring of story has long been the farmers' market; its people, ingredients, and seasons are what inspired my first book, *The Santa Monica Farmers' Market Cookbook*. It's a logical step, a quick hop really, to the next level of meaning in food in *The Seasonal Jewish Kitchen*.

THE STORY TOLD THROUGH PICTURES

The evocative photography by Staci Valentine weaves all the strands of the book together visually. The farm- and seasonal market-scapes link us to the cycles of the year. (A few of my husband's images and mine are also woven in.)

Staci's beautiful recipe photographs tell the story of my family with its diverse flavors and its mementos: the white linen tablecloth embroidered by my grandmother Mina; my aunt Rena's wire cooling rack; the colorful Bedouin needlework on the dress I bought in the souk in East Jerusalem in 1969. You can see where my history joined my husband's: the silver candlesticks his maternal great-grandmother threw into the wagon at the last moment when her daughter left the Russian shtetl for America; his paternal grandmother's green bread bowl and *hockmeisser* (chopping blade); and our kiddush cup collection built over many life cycle events through the years. I hope that these stories, pictures, and more than 150 recipes—new dishes rooted in tradition, updated family classics, and recipes shared by the people you will meet in the book—inspire you to think about your own history and how it influences what you cook and eat today.

WHAT IS JEWISH FOOD?

There is no single answer to that question. In a literal sense, Jewish food is a cuisine defined by the religious dietary laws of kashrut. But that only begins to tell the tale. One thing is certain: one person's Jewish food—matzah ball soup, pastrami on rye—is not necessarily someone else's—couscous, *tagine*. There are as many true and opinionated interpretations as there are Jewish communities, (which are pretty much everywhere in the world). And the history of any cuisine is also the story of local ingredients.

Jews and their food have been on the move since the first Exodus, roughly thirty-five hundred years ago. Subsequent expulsions, dispersions, and migrations across the millennia—into ancient Babylon (Iraq), Spain, Russia, Poland, and Germany and then back out again, to name just a handful of stops—have influenced Jewish food tradition and required its adaptation. The most recent significant migrations, into the United States and Israel, are the ones that most influence our current perceptions. That's why so many people in the United States, Jewish or not, associate Jewish cooking with the smoked fish, deli meats, and poultry dishes that the Russians and Germans brought to the United States beginning in the late-nineteenth century. It is also why the twentieth-century influx of Moroccans, Tunisians, Russians, and Ethiopians into Israel has raised the vibrant diversity of, and our interest in, contemporary Israeli food to new heights.

DIFFERENT ROUTES, DIFFERENT FOODS

The early centuries of the Diaspora gave rise to two main strands of Jewish identity. Jews who followed a more southerly route into North Africa, the Levant, and southern Europe—lands of olive oil, rice, citrus, and the bounty of the spice route—became known as Sephardim. The term comes from the Hebrew for Spain and technically refers to Jews from the Iberian Peninsula, though today it typically means everyone who is not an Ashkenazic (European) Jew. (With apologies to the Mizrachic Jews of the eastern Mediterranean, whom I am folding into the broader term for the purposes of this book.) The Sephardic cultures developed in a primarily Muslim world that reached from the Indian Ocean to the Atlantic coast of Moorish Spain and Portugal. Sephardim primarily spoke (and speak) Arabic, Hebrew, Farsi, Spanish, and Ladino, a Spanish-Hebrew language.

Jews who were pushed northward in the tenth century developed Ashkenazic traditions in a primarily Christian Europe of cold-weather crops—wheat, buckwheat, root vegetables, and preserved fish—that could be carried to landlocked areas. Ashkenaz, a descendant of Noah, was the name given to the area in western Germany and northern France that was the center of Jewish life in the region. By the sixteenth century, the greatest concentration of European Jews had shifted eastward to Poland, Lithuania, and Bohemia. Yiddish, a south German dialect written in Hebrew script, is the Ashkenazic language spoken by northern and eastern European Jews. As with the word *Sephardic*, Ashkenazic is an umbrella term that doesn't distinguish among its many branches, but will be used here.

Jewish communities prepared regional foods filtered through a Jewish lens. Even interpretation of kashrut, which kept Jewish food and Jews separate from local cuisines and communities, was influenced by local custom and ingredients. Sephardic custom allows consumption of rice and legumes during Passover; Ashkenazic custom does not. For Ashkenazim, the swelling of these grains and pulses during cooking makes these items too close to the holiday's prohibited "leavened foods." Ethiopian Jews define the biblical law "do not boil a kid in its mother's milk" narrowly. Like Ashkenazim and Sephardim, they, too, eat no milk-braised meat dishes but allow dairy and meat to be served on the same plate, unlike other observant Jews.

DELICIOUS CROSS-POLLINATION

Like cooks everywhere, Jewish cooks have always relied on the ingredients that were available to them, adopting and adapting them as their own. Ashkenazim used goose, then chicken, fat—schmaltz—in place of the pork fat commonly used in that part of Europe, and cured goose and duck breast meat instead of ham. European Jewry used plentiful potatoes and beans in *cholent*, the all-night Sabbath stew, while Sephardim used rice in *adafina* and *tbit*. *Zengoula*, traditional Iraqi funnel cakes (page 117), were adopted as a Hanukkah sweet by Iraqi Jews in the Middle Ages. Today, the syrup-soaked coils are found in every Arab bakery, as well as every North African and Middle Eastern Jewish one, and are called *jalebi*, in Indian sweets shops.

The food exchange was a two-way street. Dr. Abraham Marcus, director emeritus of the Center for Middle Eastern Studies at the University of Texas, says "people mistakenly believe there is a bubble of discrete Jewish cookery surrounded by Arab culture. It's just not so." Not only did they adapt to their surroundings, but many Jews were merchants and traders who introduced foods into new areas. And as whole Jewish communities moved, they carried their foods with them. Citrus-growing, for instance, was primarily a Jewish enterprise for many centuries, evolving from the religious use of the *etrog*, the citron important in the celebration of Sukkot (page 60).

All the same, Jews and their Jewish food traditions were essentially isolated from the rest of local society through ghettoization and by choice to maintain their identity and observe Jewish law. It wasn't until the period of European Jewish enlightenment and emancipation, the *haskalah*, culminating in the late nineteenth century, that secularization allowed greater cross-pollination of foods and flavors. Some of these culinary exchanges are surprising to us, such as fennel and eggplant moving *from* Jewish cooking *into* mainstream Italian cuisine. It's remarkable to think, as Claudia Roden writes in *The Book of Jewish Food*, that Sephardic and Ashkenazic food traditions didn't meet or mingle until the twentieth-century Jewish migrations into the United States and Israel. The migratory flow continues—notably of Iranian Jews in the late 1970s and Russian Jews in the 1980s and 1990s—altering the culinary landscape and raising our awareness of the diversity of Jewish food.

THE ISRAELI MELTING POT

Like the United States, Israel is a cultural melting pot, only in concentrated form. Some 6.5 million Jewish Israelis (native and from Morocco, Russia, Tunisia, Romania, Ethiopia, Poland, Germany, and elsewhere), 1.5 million Muslim Israelis (Druze, Bedouins, and others), and 400,000 Christian and other Israelis—live, work, and share food in a space 290 miles long (from the base of the Negev Desert in the south to the top of the Golan in the north), 85 miles across at its widest and 9 miles at its narrowest, from the Mediterranean Sea to the West Bank.

Israel is the crossroads where all the flavors of the region and Jewish cooking the world over meet. Stroll three blocks in Tel Aviv and you are likely to pass a *hummuseria*, a Paris-trained chocolatier's boutique, and a *boureka* shop specializing in Balkan hand pies (not to mention a sushi bar and an Italian or Chinese restaurant). Walk Tel Aviv's hundred-year-old, blocks-long Levinsky or Carmel market, or the warren of stalls in the venerable Mahane Yehuda market in Jerusalem, and you will find people of every background selling and buying everything from halvah to herring. This is how hummus, the chickpea and tahini spread, and falafel, chickpea patties commonly stuffed into pita, can be simultaneously considered national Israeli dishes, Jewish food, and staples of Arab cuisines. If anything exists in Dr. Marcus's culinary bubble, it's *regional* cuisine, a delicate emulsion of traditions too often broken by politics.

Jewish cooking has always been a product of local ingredients and the many flavors of a migratory past. But because of the narrowness of our own experiences or because we live in a melting pot world, we often lack the backstories of the food we eat. Too often, Jewish or not, observant or not, we find ourselves saying, "That's Jewish food? Who knew?"

HOW TO USE THIS BOOK

Before you start shopping and cooking, please take a moment to read this section, which contains descriptions of traditional ingredients, a list of handy kitchen tools, and a guide to techniques used throughout the book. This section also includes a handful of recipes that are go-to flavor builders of Sephardic and Ashkenazic cooking.

The six two-month recipe chapters begin with September and October, the start of the Jewish year and the fall harvest, and each chapter contains information about the holidays and ingredients that occur during that period. The recipes in each chapter flow from starters, salads, and soups to side dishes, mains, and desserts. At the back of book, you will find all the recipes listed by category. To make the recipes very versatile, I offer suggestions on how to adapt them to other uses and other seasons.

When you shop, keep in mind that the change of seasons is a natural phenomenon and even the word *season* itself is an imprecise term (that's why I find two-month divisions so helpful). Exactly when, where, or if a crop shows up depends on the local climate (and microclimate) and the particular weather conditions of a given year. Whenever possible, seek out foods that are grown nearest you, for they are, by definition, in season and at their freshest and tastiest (and at the best price). They will make the dishes you cook more delicious and much easier to prepare. If you live in the Northern Hemisphere, at the very least, avoid stone fruit in February. If you live where avocados and citrus don't grow, purchase them when they are in season closest to you. Lastly, embrace the fact that each crop has early-, mid-, and late-season attributes (firmness, degree of sweetness, and so on); I will show you how to use these distinctions to your advantage.

About measurements, ingredients are often listed by the piece, because a lot of cooking is just that forgiving: a little more or less onion isn't going to make a big difference. When size, weight, or volume matter, I offer specific cues, such as "2 medium eggplants, about 1¼ pounds (570 g) total." Weights are given in imperial (pounds and ounces) and metric (grams and liters) values, and dry ingredients

commonly given by volume (1 cup) in baking are also listed by metric weight, which is a far more accurate measure. For oil, salt, spices, fresh herbs, and the like, you will find a specific quantity if it matters. Otherwise, I give a range or simply the item, because amounts are often a matter of personal taste. Even in baking recipes that rely on precise chemistry, you will often see a range for sugar or lemon when fruit is involved, because how the natural fruit tastes will determine how to season it. It's my hope that you'll feel comfortable cooking as our grandmothers did—a little of this, a pinch of that—and become a confident cook.

At the back of the book, I've listed some of my favorite shopping resources and more, all of which I hope will enrich your experience of this fresh take on Jewish foods.

THE KOSHER QUESTION

There are many dietary laws that govern how observant Jews prepare and consume food. *The Seasonal Jewish Kitchen* is not a kosher cookbook, but it does follow these basic precepts: no mixing of dairy and meat in a dish or suggested menu, and no use of pork or shellfish. For those of you who include these foods in your diet, you probably won't notice their absence from these flavorful recipes! If you do keep kosher, you will be delighted to discover the many naturally pareve options, such as Semolina and Walnut Oil Cake with Coffee Hawaij (page 243), that don't require the use of margarine, imitation sour cream, or other faux foods.

Some people reading this book follow a vegetarian or vegan diet or want to introduce more plant-based meals into their diet. I leave it to you to mix, match, and prepare these recipes according to your personal food philosophy. To let you know at a glance what type of dish it is, each recipe is clearly labeled, along with the yield, as follows.

- **PAREVE** Neutral food—that is, neither meat nor dairy—and that therefore can be paired with either meat or dairy. According to kashrut, fish is pareve, but I have created a separate category for it in this book for your convenience. Eggs are pareve and included here.
- **PAREVE/VEGAN** Neutral dish that contains no eggs, honey, dairy, or other animal products.
- **FISH** Dish that contains fish (technically, pareve) and possibly dairy. In many cases, the fish protein can be left out of a dish to yield a dairy, vegetarian, or vegan variation.

- **DAIRY** Vegetarian dish that contains milk products.
- **MEAT** Dish that contains meat. You will often find a suggestion for how to convert the dish to pareve/vegan.

An appendix in which recipes are grouped according to these kosher classifications, as well as a Jewish holiday calendar for reference, appears at the back of the book. I grew up in a secular home, so I learned a lot about kashrut while researching and developing the recipes for this book. I hope that whatever dietary guidelines you practice, you will be able to enjoy all the recipes in this book.

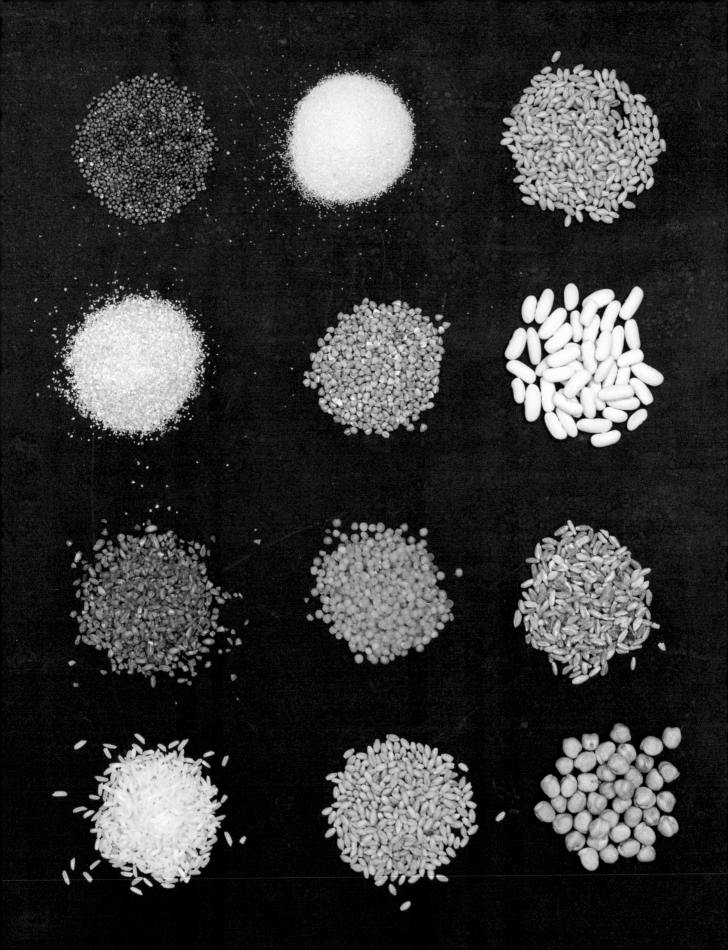

INGREDIENT ESSENTIALS

Here is a list of pantry and refrigerator ingredients that help produce the exciting flavors in this book. Many of them are basics you will already have on hand. Others may be new to you, but it doesn't mean they are hard to find. Often, they've been hiding in plain sight at your supermarket; you've just never noticed them before. Think of this as an opportunity to broaden your repertoire *and* see familiar staples in a new way.

Although many of these ingredients can be found in supermarkets, you will often find more authentic, better-quality brands in specialty shops and ethnic markets. And, of course, there's almost nothing you cannot find online these days. I've included some of my favorite resources on pages 299–300. Below are descriptions of the most essential ingredients, along with familiar substitutes when possible. You'll find out more about many of these ingredients in the recipes in which they are used.

BEANS AND GRAINS
BARLEY Most commonly sold in pearled form, which needs no soaking and cooks in about 40 minutes. Whole-grain barley must be soaked for at least 6 hours or up to overnight and requires at least twice the cooking time of pearled barley.

BEANS Fresh, dried, and canned types, such as cannellini, navy, black-eyed peas, and chickpeas. Al Wadi brand canned chickpeas come already skinned.

BUCKWHEAT GROATS In the same family as sorrel and rhubarb, these quick-cooking, gluten-free, grain-like seeds have an earthy flavor and need no soaking before cooking. Groats, also known as kasha, grow well in cold climates and are a traditional food of eastern Europe.

COUSCOUS Maghreb (Tunisia, Morocco, Algeria) semolina pasta granules traditionally steamed over simmering meat or vegetable stews and served with the stew spooned on the top. Instant couscous is available in supermarkets. Israeli couscous, also known as pearl couscous, consists of much larger toasted semolina granules. They are boiled like pasta and have a chewy texture, much like Sardinian *fregola* (which likely also originated in North Africa).

FARRO AND OTHER WHEAT BERRIES Farro, an ancient wheat (assumed by many to be the same as emmer), comes both pearled, which cooks in about 20 minutes, and whole grain, which should be soaked before cooking. Wheat berries are the whole kernels, minus the hull, and must be soaked before cooking.

FILO (ALSO PHYLLO) DOUGH Tissue-thin dough used in Balkan, Sephardic, and Middle Eastern pastries. Frozen filo dough is readily available in supermarkets.

FLOUR Use unbleached all-purpose flour to avoid the processing and off flavors of bleached flour. Whole wheat, rye, and many other flours add texture, color, and depth of flavor to baked goods. You can replace ¼ cup (30 g) of each 1 cup (125 g) of all-purpose flour with ¼ cup (25 to 30 g) of one of these alternative flours without further adjusting the recipe.

FREEKEH Fire-roasted green wheat with a slightly smoky flavor and more nutrients because it is harvested young. Available in whole-grain, cracked, and finely cracked forms. See also page 227.

LENTILS One of the oldest cultivated legumes, lentils vary in shape, size, and "melting" properties depending on type. "Caviar-size" dark green French and black lentils hold their shape when cooked. Disk-shaped red and brown lentils break down in cooking, making them good for purees and smooth soups.

MATZAH PRODUCTS Matzah farfel (precrumbled matzahs), matzah meal, and matzah cake meal are good to have on hand throughout the year.

POLENTA (AND CORNMEAL) The word *polenta* refers to medium- or coarse-grind meal from flint corn and to the Italian porridge made from it (*mamaliga* in Romania). Anson Mills in South Carolina grinds new-crop meal to order from heirloom flint corn. Cornmeal is typically produced from a softer corn and is more finely milled than polenta. For more flavor and higher nutritional value, look for meal that has not been degermed. Bob's Red Mill is a good brand. Use fine ground meal for baking.

QUINOA Native to the Andes, quinoa is an ancient plant in the same family as spinach, beets, and amaranth. Its nutritious, quick-cooking, gluten-free seeds are used like a grain or cereal. Quinoa comes in white, red, and black types; I find the latter two to be more flavorful. Although the seeds do not need pre-soaking, they should be rinsed well to remove any traces of their natural bitter coating.

CANS, JARS, MISCELLANY

BROTH Try before you commit. Look for canned and aseptic-packaged broths that taste good to you, are not overly salty, and have no metallic aftertaste. Because as these commercial products cook, their flavors concentrate, I recommend diluting them with water to half-strength.

FISH

• **ANCHOVIES** Dissolved in warm olive oil, anchovy fillets add savoriness but not fishiness, making them a great secret seasoning, especially in meatless dishes. Look for fillets packed in olive oil. Salt-packed anchovies taste even better but are more labor-intensive, requiring rinsing and filleting before use.

• **SARDINES** Use good-quality products from Spain, Portugal, or California. Angelo Parodi, Ortiz, and Matiz Gallego are good brands. The sardine population has experienced a dramatic drop in recent years, so follow your conscience.

• **TUNA** Look for water- or oil-packed tuna fillets in glass jars or in cans. Ortiz, As do Mar, and Callipo are good imported brands. American Tuna (available at Whole Foods markets nationally) is a domestic fisherman-owned company dedicated to sustainable fishing practices.

GELATIN Knox, the most familiar brand of unflavored gelatin, is meat based and nonkosher. Kosher Kolatin brand, made from beef, or KoJel brand, made from fish, can be substituted in an even exchange. How much plant-based gelatin to substitute, such as those made from seaweed (agar agar) and kudzu, depends on the other ingredients in a recipe and requires some experimenting.

HALVAH There are many types of confections with this name, which stems from the Arabic word for "sweet." The most commonly known variety in Europe and North America is the Middle Eastern sesame halvah made from the solids that remain after sesame oil production. These solids are ground with sugar or honey, often studded with pistachios or almonds, and pressed into a cake or loaf. The best halvahs are those with the highest percentage of sesame seed paste.

OLIVES Depending on variety, ripeness, and curing process (fresh-cured, salt-cured, oil-cured, brined, or cracked), olives come in many flavor profiles, from buttery sweet to peppery and bitter. Serve olives as part of a mezze or use to season a dish.

TAHINI Refers to both the ground sesame seed paste and, when thinned with water and lemon and seasoned with garlic, the traditional Middle Eastern sauce. The paste comes hulled or unhulled and raw or toasted. Unhulled tahini is darker, more robustly flavored, and more nutritious. Tahini varies in consistency according to brand, is perishable, and separates on standing. Keep refrigerated upside down to minimize separating, then bring to room temperature and stir thoroughly before using. Al Arz, produced in Nazareth, Israel, is considered one of the best brands and is available online. Al Wadi is a reliable brand found in many Middle Eastern markets.

DAIRY

BUTTER Wherever butter is called for, use unsalted butter. It allows the cook to have more control over the quality and the amount of salt in a dish.

FROMAGE BLANC Fresh French cheese that is a nice spread for bread. It doesn't hold up as well in the oven as farmer cheese or quark. I find it works best in combination with other heat-stable creamy cheeses.

LABNEH Lightly salted and drained cow's, sheep's, or goat's milk yogurt that thickens to a spreadable "yogurt cheese." Byblos is a good brand, or make your own at home (see page 22).

QUARK Low-fat, tangy fresh cheese of German origin. A common breakfast cheese spread, it also holds up well in cooking. The Israeli equivalent is *gvinah levanah* (white cheese), which comes in varying fat percentages and is a dairy staple.

RICOTTA Versatile Italian cooked fresh cheese. Sheep's milk ricotta is slightly tangy; cow's milk ricotta is sweet. Freshly made ricotta is an unforgettable milky pleasure. Urda is the Balkan version.

YOGURT Use good-quality whole-milk or low-fat plain yogurt to add tart creaminess to cold foods. It is also used in place of buttermilk to tenderize baked goods. Thick Greek yogurt has been drained of much of its whey.

SEMIHARD TO HARD CHEESES

KASHKAVAL, KASSERI, AND KEFOLATIRI Yellow Balkan sheep's milk cheeses ranging from semihard and lightly aged to long aged and sharp for grating. Kashkaval (caciocavallo in Italy) is one of the distinctive flavors of Romanian dairy cooking.

PARMIGIANO-REGGIANO The king of Italian cheeses, often imitated (Parmesan) but never equaled. It is long aged and has a sweet, nutty flavor, slightly granular texture, and good melting properties.

PECORINO Italian sheep's milk cheese made in many different regions. The most commonly stocked type is aged sharp pecorino romano for grating. Young pecorino cheese is milder, creamier, and may be sliced or grated and used in place of Swiss Emmentaler or Balkan kashkaval.

FRESH CHEESES

FARMER A dry cottage cheese commonly used in fillings for blintzes, dumplings, and baked goods. Pot cheese, which is similar, has more moisture than farmer cheese and less moisture than cottage cheese. Drain excess liquid from cottage or pot cheese to substitute it for farmer cheese.

FETA Salty fresh Greek cheese made from sheep's milk, or a combination of sheep's and goat's milk, that is drained, pressed, and brined. Similar cheeses, including sirene, brynza, and bulgarit, are made in eastern Europe, Russia, Israel, and beyond. Taste before you buy. Some versions are saltier; others, like the French sheep's milk equivalent, are creamier. Valbreso is a commonly available French brand.

RICOTTA SALATA Pressed and salted ricotta cheese. Good for grating, it is traditionally eaten in southern Italy, including Sicily, Sardinia, and Campania. Greek Mizithra is a similar salty pressed cheese. Manouri is moister and has a milder flavor.

FLAVORINGS AND SWEETENERS

CAROB MOLASSES Lebanese syrup made from roasted carob; as the syrup reduces, it develops caramel and molasses notes. Al Wadi and Salloum Bros. are two commonly available brands.

ORANGE BLOSSOM WATER Distilled from bitter-orange blossoms, this fragrant liquid lends a heady citrus note to desserts. Al Wadi and Cortas are reliable large manufacturers; Mymouné is a good specialty brand. Avoid products made with alcohol, as they can add a medicinal flavor. Fresh orange zest is a good substitute.

POMEGRANATE MOLASSES This thick, dark, tart syrup is the Middle Eastern equivalent of a balsamic vinegar reduction. Look for labels that specify that the molasses is made from 100 percent pomegranate juice.

ROSE WATER Distilled from fragrant rose petals, this highly perfumed liquid is a popular flavoring in Middle Eastern desserts. Look for labels that indicate 100 percent rose water distillate, such as the reliable Cortas brand; avoid those with additives. Rose water can be potent and overperfumed, so use sparingly. In season, make the simple rose geranium syrup on page 242.

HONEY The flavor of any honey depends on where the bees collected the nectar. Flavors range from delicate orange blossom to robust chestnut, buckwheat, or avocado. Store honey at room temperature and warm it slightly to make pouring easier. If honey crystallizes, heat it thoroughly to reconstitute it. Caramelized honey is the by-product of heating honeycomb to extract all the honey and is often available from local honey producers. The Sardinian version, *abbamele*, is lightly flavored with citrus and carries hints of toasted caramel.

SILAN The Middle Eastern equivalent of maple syrup, sorghum, or molasses, *silan*, or date syrup, is a thick reduction of fruit and water. It should taste like dates—sweet and spicy with hints of citrus. Look for Kinneret Farm brand from Israel or Moomtaz from Lebanon.

VINEGARS Red wine, white wine, sherry, cider, rice, and balsamic vinegars contribute a variety of tart flavors to salads and cooked dishes. Quality makes a difference in flavor and degree of sharpness.

OILS

MILD OILS Mild, or neutrally flavored oils, such as grapeseed, safflower, and sunflower, have a medium to high smoke point. Avocado oil, which has a very high smoke point, has a pleasant buttery quality.

OLIVE OIL One of the essential flavor elements of eastern Mediterranean and Sephardic cooking. Look for cold-pressed extra-virgin oils, filtered or unfiltered, and preferably with a harvest date on the label. Different olives, sources, and processes yield different colors and flavors, from light gold to deep green and from mild and buttery to fruity and peppery. Store away from light, ideally in a dark glass container, and use within 6 months.

SEED AND NUT OILS Sesame (raw and toasted), walnut, hazelnut, almond, and pistachio oils are used for flavoring and for dressing salads. They have a low smoke point and are highly perishable. Store in the refrigerator and use within 6 months.

SALTS

Perhaps the single most important and versatile flavoring tool, salt comes in many types, each of which delivers its own distinctive qualities to a dish. These are the types of salt I regularly use.

FINE SEA SALT Finely textured with pure flavor; especially useful in baking, where tiny crystals are desirable.

KOSHER SALT The workhorse of the kitchen, kosher salt is inexpensive and has a pure salt flavor. The best brands

(I like Diamond Crystal) contain no anticaking agents. The coarse texture of kosher salt gives it more volume, which means the cook has greater control when salting foods. Keep an open bowlful handy for easy pinches.

FLEUR DE SEL The moist sea salt crystal "blossoms" of pricey *fleur de sel* are harvested by hand from the surface of salt beds. Its sweet marine taste and delicately crunchy texture make it a wonderful finishing salt.

MALDON SEA SALT Relatively moderate in price, large-flake Maldon sea salt from England is used for both cooking and finishing. It is especially nice crushed between your fingertips over salads.

SEL GRIS Harvested from the Brittany coast and the Bay of Bombay, this moderately priced gray sea salt has large, damp crystals, a high mineral content, and a briny flavor, making it great for both cooking and finishing.

SMOKED SALT This versatile salt adds a deep, complex flavor to egg and vegan dishes as well as to meats. Its aroma and flavor vary depending on the type of wood used for smoking. Maldon makes a nice, moderately priced smoked large-flake sea salt. Store tightly closed to retain the aroma.

SPICES

CARDAMOM Sold as dried small green pods, as whole seeds, or ground. The dark, oily seeds have a spicy-sweet flavor and pungent eucalyptus notes. A member of the ginger family, cardamom is native to India, where it is one of the spices used in masala and curry blends. Crushed seeds are traditional in Druze and Bedouin coffee, and whole pods are cracked and dropped into savory stews or fruit compotes. When bleached, cardamom pods whiten and the seeds become more delicately flavored. These milder seeds are favored in Europe for baking, especially in Scandinavia.

CHILES Dried and/or smoked peppers range in flavor from fruity to bitter and from mild to searingly hot.

• **ALEPPO PEPPER** Versatile Syrian red pepper flakes have a sweet, warm, earthy heat. They add color and richness to many foods. Due to the continuing war conditions in Syria, the peppers now come from just across the border in Turkey and are called maras peppers, after Kahramanmaras Province where they are grown. But as Cambridge, Massachusetts, chef and eastern Mediterranean cooking expert Ana Sortun explains, "Aleppo has become the brand or generic name for coarsely ground, oily, sweet and spicy red chiles from the region." Depending on where you shop, you may find this spice identified as Aleppo-style pepper or maras pepper.

- **ÁRBÓL CHILE** Small, relatively mild chiles, most often found dried, are used whole to add depth and broken to add zing.
- **CAYENNE** Ground blend of dried small hot red chiles.
- **CHIPOTLE** The smoke-dried ripe jalapeño, or chipotle, adds a smoky flavor and moderate heat to stews and condiments. Whole dried chipotles are available at some supermarkets, in Latin groceries, and occasionally at farmers' markets. Do not confuse them with canned chipotles in adobo sauce.
- **PAPRIKA** Finely ground high-quality sweet paprika adds a heady vegetal complexity to foods. Half-sharp (medium-hot) paprika is one of my favorite spices, and sharp (hot) paprika packs a lot of heat. Go beyond the regular supermarket brands and you'll understand how paprika can contribute more than just bright color. A traditional seasoning in Hungarian and Romanian stews.
- **SMOKED PAPRIKA** The Spanish version, *pimentón*, is especially delicious and ranges from sweet (*dulce*) to bittersweet (*agridulce*) to hot (*picante*). I like La Dalia brand.

CORIANDER The seed of the cilantro plant, sold whole and ground, doesn't taste like fresh cilantro. It adds refreshing herbaceous notes to eastern Mediterranean foods.

CUMIN A member of the parsley family, cumin is bold, earthy, and nutty. Noted in the Bible and used in Middle Eastern, North African, Indian, and Latin American cooking, it is available whole-seed or ground.

PEPPERCORNS Black peppercorns are the pungent, not-quite-ripe berries of a flowering vine. White peppercorns, the fully ripened skinned berries of the same plant, have a milder taste and are invisible in light-colored dishes.

SUMAC Tart, deep red berries of the sumac bush that grows wild in the Middle East. When the berries are dried and coarsely ground, the color ranges from brick red to vibrant purple and the texture is slightly moist. A favorite in Persian cooking, sumac adds spectacular color and tartness without acid or astringency. A beautiful finishing spice, especially for fish.

SPICE BLENDS

BAHARAT Aromatic, hot, Arab spice blend of black and red peppers, cloves, cinnamon, and nutmeg

CURRY POWDER Ground South Asian blends of up to twenty ingredients, including cardamom, chiles, cinnamon, cloves, coriander, cumin, fenugreek, fennel, turmeric, and red and black pepper. The blends range in heat and profile depending on the cook. The best are freshly ground, but in their absence, look for interesting small-batch blends from good spice stores rather than generic supermarket brands.

HARISSA Refers to both a ground spice mix and to a condiment paste or sauce traditional to North Africa. Heat levels and ingredients vary, but typically include dried red chiles, caraway, cumin, and coriander.

COFFEE HAWAIJ Yemeni spice blend of cardamom, ginger, and cinnamon used to flavor coffee. When finely ground, it is delicious in baked goods (see page 243).

HAWAIJ Savory Yemeni spice blend of cumin, black pepper, turmeric, cardamom, coriander, caraway, and cloves used in soups, stews, and poultry dishes. The turmeric in the mix colors the foods yellow.

RAS EL HANOUT A popular North African ground spice mix that can include dozens of ingredients, ranging from paprika, cumin, and cinnamon to allspice, nutmeg, and dried rosebuds. It has floral, spice, and heat notes and adds warm orange-brown color to foods.

ZA'ATAR Variously thought to be wild thyme, hyssop, oregano, marjoram, or even savory—conflicting claims that make sense since all the plants are members of the mint family. The perennial herb is native to the Levant and is one of its most meaningful fragrances: Hebrews used it as a brush to mark their doorposts to ward off the Angel of Death during the first Passover. *Za'atar* also refers to a dry blend of the herb, sesame seeds, sumac, and salt that is a defining flavor of Middle Eastern cuisines.

KITCHEN FUNDAMENTALS

This section covers basic techniques used throughout the book. Having these essential skills at your fingertips will help you be a confident, efficient cook.

HOW TO ZEST CITRUS. Zest, the colored part of citrus skin, contains highly flavored oils, but the white layer, or pith, that lies beneath it is bitter. To make long, thin strands, scrape a five-hole zester against the fruit, pressing deeply enough to remove only the colored portion of the skin. For tiny zest bits, use a Microplane grater, and for wide strips, use a swivel-blade vegetable peeler. Whenever possible, work over the other ingredients in the dish to catch the droplets of citrus oils that will be released as you work. Use unsprayed organic fruits to avoid an acrid taste or ingesting chemicals retained in the peel.

HOW TO PEEL AND SEGMENT CITRUS. Using a sharp, small or medium knife, cut a thin slice off the top and the bottom of the fruit, exposing the flesh. Stand the fruit upright and cut downward to remove the peel in wide strips, tracing the curve of the fruit with your knife to expose the pulp and rotating the fruit after each cut. Hold the fruit in one hand over a bowl and slice along both sides of each segment to free it from the membrane, dropping the segments into the bowl as you go. Squeeze the membrane to extract juice for use in the recipe or reserve for another use.

HOW TO SEED A POMEGRANATE. Make a cut near the blossom end of the fruit, submerge the fruit in a bowl of water, and then break it into large pieces. Use your fingers to loosen all the arils, or kernels (commonly referred to as seeds), then drain and reserve them. They will keep in an airtight container in the refrigerator for 3 to 5 days.

HOW TO PEEL AND SEED TOMATOES. Drop whole tomatoes into a pot of boiling water for 30 seconds. Immerse them only two at a time to prevent lowering the water temperature. Use a spider, slotted spoon, or tongs to remove the tomatoes from the pan. The skins will slip off easily. (The classic technique includes scoring the blossom end of the tomato before plunging it into the boiling water and then immersing the hot tomato in an ice bath. I don't find these steps necessary.) Use the tip of a paring knife to cut out the core. Cut the tomatoes in half crosswise and gently squeeze each half to remove the seeds, easing the seed sacs out with a fingertip if necessary. To capture the tomato juices, work over a sieve set over a bowl. Firm or green (unripe) tomatoes can be peeled with a swivel-blade vegetable peeler.

HOW TO STRIP HERBS AND GREENS. Leaves of woody-stemmed herbs such as thyme, bay, and rosemary can be "plucked" by grasping the top of the sprig and pulling sharply downward. For greens such as kale or Swiss chard, grasp the stem end with one hand and, with your other hand, fold the leaf in half lengthwise and pull both sides of the leaf sharply downward.

HOW TO BLANCH. A technique to heighten the color of vegetables and, in the case of dense vegetables such as carrots or fennel, infuse them with moisture to keep them tender and plump in grilling or roasting. Briefly boil vegetables in salted water until their color intensifies. Drain immediately and rinse with ice water (shock) to stop the cooking and preserve color.

HOW TO SAUTÉ AND BROWN. To sauté ingredients without browning, place them with the oil in a cold pan and heat (or melt butter briefly before adding other ingredients). When you want a sizzle and quick browning, heat the pan and the fat before adding the ingredients. If using butter, add a little oil to prevent burning..

HOW TO SEASON WITH SALT. Add a little salt at each stage of your recipe—when starting to sauté, after adding liquid, and again just before serving—to deepen the flavor of the finished dish. The final layering adds textural sparkle.

When boiling foods, salt the cooking water generously: a good handful of salt added to water for cooking pasta is only about ¼ teaspoon salt for each 1 cup (240 ml) water. That's not enough to make the pasta salty but is the bare minimum needed to add flavor.

HOW TO MEASURE FLOUR. To measure by volume, spoon flour into the appropriate dry measure to heaping full. Do not shake or tap the measure to settle the flour. Use the edge of a metal spatula or the back of a knife to sweep away the excess flour, making it flush with the rim of the measure. To measure by weight, place a bowl on a kitchen scale set to zero and pour or spoon flour into the bowl until you reach the desired weight. To add other ingredients once the flour is in the bowl, keep the bowl on the scale, adjust the "tare" button on the scale to zero, and add the correct weight of the next ingredient. Continue until you have added all the ingredients you need.

HOW TO TOAST NUTS. Preheat the oven to 350°F (180°C). Spread the nuts on a sheet pan and toast in the center of the oven until fragrant and lightly golden in the center, 10 to 15 minutes for almonds, hazelnuts, and pistachios and 7 to 10 minutes for oil-rich pecans and walnuts. Set aside to cool; the nuts will continue to take on color and crispness as they cool. To remove the skins of hazelnuts and walnuts, wrap the hot nuts in a dish towel and rub them vigorously to flake off the skins. Toast nuts the day you intend to use them to ensure freshness.

HOW TO GRIND NUTS. Use a rotary grater to turn small amounts of nuts into feathered shavings that improve the texture of baked goods. It only takes 2 tablespoons raw nuts to yield ¼ to ⅓ cup (25 to 30 g) packed grated nuts. If using pre-ground meal, use ¼ cup (28 g) not packed. If using a food processor, grind the 2 tablespoons of nuts with 1 tablespoon of the sugar called for in the recipe to get a fine crumb without turning the nuts to paste.

HOW TO COOK GRAINS. Soak whole-grain wheat berries, barley, farro, and freekeh for 2 to 6 hours or up to overnight in cool water to cover. Drain, then cook in boiling salted water until tender, from 45 to 60 minutes to 1½ to 3 hours, depending on the grain. When "pearled" to remove hulls and bran layers, farro and barley need no soaking and will cook in 20 and 40 minutes, respectively. Finely cracked freekeh may be steamed like rice, reaching tenderness in about 20 minutes. Buckwheat groats (kasha) need no soaking and cook quickly. Grains will double or triple in volume when cooked. See individual grain recipes for more information.

HOW TO COOK FRESH SHELL BEANS. Shell the beans and place in a pot with water to cover. Bring to a gentle boil over medium-high heat, reduce heat to low, cover partially, and simmer until the beans are tender but still hold their shape, 30 to 40 minutes. Add salt to taste, turn off heat, cover pot, and let the beans cool. Refrigerate the beans in their liquid. Drain before using and reserve the liquid to enrich soups and stews. Fresh beans do not expand much in cooking. You will get about 1 cup (180 g) cooked beans from ½ pound (225 g) beans in the pod.

HOW TO COOK DRIED BEANS. If you have the current season's dried beans, there is no need to soak them. Otherwise, soak beans in a bowl of cool water to cover for at least 6 hours or up to overnight. Drain, place in a pot with water, using 4 cups (960 ml) water for each 1 cup (190 g) beans. Bring to a gentle boil, reduce the heat to low, cover, and simmer gently until the beans are tender but still hold their shape, 45 to 60 minutes. Add salt to taste, turn off the heat, cover the pot, and let the beans cool in the liquid. Refrigerate the beans in their liquid. Drain before using and reserve the liquid for enriching soups and stews. Dried beans will triple in volume when cooked. With chickpeas, you'll need to peel them to make a very creamy puree. Simmer chickpeas for 15 minutes to loosen the skins. Lift from the cooking water with a spider onto a kitchen towel, fold the towel over, and rub chickpeas to remove as many skins as possible. Return chickpeas to the cooking water to finish cooking. When they are tender, skim off any additional skins that have floated to the surface. Stir the pot vigorously and skim again, but don't worry if some skins stubbornly adhere.

HOW TO ROAST WINTER SQUASH OR PUMPKINS. Preheat the oven to 375°F (190°C). To roast a large whole squash, pierce it in a few places with a knife or meat fork and place on a sheet pan. Roast the squash until it is browned, shiny, beginning to lose its shape, and is easily pierced with a knife, about 1 hour for a 5-pound (2.3 kg) squash. When cool enough to handle, cut in half crosswise and scoop out and discard the seeds and strings (or save the seeds for another purpose). Scoop the pulp from the "shell." A 5-pound (2.3 kg) squash yields about 6 cups (1.4 kg) cooked pulp. Use the pulp as is, or puree in a food processor or mash with a fork and freeze in 1-pint (500-ml) containers for convenient use throughout the season.

HOW TO ROAST A SMALL LONG SQUASH, such as a butternut. Cut in half lengthwise and scoop out the seeds and strings. Brush the cut sides with olive oil and season with kosher or sea salt. Place cut side down on a baking sheet with at least 1 inch (2.5 cm) between the halves and roast in a 375°F (190°C) oven until the skin is browned and shiny and the squash is easily pierced with the tip of a knife, about 40 minutes.

HOW TO ROAST A SMALL ROUND SQUASH, such as a Sweet Dumpling. Cut off the top, scoop out the seeds and strings, brush the cavity with olive oil, season with salt, and roast cut side down as for the small long squash.

HELPFUL KITCHEN TOOLS

I'm not a gadget-oriented cook, but I do rely on some of basic tools that I think make cooking easier and produce nicer results. A good set of heavy pots and pans and sharp knives is a given. A blender, an electric mixer, and a food processor are terrific, but as you'll see, I don't use them nearly as often as I do my knives and a simple fork for mixing.

BENRINER SLICER Inexpensive Japanese mandoline for cutting paper-thin slices of vegetables and fruits. For safety, leave 1 inch (2.5 cm) of the stem attached to hold on to as you slice.

BOX GRATER The large holes of this old-fashioned tool are perfect for grating tomatoes into instant "puree" and for grating vegetables, crisp fruits, and cheese.

FAT SEPARATOR To separate the fat that rises to the top of pan drippings and stock. There are several kinds; I prefer the liquid-measuring-cup type, with a spout set low to draw out the liquid at the bottom, leaving the fat behind.

FIVE-HOLE Zester Stainless-steel tool with five small holes at the edge to produce long, thin strands of citrus peel.

FOOD MILL Hand tool for pureeing foods; simultaneously removes the skin, seeds, and fibers. Some models have a fixed blade and others have changeable blades that range from coarse to fine grind.

GRAPEFRUIT SPOON Serrated spoon for removing an artichoke's fuzzy core and hollowing vegetables for stuffing.

IMMERSION BLENDER Also known as a stick blender, a handheld electric blender for pureeing soups or other dishes right in the pot.

KITCHEN SCALE Accurate, battery-operated scales convert between imperial and metric values; "tare" feature allows you to subtract the bowl's weight and add multiple ingredients to the same bowl. OXO brand makes an easy-to-use 11-pound capacity scale.

LONG-BLADED SERRATED KNIFE Offset handle gives better leverage when slicing bread, tomatoes, meat, and cakes.

MICROPLANE GRATER An easy-to-use fine rasp to produce small bits of citrus zest.

MORTAR AND PESTLE For pulverizing garlic, spices, and herbs.

MOULI GRATER Small, rotary French hand grater; ideal for nuts and cheese.

OFFSET SPATULA Large metal blade (3 x 10-inches/ 7.5 x 25 cm) with an offset (bend) and a short handle for turning fish or lifting pastry.

OYSTER KNIFE Why is there an oyster knife in a Jewish cookbook? Because its stubby blade and wide guard make it a great tool for coring quince and chunking cheese.

PARCHMENT PAPER Handy for lining sheet pans (instead of greasing them) to speed cleanup, and for twisting into cones for piping. Unlike waxed paper, it is not coated.

PEPPER MILLS Have one for black and one for white peppercorns. The difference between freshly ground pepper and long-stored preground pepper is like night and day. Peugeot brand is recommended.

REAMER Small, handheld conical tool for juicing citrus.

SCISSORS Heavy-duty pair for everything from snipping chives to splitting a chicken.

SHEET PANS Heavy-duty pans with 1-inch (2.5-cm) rims, indispensable for roasting, baking, carrying, and organizing. Popular sizes are the half sheet (12 x 18 inches/30.5 x 46 cm) and quarter sheet (9 x 12 inches/23 x 30.5 cm).

SPIDER Shallow "webbed" skimmer for removing foods from boiling water or hot oil.

TONGS Have both long and short easy-to-squeeze tongs.

VEGETABLE DRILL Despite its high-tech name, a hand tool for hollowing out vegetables that comes with several sizes of bits. Also great for coring apples.

SEVEN BASIC RECIPES

These seven evergreen recipes are part of the foundation flavors of cooking throughout the Jewish Diaspora. You'll see them referred to frequently: Sephardic rice, tahini and lemon sauces, lightly pickled cabbage, and *labneh*, and Ashkenazic schmaltz and *gribenes*. You'll find additional flavor basics in their seasonal chapters.

BASIC WHITE RICE, SEPHARDIC STYLE

MAKES 3 CUPS (475 G)

PAREVE/VEGAN

Despite worries to the contrary, basic steamed rice isn't difficult to make and doesn't require special equipment beyond a heavy pot with a tight-fitting lid. That being said, there are so many "right" ways to make this daily staple, it's no wonder that many cooks lack confidence when making rice. Even members of my Iraqi family disagree on the specifics (and I'm sure I'll hear from all of them after they read this recipe).

One thing is certain, however: Sephardic-style rice means that the cooked grains must be separate. You can achieve this several ways, starting with using a long-grain rice (long-grain, basmati, and jasmine are all good). Some cooks wash the raw rice in several changes of water to remove excess starch. Others begin by briefly stirring unwashed rice in a little hot oil to seal the grains before adding water to the pot. Either step will produce a more elegant pot of rice, but I confess that when I'm in a hurry, I don't bother. A basic ratio of 1 cup (185 g) rice to 1½ cups (360 ml) water produces consistent results and may be multiplied as needed. Each cup (185 g) of raw rice yields about 3 cups (475 g) cooked rice. Both basmati and jasmine rice are known for their fragrance, but all good-quality rice varieties have a slightly floral, buttery perfume. Here are two good ways to cook white rice.

1½ cups (360 ml) water

½ to 1 teaspoon salt

1 cup (185 g) long-grain white rice, picked over and rinsed or not rinsed

2 tablespoons mild oil, if using second method

METHOD ONE

Bring the water to a boil in a deep 2-quart (2-L) pot fitted with a lid. Add the salt to taste and stir in the rice. Cover, reduce the heat to medium-high, and return the water to a boil, watching so that the rice doesn't boil over. Reduce the heat to low, stir the rice briefly to loosen the grains, and cover the pot again. Cook the rice until all the liquid is absorbed and the grains are tender and fragrant, about 15 minutes, stirring once during cooking.

Remove from the heat and let stand, covered, for 5 minutes to allow the grains to firm slightly, then fluff with a fork. If making a double or triple batch, plan on 20 minutes or longer cooking time.

METHOD TWO

Heat the oil in the pot over medium-high heat. Add the rice and stir constantly for 1 minute. Add *hot* water and the salt, reduce the heat to low, cover, and steam as directed in the Method One.

VINEGARED CABBAGE

MAKES ABOUT 1 CUP (150 G)

PAREVE/VEGAN

Pickled or fermented cabbage is another common sour accent in Middle Eastern foods, especially in salads and sandwiches. I prefer the more delicate result of quick "vinegaring." This recipe can be doubled or tripled and will keep in the refrigerator for about one week.

5- to 6-ounce (140- to 170-g) wedge green or Savoy
    cabbage, cut crosswise into narrow ribbons
2 tablespoons cider vinegar or white wine vinegar
2 tablespoons water
½ teaspoon salt

Bring a saucepan filled with water to a boil. Add the cabbage and cook until wilted, about 2 minutes. Drain well and place in a bowl; you should have about 1 cup (150 g). Stir in the vinegar, water, and salt. Let stand for at least 15 minutes before using.

LABNEH

MAKES 2 CUPS (450 G)

DAIRY

Labneh is lightly salted and drained cow's, sheep's, or goat's milk yogurt that becomes tarter, thicker, and creamier in the process of removing the liquid. A favorite accent food throughout the Levant and the Arabian Peninsula, it is indispensable for making Shanklish (page 101) and as a cooling condiment for spicy regional dishes such as Shakshuka (page 62). Try a "shmear" of *labneh* instead of cream cheese on bagels. *Labneh* continues to thicken the longer it drains; after two days, it will be firm enough to roll into balls and marinate in olive oil and herbs, which will keep for a couple of weeks. Commercial *labneh* is available at supermarkets and Middle Eastern groceries, but it's hard to beat the homemade version, which has no thickeners or stabilizers.

2 pounds (900 g) plain yogurt, either whole milk
    or low-fat
½ teaspoon salt
Za'atar for rolling balls
Olive oil for covering balls

Stir together the yogurt and salt. Line a fine-mesh sieve with several layers of cheesecloth (or one layer of kitchen muslin) large enough so that the ends overhang the sieve. Rest the sieve over a bowl. Spoon the yogurt into the sieve, then cover with the ends of the cheesecloth. Refrigerate for at least 6 hours or up to 24 hours.

Scrape labneh into a bowl, cover tightly, and refrigerate for up to 4 days. Discard the whey or refrigerate it and use to thin and add tartness to soups.

Alternatively, drain the yogurt until it is stiff enough to roll into balls, 2 to 3 days. Roll into 1- to 2-inch (2.5- to 5-cm) balls, roll the balls in za'atar and place in a clean jar. Pour in olive oil to cover. Cap tightly and refrigerate for up to 2 weeks. Bring to room temperature to serve.

TAHINI SAUCE

MAKES ¾ TO 1 CUP (180 TO 240 ML)

PAREVE/VEGAN

Tahini refers to both the sesame paste and the sauce created when the paste is seasoned with garlic and thinned with lemon juice and water. It is as ubiquitous in the Middle East as ketchup or mayo in the United States and *chimichurri* in Argentina. Use tahini sauce whenever you need a nutty, creamy accent to Mediterranean food.

⅓ cup (80 g) raw tahini
2 to 3 tablespoons fresh lemon juice
1 to 2 cloves garlic
¼ cup (60 ml) water, plus more as needed

Stir together the tahini and 2 tablespoons lemon juice. Crush the garlic through a press into the tahini mixture. Whisk in the water. The mixture will stiffen. Gradually whisk in more water until the sauce is creamy. The consistency is a matter of preference: anywhere from heavy to softly whipped cream. Add more lemon juice as desired.

LEMON SAUCE

MAKES ½ CUP (4 FL OZ/120 ML)

PAREVE/VEGAN

This condiment adds a nice jolt of acid to Arab-style hummus and grilled fish and meats. My version is based on one I had at Abu Hassan in Jaffa, reputedly one of the best *hummuserias* in Israel.

1 to 2 large lemons
2 teaspoons mild oil, such as grapeseed or safflower
½ teaspoon kosher or sea salt
½ teaspoon Aleppo pepper

Squeeze enough lemons to yield ½ cup juice (4 fl ounces/ 120 ml). Stir in the oil, salt, and Aleppo pepper. Serve individual portions in small bowls.

SCHMALTZ AND GRIBENES

MAKES ABOUT 1 CUP (200 G OR 250 ML) SCHMALTZ
AND 1 CUP (120 G) GRIBENES

MEAT

I didn't grow up with schmaltz or *gribenes*, but I've long relied on the pan drippings from my roast chicken to make decadent potatoes or begin a gravy. And I couldn't do without the flavorful fat that congeals at the top of homemade chicken soup when I make matzah balls. How different could those fats be from the mystical schmaltz of memory?

Different enough to be worth the effort. Making schmaltz isn't difficult, but it does take time. The simmering pot needs to be tended to keep the bits from sticking and the bubbling fat from darkening. It's kind of a miracle actually; you end up with clear golden liquid and crisp mahogany cracklings that can be used in many ways. I've given you ten at the end of this recipe to get you started.

Use fat and skin from good-quality chickens and ducks. Ask your butcher for trimmings or get them from your poultry farmer if he or she sells cut-up birds. Otherwise, collect the raw bits of fat and skin each time you trim a bird and freeze these bits until you have enough to make a good batch of schmaltz. The recipe here may be halved or multiplied, keeping the same proportions, but I wouldn't start with more than 1½ pounds (680 g) of fat and skin, as it takes time to cut everything. One 4-pound (1.8-kg) chicken stripped bare yields ½ pound (225 g) skin and fat for making schmaltz and *gribenes*.

1 pound (450 g) chicken or duck fat and skin
   (with more fat than skin)
½ onion, chopped
¼ cup (60 ml) water

Schmaltz, chicken or duck fat cooked low and slow with onions, and *gribenes*, cracklings made from poultry skin and onions, are at the core of the Ashkenazic food identity. Over the decades, they have gotten a bad rap by some, as unhealthful, outdated, and overused. I have three words for you: duck-fat fries. When used with a light hand and made from quality ingredients, rendered and seasoned poultry fat is a marvelous culinary essence.

If using fresh fat and skin, place them in a shallow layer on a plate and freeze until partially frozen, about 45 minutes. If you are starting with bits you have frozen, partially thaw them to make them easier to cut. Chop or use scissors to cut the fat and skin into ½-inch (12-mm) pieces. Put the pieces in a 2-quart (2-L) pot along with the onion and water, place over low heat, and cook until all the fat is rendered and pale gold and the bits of skin and onion are rich mahogany brown, about 2 hours. Throughout the cooking, keep the fat bubbling and stir the mixture often to keep the bits from sticking. Be careful not to let the fat darken.

Strain the schmaltz through a fine-mesh sieve into a glass jar, then drain the gribenes on paper towels. You should have ¾ to 1 cup (180 to 240 ml) schmaltz and a generous 1 cup (120 g) *gribenes* (more of each if using duck trimmings). Tightly cap the schmaltz. Season *gribenes* with salt if desired, place in a paper towel–lined container, and cover tightly. Store schmaltz and *gribenes* in the refrigerator for up to 1 week or in the freezer for up to 2 months.

"INSTANT SCHMALTZ"

Make a pot of chicken soup (page 44), then strain and chill the broth. Remove the hardened layer of fat from the top—voilà, "schmaltz." Although technically not the real thing, and sans *gribenes*, this lovely rendered fat is infused with the flavors of the vegetables you used to make the soup.

Alternatively, roast a chicken, then deglaze the pan. Save the fat you skim off (or that gets left behind) in a fat separator and use to make delicious roasted potatoes.

TEN DELICIOUS THINGS TO DO WITH GRIBENES

1. Use in Rustic Chopped Chicken or Duck Livers (page 35).
2. Add to Rapini and Rice Soup along with poached eggs (page 179).
3. Add to Cabbage, Rice, and Green Garlic Porridge with Meatballs (page 135).
4. Scatter over Sarah's Steamed Potatoes (page 221) that you've cooked in schmaltz.
5. Scatter over Cauliflower "Steaks" with Hawaij and Tahini (page 263).
6. Add to Winter Greens Sauté (page 102).
7. Roast Brussels sprouts with schmaltz, salt, and pepper. Add a handful of *gribenes* to the pan during the last 10 minutes of roasting (see page 137 for how to roast perfect Brussels sprouts).
8. Add to a meat version of Buckwheat, Bow Ties, and Brussels Sprouts (page 137).
9. Add to sautéed green beans.
10. Add to salads—Jewish bacon bits!

PAREVE/VEGAN "SCHMALTZ AND GRIBENES"

MAKES ABOUT 1 CUP (210 G)

Ashkenazic Jews use oil-braised onions in place of schmaltz and *gribenes* to flavor dairy dishes, rice, and noodles, as well as chopped liver. These deeply cooked onions are also delicious stirred into labneh.

Put 3 large onions, finely chopped, in a large skillet, sprinkle with a little black pepper, and cover with about 1 inch (2.5 cm) of vegetable oil. Place over medium-high heat and cook, stirring constantly, until the onions are light golden, 7 to 10 minutes. Reduce the heat to low and cook, stirring frequently, until the onions are brown, 20 to 30 minutes. Strain the onions, reserving the oil. Transfer the onions to a glass container, add enough of the cooking oil to keep them moist, and cover tightly. To use, take a spoonful or two of the onions, as needed, allowing excess oil to drip back into container. The onions will keep in the refrigerator for 1 to 2 months.

September & October

ENDINGS AND BEGINNINGS

The Jewish year begins with an ending, the conclusion of the main growing season. The autumn harvest includes the biblical seven species of Israel named in Deuteronomy 8:8—wheat, barley, and in Mediterranean climates, pomegranates, dates, olives, and the last of the figs and grapes. It's also the season for quince, thought by many to be the biblical fruit in the Garden of Eden. In short, these two months are filled with symbolic foods.

Late summer and early fall are marked by great transition. It is a time of thanksgiving for the bounty of the previous year, hope for a sweet and good year ahead, and a period of reflection and atonement during the ten days between Rosh Hashanah and Yom Kippur, and for some, to the holidays of Sukkot and Simchat Torah that follow. At this point in the year, the annual cycle of reading the Torah ends and begins again.

These two months are a shoulder season, when late-summer tomatoes, summer squash, and eggplants mingle with new-harvest winter squash, dates, and nuts in market stalls and in the kitchen. Because the Jewish year also begins in many parts of the world with the onset of the rainy season after a hot, dry summer, this chapter is filled with dishes that suit our mood as it shifts from outdoors to a more interior life.

September & October

TUNISIAN LEMON RIND SALAD

MAKES ABOUT 2 CUPS (460 G), 6 TO 8 SERVINGS

PAREVE/VEGAN

When life gives you lemons, make lemonade *and* this cooked salted lemon salad. I learned this clever way to repurpose lemon rinds from my Tunisian cousin-by-marriage, Edna Brayer. She begins by blanching the rinds to tenderize them and remove harsh flavors. Be sure to use top-quality organic lemons here; waxed industrial lemons leave a harsh aftertaste even after three blanchings. This dish can be used in place of traditional preserved lemons and is a great accent with grilled chicken and fish and as a condiment on a mezze table. Tunisians are fond of spicy food, and since *harissa* blends vary in heat, use as little or as much as you like.

6 lemons, about 2 pounds

3 tablespoons extra-virgin olive oil

1 tablespoon kosher or sea salt

1 tablespoon minced garlic

1 to 4 teaspoons harissa paste (optional)

Bring a large pot of water to a boil. Juice the lemons and measure out ⅔ cup (165 ml) of juice. Reserve the remaining juice for another use. Place the lemon rinds in a medium pot and add cold water to cover. Bring to a boil, cook for 1 minute, and drain.

Return the lemon rinds to the pot, pour some of the boiling water over the rinds, and repeat the blanching process. Do this step a third time and drain the lemon rinds well and let them cool.

Dice the rinds into ½-inch (12-mm) pieces and place them in a clean pot. Add the lemon juice, olive oil, salt, garlic, and the harissa to taste and place over medium heat. Cook uncovered, stirring occasionally, until thick and creamy looking, about 15 minutes. If it seems too dry, add a little water, possibly ¼ to ½ cup (60 to 120 ml).

Remove from the heat, let cool, and taste and adjust the seasoning with salt, lemon juice, and/or harissa if needed. Serve at room temperature. Store in an airtight container in the refrigerator for up to 5 days.

MATBOUCHA

MAKES ABOUT 2½ CUPS (800 G)

PAREVE/VEGAN

There are almost as many variations of and uses for the spicy tomato jam condiment known as *salade cuite*, or "cooked salad," as there are people in Israel, Morocco, or Tunisia. When my cousin Pazit married Moroccan Israeli soccer hero Avi Gabai, she learned from his sisters how to make all his favorite foods, including this version of *matboucha*. It adds zest to many a dish, including hummus, and is the foundation for that other Israeli-Tunisian-Moroccan favorite, the egg dish *shakshuka* (page 62). Be sure to try it with black-eyed peas (page 51). Sauce tomatoes such as Roma, San Marzano, or Costoluto Genovese work best here. When good fresh tomatoes aren't available, use canned crushed tomatoes instead. This recipe can be easily doubled and freezes well.

2½ pounds (1.2 kg) meaty tomatoes, such as
    Roma, San Marzano, or Costoluto Genovese,
    or 1 can (28 ounces/800 g) crushed
    tomatoes
2 to 4 chiles, such as jalapeño or habanero or a
    mix, 2 to 4 ounces (55 to 115 g) total
8 cloves garlic, minced
1 tablespoon sweet paprika
1½ teaspoons hot paprika, or to taste
¼ cup (2 fl ounces/60 ml) grapeseed or other
    mild oil
Kosher or sea salt
Sugar

To peel the tomatoes, either use a swivel-blade vegetable peeler or immerse them in boiling water and slip off the skins as directed on page 17. If you like, cut the tomatoes in half and squeeze them to remove the seeds. Skip this step if the seeds don't bother you. Chop the tomatoes into ½- to 1-inch (12-mm to 2.5-cm) pieces. You should have 3¼ to 3½ cups (585 to 630 g) altogether. Place them in a wide pot or a deep sauté pan.

Mince the chiles and add them to the pan along with some or all of their seeds for added heat. Add the garlic, stir in the paprika, and pour the oil over all. Start cooking the mixture over medium-high heat, stirring occasionally to prevent sticking. Once the mixture comes to a boil, reduce the heat as necessary to keep it bubbling without burning, and cook until very thick and glossy, about 1 hour. Use a splatter screen to keep your stove clean, if you like.

Remove from the heat and season to taste with salt and sugar, adding about 1 teaspoon of each. Let cool and transfer to 1 or 2 tightly capped jars. The condiment will keep in the refrigerator for up to 1 week and in the freezer for up to 2 months.

SMOKY HARISSA

MAKES 1 CUP (260 G)

PAREVE/VEGAN

As the season for tomatoes and peppers winds down, many farmers dry and smoke the remaining abundance to stretch the season and turn both crops into convenient pantry items to flavor fall and winter foods. Here's a smoky approach to the classic Moroccan and Tunisian spice paste. Dried smoked tomatoes are available at some supermarkets and specialty stores. Chipotle chiles, which are smoke-dried jalapeños, are available at some farmers' markets, supermarkets, and Latin groceries.

4 large or 8 small chipotle chiles

¼ cup (25 g) smoked dried tomatoes

¼ cup (25 g) dry-packed sun-dried tomatoes

½ teaspoon caraway seeds

½ teaspoon cumin seeds

1½ to 3 cups (360 to 720 ml) boiling water

2 large cloves garlic

1 teaspoon salt

1 teaspoon hot paprika or cayenne pepper

¼ cup (60 ml) olive oil

In a medium heatproof bowl, combine the chiles, smoked dried and sun-dried tomatoes, and caraway and cumin seeds. Pour in the boiling water to cover and let stand until the chiles and tomatoes have softened, 30 to 45 minutes. Strain and reserve the soaking liquid.

Cut the tomatoes into small pieces. Remove and discard the stems from the chiles. Cut the chiles into small pieces and reserve as many chile seeds as you like for added heat (harissa is traditionally very spicy).

Fit a food processor with the metal S blade. With the motor running, drop in the garlic to mince. Turn off the processor, add the tomatoes and chiles, the caraway and cumin seeds clinging to the sieve, the salt, and the paprika and pulse until the mixture is finely ground. With the motor running, slowly pour in the olive oil, processing until a thick paste forms. Then add enough of the soaking liquid (about ½ cup/120 ml) to make a thick, smooth puree, stopping to scrape down the sides of the work bowl often.

Transfer to a container. It will keep for a good week or more in the refrigerator and can be frozen up to 1 month.

Rosh Hashanah

HEAD OF THE YEAR

Rosh means "head" in Hebrew, as in important, which indeed this holy day is. Traditionally thought to mark the creation of the world, it begins a ten-day period of introspection about the past year that culminates in the holiest day of the year, Yom Kippur, the Day of Atonement. But Rosh Hashanah doesn't fall on the first day of the first month of the Jewish calendar. It occurs in the *seventh* month, a sort of Sabbath of the year. It's also the beginning of the fall harvest and rainy season. (The first month of the Jewish year is in spring.)

As with new-year traditions in other cultures, Rosh Hashanah comes with a cornucopia of "good luck" foods to symbolize wishes for a sweet year filled with blessings and virtuous deeds. It is customary to begin the year by tasting a "new" food, usually first-of-the-season fruits and vegetables. Such moments of anticipation and gratification have become a way of life for today's local-foods enthusiasts. Isn't it nice to know we are simply returning to an ancient tradition?

Autumn crops such as apples, quinces, pomegranates, winter squashes, dates, winter greens, and root vegetables figure prominently in holiday menus and pre-meal blessings. One of today's most popular customs, dipping apples in honey before the meal, had its beginnings in twelfth-century France. The other widely known tradition, breaking open a pomegranate to share with guests, offers the hope that the new year will be filled with as many good deeds and

blessings as the biblical fruit's multitude of kernels (arils). Pomegranates also symbolize fertility and abundance.

There are also "anti-good-luck" foods. Some people avoid sour foods or black ones (olives, raisins, eggplant, coffee, chocolate), the color of mourning. I leave it to you to decide how much "insurance" you need.

———

A ROSH HASHANAH MEAT MENU

Rustic Chopped Chicken or Duck Livers with Parsley and Celery Salad (page 35)

My Mother's Chicken Soup with Special Noodles (page 44)

Pure and Simple Brisket (page 65)

Roasted Carrot and Sweet Potato Tzimmes (page 47)

Winter Greens Sauté (page 102)

Pomegranate-Orange Gelée with Citrus Salad (page 70)

Aunt Sarah's Honey and Apple Cake (page 77)

A ROSH HASHANAH VEGETARIAN MENU

Sweet Potato and Butternut Squash Mini-Latkes (page 96)

Rapini and Rice Soup (page 179)

Toasted Israeli Couscous in Winter Squash Cases (page 104)

Autumn Slaw with Beets, Carrots, and Kohlrabi (page 41) or Carrot, Date, and Preserved Kumquat Salad (page 129)

Roasted Autumn Fruit (page 68)

Aunt Sarah's Honey and Apple Cake (page 77)

RUSTIC CHOPPED CHICKEN OR DUCK LIVERS
WITH PARSLEY AND CELERY SALAD

MAKES ABOUT 3 CUPS (625 G), 8 TO 10 APPETIZER SERVINGS
OR 6 TO 8 MAIN DISH SERVINGS

MEAT

I could easily devour this rustic, yet sophisticated take on the traditional Ashkenazic starter as my main meal. Divine on toasted marble rye, this spread is best made a day ahead to allow flavors and textures to meld, then reheated to serve. Chicken livers tend to be softer and more susceptible to overcooking than duck livers. When overcooked or steamed from being crowded in too-small a pan, they can turn chalky and bitter. The addition of acid (vinegar) preserves the livers' creamy texture and contrasts well with their richness. If you don't have schmaltz or *gribenes*, make this dish anyway.

1 pound (450 g) chicken or duck livers

2 onions, thinly sliced (3 cups/245 g)

Kosher or sea salt and freshly ground black pepper

5 to 6 tablespoons (75 to 90 g) schmaltz (page 24), rendered fat from chicken soup or roast chicken, or olive oil

About 4 tablespoons (60 ml) sherry vinegar or red wine vinegar

⅓ cup (40 g) gribenes (page 24)

3 tablespoons finely chopped fresh Italian parsley

Rye, pumpernickel, or country bread, toasted or grilled

Parsley and Celery Salad (recipe follows)

Pat the livers very dry, and if you have time, air-dry them in the refrigerator for 1 hour on a paper towel–lined plate or tray. Turn the livers out onto a work surface. You'll notice a prettier "right" side and a less appealing "wrong" side of each liver. Place the livers right side down to expose the connective tissue and vein matter. Remove any bits of fat and vein. If you like, remove the connective tissue that joins the two lobes: Using a paring knife, make a small diagonal cut to free the connective tissue. Then, holding the knife parallel to the work surface, cut across the liver and under the vein, pulling the connective tissue to help remove it as you cut. Or, use kitchen scissors and slip one of the blades under the connective tissue to loosen and pull it up so that you can cut it away.

In a 12- to 14-inch (30.5- to 35.5-cm) skillet, cook the onions with a little salt in 3 tablespoons of the schmaltz over medium-low heat until tender and pale golden, lowering the heat as needed to keep them from browning, about 15 minutes. Transfer the onions to a bowl large enough to hold all the ingredients.

Return the pan to medium heat and add 1 tablespoon of the schmaltz. When the schmaltz sizzles, add one-third to one-half of the livers, right side down, to the pan. Season with salt and pepper and sauté until browned on the first side, about 3 minutes. Turn the livers and cook until they barely reach desired doneness, 1 to 2 minutes for medium and 3 to 4 minutes for medium-well. The timing will depend on the consistency and size of the livers. Using a slotted spoon, add the livers to the onions; the livers will continue to cook from their own heat to reach desired doneness. Repeat with the remaining 1 to 2 tablespoons schmaltz and the livers and transfer the livers to the bowl. Turn off the heat under the pan.

continued »

Add 3 tablespoons of the vinegar to the pan and turn the heat to medium-low. Cook and stir, scraping up any brown bits, until the sharp smell of vinegar has diminished and the liquid has reduced slightly, about 1 minute. Scrape the drippings into the onion-liver mixture.

Add the gribenes to the liver-onion mixture. Using a sharp knife—not a food processor—finely chop the onion-liver mixture. Taste and adjust the seasoning with the remaining 1 tablespoon vinegar and salt and pepper as needed. The dish should be prepared to this point at least several hours or up to 1 day ahead of serving (refrigerate if holding more than 1 hour). When ready to serve, stir in the parsley and reheat over low heat.

To serve, mound about ¼ cup (50 g) chopped livers on each slice of bread and accompany with the salad.

SHOPPING TIP: Buy livers from a butcher or small farmer who raises naturally fed, free-range birds. Chicken livers come in multiple shades from a tawny gold to pinkish to dark reddish brown and from very soft to plump and firm. There many opinions about why the colors vary and which are more desirable. Some believe that the rarer light-colored livers are a sign of a hen's fattier diet and have a creamier texture. My best advice is to look for livers that are intact and have a fresh smell.

KITCHEN NOTE: A *hockmeisser* and a wooden bowl were once the go-to tool kit for chopping. Similar to the two-handled Italian *mezzaluna*, the half-moon shape of the single-hand *hockmeisser* was designed to cut against the curve of the bowl.

PARSLEY AND CELERY SALAD

MAKES 8 SERVINGS

PAREVE/VEGAN

Light and bright green leaves intermingle in a palate-cleansing, refreshing side salad for rich meats, such as the chopped chicken or duck livers, above, and as a refreshing counterpoint to ripe, salty, rich cheeses, such as Saint Agur or Cabrales. This also makes a beautiful first course to a vegetarian or fish dinner.

1 bunch celery
1 bunch Italian parsley
Extra-virgin olive oil
Red wine vinegar
Kosher or finishing salt, such as Maldon sea salt,
    and freshly ground black pepper

Cut the root end off the celery. Pull apart the bunch until you reach the tender, whitish ribs and pale green inner leaves. Use these small ribs and tender leaves first and move to the larger ribs as necessary to achieve the needed measure, removing the strings from the larger ribs with a vegetable peeler before slicing them. Using a sharp knife or a Japanese mandoline, thinly slice the ribs and young leaves on the diagonal until you have 3 cups (300 g). Place the celery in a salad bowl, tearing any large leaves.

Pluck enough parsley leaves to measure 1¼ cups (35 g). Add to the celery, tearing some of the leaves to give textural variety. Toss with 1 to 2 tablespoons olive oil and season to taste with vinegar, salt, and pepper. Allow the salad to stand for 30 minutes and up to 1 hour before serving.

HERRING, POTATOES, AND EGGS

MAKES 8 SERVINGS

FISH

For centuries, herring was one of the most important fish in the regions bordering the North and Baltic Seas. Since the fifteenth century, when the Dutch began salting the oily fish to prevent it from going rancid, herring has been a protein staple throughout central and northern Europe. After being salted, herring is commonly marinated or pickled, and German, Dutch, Scandinavian, Russian, and Polish cuisines—Jewish or not—favor a sweet-and-sour approach to the preserved fish.

Back when all Jewish food stores observed kashrut, Jewish delicatessens sold only meat and pareve products. Cured, smoked, and pickled fish, which could be served with dairy products, were the provenance of another sort of deli, called an "appetizing store" in New York. With the great influx of eastern European Jews to the United States in the late nineteenth and early twentieth centuries, New York could claim an appetizing store in every neighborhood. Most of these shops have disappeared, but two of New York's most famous from that era, Barney Greengrass and Russ & Daughters, continue to thrive, and a new wave of shops is opening, such as Mile End Deli in Brooklyn and Wexler's Deli in Los Angeles, that smoke and hand slice their own fish.

Pickled fish is a classic component of a break-the-fast meal at the conclusion of Yom Kippur. It is especially gorgeous served as a composed salad, accompanied with toasted challah, pumpernickel, or bagels. Use good-quality pickled herring, such as those from Russ & Daughters or the Blue Hill Bay brand marketed by ACME Smoked Fish, or make your own (see page 40). Serve with iced vodka, aquavit, or sake for a terrific "herring pairing," as Russ & Daughters would say.

½ pound (225 g) waxy or all-purpose potatoes, such as Russian Banana, La Ratte, French, or Rose Finn Apple fingerlings or Yukon Gold, boiled

2 hard-boiled eggs, peeled

3 or 4 red radishes, trimmed

1 tart apple, halved and cored

¼ pound (115 g) beets (about 2), roasted, peeled, and cooled

½ pound (225 g) pickled herring

2 tablespoons rice vinegar

Sugar

2 tablespoons chopped fresh chives

Sel gris or kosher salt

Challah, bagels, bagel chips, and/or pumpernickel (fresh or toasted)

FOR A PLATED SALAD: Peel the potatoes if you like and slice them into thin rounds or half-moons; halve small fingerlings. Quarter the eggs lengthwise, thinly slice the radishes and apple, and dice the beets. Arrange these ingredients and the herring on a platter or on individual plates. Be sure to include some of the onions from the herring. Whisk together the vinegar with sugar to taste. Drizzle some or all of the sweetened vinegar over the salad ingredients, then sprinkle with the chives and crush a little sel gris over all. Serve with the breads.

FOR A CHOPPED SALAD: Working with one ingredient at a time, chop the potatoes, eggs, radishes, apple, beets, and herring into ¼- to ½-inch (6- to 12-mm) pieces. At least 30 minutes or up to 3 hours before serving, toss together all the chopped ingredients. In a small bowl, whisk together the vinegar with sugar to taste. If you prefer, hold back the beets and instead scatter them over the salad just before serving to prevent tinting the salad pink. Cover and refrigerate until ready to serve. Taste and add vinegar, sugar, or salt as desired. Serve with the breads.

CURING AND PICKLING YOUR OWN FISH

MAKES 6 SERVINGS

FISH

This little project is fun and not difficult, even when you fillet the fish yourself. Use very fresh, sustainably caught oil-rich fish such as herring, sardines, or mackerel.

FOR THE FISH

1½ pounds (680 g) whole small oily fish
   (about 6 sardines or herrings, about
   4 ounces/115 g each)
2 tablespoons kosher salt

FOR THE PICKLING BRINE

½ cup (120 ml) dry white wine
½ cup (120 ml) distilled white or white wine
   vinegar
¼ cup (50 g) sugar
½ small onion, thinly sliced
1 teaspoon white peppercorns

TO PREPARE THE FISH: Ask your fishmonger to clean and fillet the fish, or do it yourself: Gently scrape the fish from the tail toward the head with the back of a paring knife to remove the scales. Rinse the fish under cool running water to wash away any scales. Insert the knife tip at the tail end of the underside of the fish and cut the fish open up to the head. Use your finger to scoop out and discard the entrails. Rinse the fish thoroughly. Tear off the head by pulling it up toward the backbone of the fish and discard. Flatten the fish, skin side down, on a work surface. Gently run your finger along each side of the backbone to separate the flesh from the bone. Pull the backbone and ribs up from the flesh and toward the tail, then pull or cut off the backbone with the tail attached and discard. Repeat for the remaining fish.

Place 3 butterflied fish, skin side down, in a shallow nonreactive pan or dish (a Pyrex pie plate works well). Sprinkle the salt evenly over the fish. Top with the remaining 3 fillets, skin side up. Cover with plastic wrap. Lay two or three 1-pound (450-g) cans side by side in a 1-gallon (4-L) resealable plastic bag and use as a weight on the covered fish. Refrigerate the fish for 8 to 12 hours. They will feel firm and a little brine will have formed.

TO MAKE THE PICKLING BRINE: In a small pot, mix together the wine, vinegar, sugar, onion, and peppercorns. Place over high heat and bring to a boil, stirring to dissolve the sugar. Remove from the heat and let cool completely.

TO PICKLE THE FISH: Remove the weight and the plastic wrap, then rinse the fillets to remove the excess salt and pat dry. Place in a clean glass or other nonreactive container. Pour the pickling brine over the fish to submerge completely. Cover and refrigerate for 24 hours before serving. (The fish will keep up to 5 days.)

Remove the fish from the brine and cut on the diagonal into thick slices. Scatter the pickled onions over the fish and add a little of the pickling juices, if you like.

AUTUMN SLAW WITH BEETS, CARROTS, AND KOHLRABI

MAKES 8 SERVINGS

PAREVE OR PAREVE/VEGAN

Most Americans don't know what to do with kohlrabi, a Martian spacecraft–lookalike tuber that offers a crisp nutlike flavor reminiscent of water chestnuts. In Israel, it is a popular addition to salads and pickled vegetable mixes. This is my cousin Michal Brayer's favorite salad, and now one of mine, too. This refreshing magenta-and-orange slaw will take you through the fall and winter seasons. Use agave instead of honey for a vegan salad (see photo, page 86).

FOR THE SLAW

½ pound (225 g) carrots (about 3)

½ pound (225 g) kohlrabi (about 1 medium-large)

1 to 2 tart apples, such as Granny Smith, Spitzenberg, or Pink Lady, ½ pound (225 g) total

½ pound (225 g) beets (about 3)

¼ cup (10 g) fresh Italian parsley or celery leaves, torn

FOR THE DRESSING

¼ cup (60 ml) mild oil, such as safflower or grapeseed

1 teaspoon raw or toasted sesame oil

¼ cup (60 ml) fresh lemon juice (from about 1 lemon)

2 teaspoons honey or agave, warmed

Kosher or sea salt and freshly ground black pepper

TO MAKE THE SLAW: Fit a food processor with the grating disk. Peel the carrots and kohlrabi, then grate them in the processor and transfer to a salad bowl. Peel the apples, if desired, then quarter, core, and grate in the processor and add to the bowl. Peel the beets, grate them, and add to the bowl. You can prepare the salad up to this point early in the day, cover, and refrigerate it. In this case, store the beets separately from the other ingredients, and cover the grated apples with the carrots and kohlrabi to keep them from turning brown.

TO MAKE THE DRESSING: In a small bowl, whisk together the vegetable and sesame oils, lemon juice, honey or agave, about 1 teaspoon salt, and several grinds of pepper. Pour over the salad and toss to coat.

Add the parsley leaves to the salad and toss again. This sturdy salad will stay fresh at room temperature for up to 3 hours, and the leftovers are delicious the next day.

SHOPPING TIP: Look for juicy-looking carrots, beets, and kohlrabi. The moisture factor is more important than their size, especially when you want to use them raw.

ARUGULA WITH FRESH GOLDEN BARHI DATES, DRIED APRICOTS, NECTARINES, AND SUMAC

MAKES 8 SERVINGS

PAREVE/VEGAN

In date-growing regions, the harvest begins in late summer or early autumn. Barhi dates are the first variety to be brought to market, still on the stem, a beautiful shade of soft gold, and crisp (see photo, page 29). Their flavor hovers between sweet and astringent. Golden Barhis, known as "fresh" or *khalal*, the second of four stages of ripeness, are lovely with late-season nectarines or mangoes in a distinctive early autumn salad. Any astringency in the fresh dates is tamed by the use of orange juice, sweet nut oil, and tart sumac in the dressing. Fresh Barhi dates are available at Middle Eastern markets, California farmers' markets, and by mail order for a few brief weeks in the fall. They are a rare treat, but now you know what to do with them. The basic structure of this salad lends itself to many seasonal combinations of dried and fresh fruits. Try Fuyu persimmons and pears in place of the dates and nectarines and contrast their sweetness with additional tart dried fruits and early mandarins.

½ pound (225 g) crisp golden Barhi dates
    (about 16)
½ cup (55 to 85 g) moist dried apricots
    (about 16; 2 to 3 ounces)
2 ripe nectarines or juicy pears, about ½ pound
    (225 g) total
½ pound (225 g) arugula
1 to 2 tablespoons nut oil, such as walnut,
    pecan, almond, or pistachio
1 Valencia orange
Finishing salt, such as fleur de sel or
    Maldon sea salt
Ground sumac

Cut the dates in half lengthwise and remove the pits, then cut each half into thin crescents and place in a salad bowl. Use kitchen scissors to snip apricots into strips and add to the bowl. Halve the nectarines or pears and pit the nectarines or core the pears. Cut into thin crescents and add to the bowl along with the arugula.

Drizzle the oil to taste over the salad and toss lightly. Using a five-hole zester, and working over the salad bowl, remove the zest from the orange in long strands, getting both the zest and the spray of citrus oils into the bowl. Give the salad a healthy squeeze of orange juice and season to taste with salt and sumac. Toss the salad and sprinkle with additional sumac for color and added tartness.

KITCHEN NOTE: To quickly ripen khalal-stage Barhi dates for another use, freeze them for at least 24 hours. When thawed, they will have turned light brown and have become soft and sweet. This is the same freezing technique that works with astringent Hachiya persimmons, the oblong variety that must be meltingly ripe to be eaten.

> ### THE LIFE OF A DATE IN FOUR STAGES
>
> **KIMRI** unripe, green
>
> **KHALAL** fresh, crisp, golden
>
> **RUTAB** moist, sweet, very ripe, and brown
>
> **TAMAR** (literally "date" in Hebrew and Arabic) sweet, chewy, and dried

MY MOTHER'S CHICKEN SOUP

MAKES 9 TO 10 CUPS (2 TO 2.5 L)

MEAT

My mother Serilla, an artist and scholar, didn't know how to boil the proverbial pot of water, let alone make a delicious chicken soup, when she married my father, Ben, and moved from Israel to California. The youngest of four girls, she had had no need to learn to cook. Her older sisters helped their mother, while my mother roamed the house, reading.

But, as is so often the case in the Diaspora, food memories proved a powerful teacher. My mother never attempted the exquisite baking that her mother, Mina, and sister, Sarah, managed on the family's meager income, but she did remember how certain dishes tasted—chopped liver, braised chicken, fire-roasted eggplant, calf's brains, a good hummus, and chicken soup—and recaptured the flavors of her childhood for us.

Recently, my mother switched to kosher chicken parts for her soup, not because my parents are observant, but because the brined flavors remind her more of her own mother's soup. I prefer to use chickens from small local producers, removing the breast meat from two or three birds for another use and making soup from the bony parts and dark meat. Either way, this soup is a rich gold, infused with the many vegetables my mother likes to use.

It is also quite refined in its way. My mother strains it through cheesecloth to yield a beautifully clear broth. Her system involves three bowls and sieves, but after trying her method, I have to agree, it is genius.

My mother usually simmers cooked fine egg noodles, matzah balls (page 178), or our family's "special noodles" in the broth to soak up its flavor. But on Rosh Hashanah, she likes to add immature chicken eggs to the soup (the Jewish New Year is also considered the anniversary of Creation). These unhatched eggs (basically the yolks, before the albumen and shell have formed) are sometimes found inside a slaughtered hen. They come in varying sizes, from pea size to a more common yolk size and are often still strung together like pearls. When cooked, their texture is creamier, and the flavor more intensely eggy than the mature yolks we are used to eating. Once commonly available at supermarkets, they are now found at kosher, Italian, and Asian markets or butcher shops.

5 pounds (2.3 kg) chicken (from 2 whole chickens,
 or from one 4-pound/1.8 kg chicken, cut up, plus
 3 pounds/1.4 kg thighs, drumsticks, and wings)

2 onions, about 1 pound (450 g) total, peeled

1 leek, split lengthwise, then cut crosswise into large
 pieces (about 2 cups/200 g)

3 large carrots, ¾ pound (340 g) total, peeled

3 ribs celery with leaves, about 6 ounces (170 g) total

1 parsley root, peeled

1 parsnip, peeled

½-pound (225-g) piece winter squash, peeled and
 cut into large chunks, or ½ pound (225 g) yellow
 zucchini or crookneck squashes

½ to 1 bunch Italian parsley, about 3 ounces (85 g)

A few dill sprigs (optional)

Kosher or sea salt

Pat the chicken dry. Trim off any excess fat and skin and freeze for making schmaltz and gribenes later (page 24). Cut the whole chicken(s) into quarters, remove the breast meat from the bones, set the bones aside for the broth, and reserve the meat for another use. (You can also remove skin from breast meat to use for schmaltz and gribenes.)

Place the chicken pieces and bones in an 8-quart (8-L) pot and pour in water to cover the chicken (about 3 quarts/3 L). Cover the pot partially and bring to a simmer over medium heat, skimming off any foam that bubbles up to the surface. Do not bring the water to a true boil or the soup will end up cloudy. Adjust the heat as necessary to maintain a simmer.

When no more foam appears, add the onions, leek, carrots, celery, parsley root, parsnip, and squash, pushing them down into the liquid as best you can. Don't worry if they are half out of the water; they will reduce in volume as the soup cooks. Adjust the heat to keep the soup at the gentlest simmer; you should see bubbles occasionally rise at the edges of the pot. Cook, uncovered, until the soup is golden and the vegetables and chicken are extremely tender, about 3 hours is ideal, adding the parsley and dill during last 15 minutes of cooking.

Turn off the heat and let the soup stand until just cool enough to handle. Place a sieve over a medium bowl and transfer the vegetables to the sieve. Place a large sieve or colander over a large bowl and transfer the chicken to this sieve. Line a third sieve with a double layer of cheesecloth or a large coffee filter and set over a large bowl. Ladle the soup from the pot through the cheesecloth-lined sieve, then pour any soup that collects in the other 2 bowls through the cheesecloth. Finally, squeeze the cheesecloth to extract any soup. You should have 9 to 10 cups (2 to 2.5 L) soup. Discard the chicken and vegetables, or save any good bits for garnishing the soup later.

Season the soup with salt. If serving the soup immediately, use a large spoon to skim off the fat from the surface, then reheat the soup to serving temperature. If not using immediately, let cool completely, cover, and refrigerate until well chilled, then lift off the congealed fat. You may use this flavorful fat for cooking or for matzah balls (page 178). The soup can be refrigerated in an airtight container for up to 4 days or frozen for up to 3 months.

SPECIAL NOODLES

Call this Jewish egg drop soup: lightly whisked eggs thickened with wheat or rice flour to give the "noodles" a more substantial, yet still delicate quality. I watched my mother make these noodles, and my three children in turn learned by watching me. The success is all in the wrist.

To make enough for 4 servings, lightly whisk 2 eggs with a fork until barely blended, then stir enough flour into the eggs until the mixture reaches the consistency of heavy cream with lots of little lumps. Drop batter by the forkful into 4 cups (960 ml) simmering chicken soup and simmer until cooked through, about 2 minutes. You'll have a raft of fluffy noodles enriched with the flavors of your soup.

ROASTED CARROT AND SWEET POTATO TZIMMES

MAKES 8 TO 10 SERVINGS

PAREVE/VEGAN

Tzimmes is an eastern European stew of carrots and/or sweet potatoes and prunes traditionally cooked with beef flanken, often sweetened with brown or white sugar, and sometimes thickened with flour. In Yiddish, the word *tzimmes* means "a big fuss," probably because of all the work required to make the old-style dish. This version couldn't be easier: Skip the meat, sugar, and flour and instead roast carrots, sweet potatoes, and dried Santa Rosa–type plums (or common dried prunes) in fresh orange juice until they are tender, browned, glazed with citrus, and deliciously infused with orange. Tzimmes is a great companion to brisket or chicken and is also a good accompaniment to farro or quinoa for a pareve/vegan main course. It can easily be made a day ahead and reheated and is often served in the fall for Rosh Hashanah and in the spring for Passover. It is also a lovely addition to any festive meal during these times of the year. Both seasons yield sweet carrots, especially in the spring. In the fall, use new-season white- or orange-fleshed sweet potatoes.

6 to 8 oranges
1 lemon
2 pounds (900 g) carrots
3 pounds (1.4 kg) sweet potatoes
1 pound (450 g) shallots (about 8 large)
½ to ¾ pound (225 to 340 g) dried plums or
    pitted prunes (vary the amount depending on
    how sweet and fruity you want the dish)
3 to 4 tablespoons extra-virgin olive oil
Kosher or sea salt and freshly ground white or
    black pepper

Preheat the oven to 400°F (200°C). Using a swivel-blade vegetable peeler, remove the zest in large strips from 2 of the oranges and the lemon. Be sure to press down only hard enough to capture the colored part of the skin, not the bitter white pith. Juice enough oranges to yield 2½ cups (600 ml) juice. Reserve the lemon for another use.

Peel the carrots and cut them crosswise into 2-inch (5-cm) chunks or lengthwise into 2-inch (5-cm) chunks (if carrots are very fat, first halve them lengthwise). Peel and cut the sweet potatoes into large bite-size chunks. Peel and quarter the shallots lengthwise. Use kitchen scissors to snip the dried fruits in half.

Use a roasting pan large enough to hold all the vegetables in more or less a single layer. Place carrots, sweet potatoes, shallots, dried fruit, and lemon and orange zests in the pan. Toss with enough olive oil to coat evenly, season with salt and pepper, and pour the juice over all.

Roast the vegetables, turning them once or twice during cooking, until they are tender and are browned in places and most of the juice is absorbed, about 1¼ hours. If you want a saucier finished dish, add another ½ to 1 cup (120 to 240 ml) juice during the last 20 minutes of cooking. The juice should thicken slightly. Serve warm or at room temperature.

GVETCH: ROASTED ROMANIAN RATATOUILLE

MAKES 10 TO 12 SERVINGS

PAREVE/VEGAN

Every Mediterranean-influenced cuisine embraces the magical late-summer marriage of tomatoes, eggplants, peppers, and squash—ratatouille, caponata, and now *gvetch*, the Romanian entry. Although Romania is most often associated with its Slavic neighbors, it was once part of the Ottoman Empire, and its cuisine has a distinct eastern Mediterranean quality to it. There are endless *gvetch* variations, some with meat and others with a dozen different vegetables. My family has always stuck to the classic Provençal ingredients. Paprika is a Romanian note; the cumin may have found its way into the dish during my family's three generations in melting-pot Israel.

My aunt Sarah taught me her easy stove-top *gvetch*; I like my oven variation even better. Roasting the vegetables concentrates their flavors and reduces the juices to a thick, caramelized sauce. Use meaty Roma tomatoes or another Italian sauce variety, such as Costoluto Genovese, for the best results. Ten minutes of active work yields a big batch you can use in a multitude of ways. And, its flavors improve over a few days.

2 pounds (900 g) fleshy sauce tomatoes, such as
    Roma or Costoluto Genovese

4 to 6 medium-size green or white (Lebanese)
    zucchini or marrow squash, about 1½ pounds
    (680 g) total

2 medium eggplants, about 1½ pounds (680 g) total

3 or 4 sweet red peppers

1 or 2 onions, peeled

6 to 8 large garlic cloves, peeled

1 tablespoon sweet or hot paprika, or a mix

¼ teaspoon ground cumin

2 bay leaves

Extra-virgin olive oil

Kosher or sea salt and freshly ground black pepper

Preheat the oven to 400°F (200°C).

Roughly chop the tomatoes, zucchini, eggplants, sweet peppers, and onions into about 1-inch (2.5-cm) pieces. Transfer the vegetables to a large roasting pan (about 12 x 15 inches/30.5 by 38 cm) along with the garlic cloves, paprika, cumin, bay leaves, a good glug of olive oil (3 to 4 tablespoons), about 2 teaspoons salt, and several grinds of pepper. Toss to mix, then spread the mixture in a even layer in the pan. It should be about 2 inches (5 cm) deep.

Roast without stirring until the vegetables are very tender and browned in places and the tomatoes have melted into a thick sauce, about 1 hour. Serve warm or at room temperature.

FIVE SMART THINGS TO DO WITH LEFTOVER GVETCH

1. Stuff into pita with sliced hard-boiled egg; top with Fresh Chile Oil (page 281).

2. Chop or pulse it finely and use as a filling in a bialy (*pletzel*) sandwich with cheese, pickles, tomatoes, and cucumbers, as Delicatessen Sacha Finkelsztajn in the Marais—the Jewish quarter of Paris—does, or with leftover brisket.

3. Turn it into a *pashtida*: Use 3 cups (500 g) gvetch for 1 pound (450 g) pasta. Toss with kashkaval cheese, olive oil, and some of the pasta cooking water and bake.

4. Fold into an omelet, with cheese.

5. Turn it into a spread: Chop or pulse in a food processor with capers, olives, a bit of red wine vinegar, and minced fresh chile or red pepper flakes to taste. Cook over medium heat until very thick.

SUMMER SQUASH LATKES
WITH LABNEH, SUMAC, AND THYME

MAKES ABOUT 30 LATKES, 8 SERVINGS

DAIRY

Most people think of latkes only for Hanukkah and made only with potatoes, but the basic ratio of 1 egg to 2 cups shredded vegetables works throughout the year, especially during zucchini season. Serve these pancakes as a late-summer or early-fall vegetarian main course or as a starter for a fish dinner. Stuff leftover latkes, *labneh*, and chopped tomato into pita for a delicious lunch the next day. You can skip the *labneh* for a neutral, nondairy dish. This recipe may be easily multiplied. See *The Art of Perfect Latkes*, page 97, for cooking tips.

2 pounds (900 g) green or white (Lebanese) zucchini or marrow squash

2 teaspoons kosher or sea salt

½ onion

1 large clove garlic

6 tablespoons (47 g) unbleached all-purpose flour or (55 g) potato starch

1 tablespoon chopped fresh thyme, plus more for finishing

3 teaspoons ground sumac

2 eggs, lightly beaten

Mild oil with a medium-high smoke point, such as grapeseed or avocado

1 teaspoon finishing salt, such as fleur de sel or Maldon sea salt

1 cup (225 g) labneh, homemade (page 22) or store-bought, or Shanklish (page 101)

Using large holes of a box grater or a food processor fitted with the grating disk, grate the zucchini. Place in a colander set over a bowl, toss with 1 teaspoon of the kosher salt, and let stand for 30 minutes to drain. In batches, place the zucchini in a dish towel and wring dry to remove all liquid. (This step can be done up to 1 day ahead and then the zucchini can be covered and refrigerated.) Grate the onion on the large holes of the box grater and mince the garlic, or push the onion and garlic clove through the feed tube of the processor to grate.

In a large bowl, toss together the zucchini, onion, garlic, flour, thyme, 2 teaspoons of the sumac, and the remaining 1 teaspoon kosher salt. Stir in the eggs. The batter can be made up to 1 hour ahead and held at room temperature.

Line 2 or 3 sheet pans with paper towels. Place the prepared pans, the latke batter, a large spoon, and a spatula near the stove. Heat 1 or 2 large skillets over medium heat. Generously film the skillet(s) with oil (not more than ¼ inch/6 mm deep). When the oil is shimmering (a tiny bit of batter dropped into it should sizzle on contact), start spooning in the latke batter, making sure to add both solids and liquid. Flatten each spoonful with the back of the spoon into a circle 3 inches (7.5 cm) in diameter. Do not crowd the latkes in the pan(s). You'll get 4 or 5 pancakes in a 12-inch (30.5-cm) skillet.

Cook the latkes, flipping them once, until golden on both sides, 5 to 6 minutes total. Transfer the latkes to a prepared sheet pan. Cook the remaining batter in the same way, stirring the batter before adding more to the pan. Add more oil to the pan as needed to prevent sticking, and from time to time, remove and discard any little brown bits that accumulate in the pan as you cook.

In a small bowl, stir together the finishing salt and the remaining 1 teaspoon sumac. Serve the latkes hot, each one topped with a dollop of labneh and sprinkled with the salt-sumac mixture and thyme.

FRESH BLACK-EYED PEAS AND MATBOUCHA

MAKES 8 SERVINGS

PAREVE/VEGAN

Fresh shell beans of all sorts show up in late summer and early fall, looking like a jeweler's workbox full of gems. I'm especially fond of the flavor and creamy texture of fresh black- and pink-eyed peas. Simmer them in spicy *matboucha* and serve them over rice for a sort of Tunisian-Moroccan-Louisianan version of Jewish comfort food. Romano and Chinese long beans cut crosswise into pea-size bits are also delicious here. I've used vegetable stock in the recipe, but meat stock or water also works well.

2½ cups (800 g) Matboucha (page 32)

1 to 2 cups (240 to 480 ml) homemade vegetable stock (page 92) or canned

2 pounds (900 g) fresh black- or pink-eyed peas in the pod, shelled (about 4 cups/600 g)

2 tablespoons chopped fresh cilantro

Kosher or sea salt

Basic White Rice (page 21) for serving

In a wide pot, stir together the matboucha and 1 cup (240 ml) of the stock and bring to a simmer over medium heat. Add the peas, cover, reduce the heat to medium-low or low, and simmer gently until the beans are tender and the sauce has increased in volume, about 25 minutes. There should be ample sauce. Stir in the remaining 1 cup (240 ml) stock if needed.

Stir in the cilantro and season with salt. (At this point, the dish can be cooled, covered, and refrigerated for up to 1 day, then reheated over low heat.) Serve over rice.

TO MAKE THIS DISH WITH DRIED BEANS: If the beans are not current crop, soak them as directed in How to Cook Dried Beans on page 18, then cook them in water until tender, about 45 minutes. Drain, saving the cooking liquid to enrich the sauce, and begin the recipe.

SHOPPING TIP: Look for bean pods that are still greenish but starting to become yellow and dry. The peas inside should range from a glossy pale green to cream color and have the familiar "black eye." Dark green pods are more difficult to open and the peas are often too tiny. Fully brown dry pods contain the more familiar matte-beige mature bean, which has a hearty texture and flavor.

Yom Kippur

FOOD TRADITIONS

Yom Kippur may be a day of fasting and repentance, but you must eat before and after. In fact, it's considered a bigger *mitzvah* (good deed) to feast before Yom Kippur than to fast for the entire day. Sure enough, there are delicious traditions to guide us. Pre-fast meals focus on protein foods, such as chicken and chicken soup, to sustain you through the 25-hour fast. Spicy, salty, overly sweet, or fried foods that stimulate the appetite or make you thirsty are avoided, as are nuts and legumes.

Break-the-fast meals, on the other hand, are designed to restore. Sephardim often use tart flavors to reawaken the appetite: lemonade; lemon-accented dipping sauces, soups, fish, and meat; or yogurt-and-cucumber-based dishes such as Greek *tzatziki* and Bulgarian *tarator*. European-style break-the-fast menus most often resemble a dairy brunch buffet that is easy to prepare ahead: bagels, cream cheese, smoked or pickled fish to replenish minerals lost during fasting, egg salads, blintzes, kugels, and sweets.

PRE-FAST RECIPE SUGGESTIONS

Hamut: Syrian Lemon Chicken Fricassee (page 53)

Raquel's Rice and Fideo (page 54)

Oven-Braised Romanian Chicken (page 189)

Aunt Sarah's Steamed Potatoes (page 221)

BREAK-THE-FAST RECIPE SUGGESTIONS

Herring, Potatoes, and Eggs (page 38)

"Manta Ray" Ceviche (page 212)

Safta Rachel's Sesame Seed Bageleh (page 85)

Arugula with Fresh Golden Barhi Dates, Nectarines, Dried Apricots, and Sumac (page 42)

Tomato-Braised Romano Beans and Salt Cod (page 61)

Cheese Blintz Soufflé (page 233)

Cozonac: A Simple Sweet Yeast Cake (page 113)

Tahini Butter Cookies (page 149)

Poppy Seed Shortbread Cookies (page 290)

HAMUT: SYRIAN LEMON CHICKEN FRICASSEE

MAKES 6 TO 8 SERVINGS

MEAT

There are many versions of *hamut* (pronounced the Arabic way, with the accent on the first syllable), even some without chicken, but none that I've seen without the defining flavor of lemon. This is the way the Weiser family makes it for Shabbat. Eighty-two-year-old Raquel Weiser, matriarch of Weiser Family Farms in Tehachapi, California, was born and raised in Mexico City's large Jewish community, where her Syrian-born parents had fled after the fall of the Ottoman Empire. Ninety-year-old farm patriarch Sid Weiser grew up in Boyle Heights, Los Angeles's first Jewish community, and was swept away by the diminutive blue-eyed Aleppine beauty on a visit to Mexico. The couple settled in the Los Angeles area, where they raised three children. Raquel cooked a mix of Syrian, Mexican, and American foods, and Sid taught chemistry until the family could realize its dream of starting a farm (today, their youngest son, Alex, is the farm's creative force). Like the busy farmer's wife that she still is, Raquel often cooks *hamut* as you would a chicken soup—everything thrown together in one pot and left to simmer. She confesses that her mother took more care, cooking the dish in stages, as I've done here. Serve the fricassee with Raquel's favorite rice (recipe follows).

6 whole chicken legs (thigh and drumstick), about 3 pounds (1.4 kg) total
Kosher or sea salt and freshly ground black pepper
2 tablespoons extra-virgin olive oil
1 onion, chopped
2 cups (245 g) sliced carrots
2 cups (200 g) chopped celery ribs and leaves
3 cloves garlic, minced
4 tablespoons (25 g) fresh mint leaves, finely chopped

¾ cup (180 ml) fresh lemon juice (from 3 to 4 lemons)
1 pound (450 g) meaty sauce tomatoes, such as Roma, San Marzano, or Costoluto Genovese, peeled (see page 17) and diced, or 1 can (8 ounces/225 g) tomato sauce
1 cup (240 ml) water or chicken stock
1 small potato, peeled and grated, if needed
Raquel's Rice and Fideo (recipe follows), Basic White Rice (page 21), quinoa, or other grain for serving

Pat the chicken dry and season with salt and pepper. In a wide pot, heat the olive oil over medium-high heat. Working in batches if necessary to avoid crowding, add the chicken pieces and brown, turning as needed, until golden brown on all sides, 10 to 12 minutes. Transfer the chicken to a plate.

Pour off all but 2 tablespoons of the fat from the pot, reduce the heat to medium, and add the onion, carrots, celery, and about ½ teaspoon salt. Stir well, scraping the pan bottom to loosen the brown bits, and cook, stirring occasionally, until the onion is translucent and soft and the carrots and celery are bright in color and beginning to get tender, 7 to 10 minutes. Add the garlic and 1 tablespoon of the chopped mint, stir, and cook 1 minute more, being careful not to let the garlic brown. Remove from the heat.

Using a Microplane grater, and working over the pot, grate the zest from 2 of the lemons, capturing both the zest and the spray of citrus oils in the pot. Juice enough lemons to yield ¾ cup (180 ml) juice. Add ½ cup (120 ml) of the juice, tomatoes, and water to the pot, return to medium heat, and cook until liquid is reduced by one third, about 5 minutes. Return the chicken to the pot and spoon some of the liquid over it. Cover the pot, reduce the heat to

continued »

low, and simmer, basting the chicken occasionally with the liquid, until the chicken is very tender, about 45 minutes. The chicken should always be half submerged in the sauce as it cooks. Sauce develops as the dish cooks, so you may not need additional liquid, but add a little water or stock if needed.

Uncover the pot during the last 10 minutes of cooking to thicken the liquid. At this point, taste the sauce. It should be very lemony. Add more lemon juice as needed,

along with the remaining 3 tablespoons mint. If the sauce seems too thin, add the potato and cook until the potato dissolves and the sauce is thick, about 10 minutes. This dish can be made a day ahead, cooled, covered, and refrigerated. Reheat on the stove top or in an uncovered pan in a 425°F/220°C oven. Add the last 3 tablespoons ot mint after reheating.

Serve the hamut in shallow bowls with Raquel's Rice and Fideo or other grain.

RAQUEL'S RICE AND FIDEO

MAKES 8 SERVINGS

MEAT

Syria and Mexico are both rice cultures, and Raquel's favorite rice always includes thin noodles toasted to a golden brown. If that sounds like Rice-A-Roni, it's because the popular packaged mix was inspired by a traditional rice dish that originated in the Balkans. Raquel sometimes includes a few cooked lentils, which look like little coins, for prosperity. You may use *fideo*, traditional coiled egg noodle nests, or short fine egg noodles.

1 tablespoon mild oil, such as sunflower, safflower, or grapeseed

2 fideo nests, or ⅓ cup (15 g) short fine egg noodles

2 cups (370 g) long-grain white rice, picked over and rinsed

3 cups (720 ml) hot water, or 1½ cups (360 ml) each chicken stock and water

1 teaspoon kosher or sea salt

¼ cup (50 g) drained cooked green lentils (optional)

Have all the ingredients nearby. In a wide pot, heat the oil over medium heat. Break the fideo nests into the pot, or add the noodles, and cook, stirring frequently, until golden, about 2 minutes. Add the rice and stir until the grains have whitened, 1 to 2 minutes. Add the water and salt and bring to a boil. Reduce the heat to low, cover, and cook, stirring once about halfway through the cooking, until the rice is tender and all the liquid has been absorbed, about 15 minutes. Add the lentils, if using, during last the few minutes of cooking.

MEAT-AND-RICE-STUFFED SUMMER SQUASH

MAKES 8 SERVINGS

MEAT

Stuffed foods are typical Sukkot fare to celebrate the abundance of a fall harvest, and stuffed vegetables are an art form in traditional eastern Mediterranean cooking. The tinier the vegetable and the more intricate the process, the better. There's even a vegetable drill that makes coring a snap. To bring this classic fully up-to-date, pre-roast unfilled squashes to develop their sugars and then roast the stuffed squashes, instead of stewing them. Plan on ¼ to ½ cup (55 to 115 g) filling per squash; you may have extra filling left over. Choose shiny, firm, small-to-medium squash for this dish. Skip overgrown, woody ones that could feed an army. Small eggplants are also delicious prepared this way.

8 to 12 medium-size round summer squash,
  such as Ronde de Nice, 8-Ball, or Cannonball,
  6 to 8 ounces (170 to 225 g) each (about 3½
  pounds/1.6 kg total)
Extra-virgin olive oil
Kosher or sea salt and freshly ground black
  pepper
1 pound (450 g) ground beef or lamb
1 small onion, chopped
1 clove garlic, minced
1 pound (450 g) meaty sauce tomatoes, such as
  Roma, San Marzano, or Costoluto Genovese,
  peeled (see page 17) and chopped
2 cups (315 g) cooked rice
2 tablespoons chopped fresh Italian basil or
  Italian parsley leaves
2 teaspoons ras el hanout

TO PREPARE THE SQUASHES: Preheat the oven to 425°F (220°C). Cut the stem end off each squash where the squash starts to widen. Reserve these "caps." Using a paring knife and a small pointed spoon (a grapefruit spoon works well), scoop out the flesh from each squash, leaving a shell ¼ inch (6 mm) thick. Or, use a vegetable drill (page 20) to hollow them out. Finely chop the scooped-out flesh and reserve. (This step can be done several hours ahead.)

Brush the squash cases and caps, inside and out, with olive oil and season with salt. Place cases and caps, cut side down, on a sheet pan without crowding. Roast until just tender and the cut edges are browned, 15 to 18 minutes. Lift the edge with a spatula or pancake turner to check doneness. Turn the squash cut side up to cool while you make the filling. (This step can be done a couple of hours ahead and the squash kept at room temperature.) Reduce the oven temperature to 375°F (190°C).

TO MAKE THE FILLING: Place a large skillet over medium-high heat. Add the meat, season with a little salt and pepper, and cook, breaking it up with a large slotted spoon, until browned, 5 to 7 minutes. Using the slotted spoon, transfer the meat to a bowl.

Pour off all but 1 tablespoon of fat from the pan and return to medium heat. Add the onion and a little salt and cook, stirring occasionally, until the onion is soft and translucent, 5 to 7 minutes. Stir in the garlic and cook for 1 minute. Stir in the chopped squash and half the tomatoes and cook, stirring often, until the squash is tender and the vegetable juices have thickened, 5 to 10 minutes. Return the meat to the pan and add the rice, basil, and ras el hanout. Stir to mix well, then taste and

continued »

add salt and pepper as needed. You should have 5 to 6 cups (1.1 to 1.4 kg) filling. (The filling can be made several hours ahead and refrigerated.)

TO ASSEMBLE THE DISH: Oil a heavy, shallow baking pan or enameled cast-iron skillet. Scatter the remaining chopped tomato over the bottom of the pan. Fill each squash with the filling, mounding it to extend above the case. Place filled squashes, cut side up and close together, in the pan and top each squash with its cap.

Bake the squash until they are very tender, the exposed filling is browned in places, and the tomatoes on the bottom of the pan have melted into a small amount of thick sauce, 25 to 30 minutes. Serve warm from the oven.

PAREVE/VEGAN VARIATION: Omit the meat and ras el hanout. Double the amount of rice and basil and add ½ pound (225 g) mushrooms, chopped, to the pan after the onion is soft. Stir in a handful of pine nuts near the end of the cooking time.

DAIRY VARIATION: Stir ½ cup (50 g) grated Parmigiano-Reggiano cheese or aged sheep's milk cheese, such as kashkaval, into the pareve variation (above), and sprinkle the filled squash with additional cheese before baking.

Sukkot

DINING UNDER THE STARS

Sukkot is a joyous thanksgiving for the autumn "ingathering of the fields" (Exodus 23:14–16). The weeklong holiday is celebrated by building and spending time in outdoor huts to commemorate the Israelites' living in makeshift structures during the Exodus from Egypt and to honor the simple shacks in which farmers camped during harvest time.

Today, Sukkot is more like "glamping." Decorated with autumn fruit, gourds, and vegetables, the *sukkah* (hut) is where everyone gathers for evenings (and sometimes nights) of storytelling, wine, and food (in particular, stuffed vegetables, dumplings, and pastries to connote abundance). The night sky is visible through a loosely thatched roof, often made of palm fronds, to recall how the stars would appear if you were standing in a date garden looking up. At the very least, Sukkot is an opportunity to enjoy the last mild evenings before colder weather sets in.

But, of course, it's more. Sukkot is one of the three agriculturally significant festivals first mandated in Exodus (the others are Passover and Shavuot). It's a time to welcome strangers and the poor to share in an abundant harvest, symbolically represented by the *lulav* (fronds and branches of palm, myrtle, and willow woven together) and the fragrant *etrog* (citron). And it's a time to read Ecclesiastes and remember the cyclical nature of things.

RECIPE SUGGESTIONS
FOR SUKKOT
THAT MOVE EASILY
FROM KITCHEN TO OUTDOORS

Meat-and-Rice-Stuffed Summer Squash
(page 57)

Toasted Israeli Couscous in
Winter Squash Cases (page 104)

Autumn Slaw with Beets, Carrots, and
Kohlrabi (page 41)

Roasted Carrot and Sweet Potato Tzimmes
(page 47)

Apples in Nightgowns (page 115)

Aunt Sarah's Honey and Apple Cake
(page 77)

Spiced Date and Walnut Oatmeal Cake
(page 153)

Simchat Torah

Sukkot is immediately followed by Simchat Torah, the jubilant conclusion of the yearlong reading of the Torah. The last passages of Deuteronomy are read, the Torah is rewound, and the opening verses of Genesis are read to begin the cycle anew. It's one of my favorite holidays: a celebration of books and learning, with music, dancing, and throwing back vodka shots to mark the end of the holiday season. What's not to like?

THE ETROG: A VERY PARTICULAR CITRON

The etrog, Hebrew for citron and the name of this variety, is the most prized of the four plant species used to celebrate Sukkot. Looking much like a large, lumpy yellow-green lemon, the citron's defining significance is its intoxicating fragrance with hints of violet that can fill a room for weeks.

The word etrog doesn't appear in the Bible, but the citron has long been thought to be the fruit specified in the description of Sukkot in Leviticus. Precisely when and where the ancient fruit native to the Himalayan foothills became known to Jews is up for debate—thirteenth century BCE Egypt, sixth century BCE Babylonia, or perhaps during the time of Alexander the Great, around 300 BCE—but it was certainly symbolically important by the time of Judah and the Maccabees around 160 BCE.

As Jews were displaced westward, they carried their citron trees with them in a sort of agricultural diaspora. In fact, for several hundred years after the fall of the Roman Empire, citrus farming in southern Italy and Greece was predominantly a Jewish endeavor. Purely culinary use, candied citron and so on, came later with the arrival of sugarcane.

Citrons aren't easy to grow. The plants are frost intolerant, require a lot of water, and have a weak root system and short life span. When the Jewish population pushed into eastern and central Europe, the etrog became even more precious, since the Ashkenazim had to import them at great expense—without refrigeration—often sharing one citron per community.

As prices rose, the physical attributes of the etrog became ever more obsessively important to discriminating shoppers, who were meticulous in their observance of this Jewish law. The perfect citron must be grown in an orchard protected from sand, wind, sunburn, and insects. It must be utterly unblemished and at least twice the size of a chicken egg, but able to fit comfortably in a man's hand. There must be a bit of stem at one end, and the remaining nubbin of blossom, the pitom, at the other (unless it fell off while the fruit was on the tree, in which case, it's okay). A number of citron varieties are allowed,; some are long and slender, others lemon shaped, and still others nipped in at the waist. The beautiful Buddha's hand fingered citron doesn't qualify (although the Jews of Shanghai found a workaround when that was all that was available to them after World War II).

Such an enterprise was bound to give rise to secrecy, intrigue, and scandal. Even today, precise locations of orchards that produce Sukkot-worthy fruits are kept under wraps. Most ritual citrons are grown in Italy, Israel, and Morocco. John Kirkpatrick is the largest producer in the United States; only a quarter of the twelve thousand or so citrons he grows on fifty acres (twenty hectares) in California's Central Valley under rabbinical supervision qualify for use by observant Jews, and some of the etrogim command astronomical prices. Much of the remaining crop is sold to distilleries to produce citron-infused vodka.

The quest for visual perfection has also led to heavy pesticide use. If you want to make infused vodka or liqueurs, candied peel, marmalade, or Tunisian Lemon Rind Salad (page 31), look for sustainably grown fruit and be happy with a few imperfections. According to citrus expert and aficionado David Karp, the large Yemenite citrons that grow to the size of footballs are thought to be best for cooking, as they have the thickest and "sweetest" pith (albedo, the white, usually very bitter, part of the citrus peel).

TOMATO-BRAISED ROMANO BEANS AND SALT COD

MAKES 8 TO 10 SERVINGS

FISH

Here is a lighter seasonal spin on fried *baccalà* in tomato sauce, a classic Italian Jewish dish. Skip the frying and use robust late-season sauce tomatoes and meaty romano beans for added depth and texture. Salt-preserved cod has long played an important role in Atlantic and Mediterranean food cultures. The fish is utterly transformed by the process, much like the difference between fresh and cured meats. Plan ahead when you want to make this dish, as you'll need to soak the cod for two days to desalt it (some specialty stores sell frozen desalted cod). Even then, the dish may not need salt, so wait until it's done to decide. The stew goes exceptionally well with Sarah's Steamed Potatoes (page 221). Without the fish, this is a delicious, hearty pareve/vegan main dish.

1½ pounds (680 g) salt cod fillet

2 pounds (900 g) meaty tomatoes, such as Roma, San Marzano, or Costoluto Genovese

1 large onion, chopped

3 to 4 tablespoons extra-virgin olive oil, plus more for finishing

3 cloves garlic, minced

2 pounds (680 g) romano beans, stemmed and cut into ½-inch (12-mm) pieces, or snap beans, trimmed and cut into 1-inch (2.5-cm) pieces

4 thyme sprigs

Kosher or sea salt, if needed, and freshly ground black pepper

Sarah's Steamed Potatoes (page 221) or Basic White Rice (page 21) for serving

Rinse the cod under cool running water, place in a nonreactive bowl, and add cool water to cover. Cover and refrigerate from 24 hours, for fillet that is 1 inch (2.5 cm) thick or less, to 48 hours, for pieces 2 inches (5 cm) thick, changing the water at least three times each day. Drain the cod and cut into pieces 2 inches x 1 inch (5 x 2.5 cm), removing any dark pieces and hidden bones.

Halve the tomatoes crosswise and scoop or gently squeeze out the seeds. Set a box grater in a large bowl and grate each tomato half on the cut side, rubbing it over the large holes until you reach the skin. You should have about 3 cups (550 g) pulp. Discard the skins.

In a wide pot, sauté the onion in 2 tablespoons of the olive oil over medium heat until softened and translucent, 5 to 7 minutes. Stir in the garlic and cook for 1 minute longer. Add the beans, raise the heat to medium-high, and cook until their color brightens, 3 to 5 minutes. Stir in the tomatoes, 1 to 2 more tablespoons olive oil, the thyme sprigs, and several grinds of pepper. Cover the pot, bring to a boil, and then reduce the heat to a simmer. Cook until the beans are just tender and the tomato juices have developed, about 15 minutes.

Add the cod to the pot, partially burying the fish in the tomato-bean mixture. Cover again and continue to simmer, spooning the juices over the fish about halfway through the cooking, until the beans are very tender, the fish flakes easily, and the tomato sauce is plentiful, about 20 minutes.

Taste the sauce. If it is too salty, add ½ to 1 cup (60 to 120 ml) water to the pot and simmer a little longer. If it is not salty enough, season to taste with salt. Ladle over potatoes in shallow bowls and drizzle each serving with olive oil.

SHOPPING TIP: Salt cod, also known as *bacalao*, is available at some supermarkets, and at Latin, Italian, Portuguese, and Greek markets. Look for the whitest fillets, about 2 inches (5 cm) thick at their thickest end.

SHAKSHUKA

MAKES 6 SERVINGS

DAIRY

Moroccans, Tunisians, and Yemenites all claim this quick egg dish as their own. Great for brunch or supper, it's the Israeli equivalent of huevos rancheros. Keep a supply of *matboucha* on hand, so you can whip up a hearty meal in minutes. The term *shakshuka* comes from either the Hebrew verb "to shake," as one does to a pan over a hot stove, or from Arabic slang for a mixture or stew. Skip the labneh for a vegan version and feel free to add spinach or cooked lamb sausage to the pan before adding the eggs for other variations.

2 cups (640 g) Matboucha (page 32)

2 tablespoons extra-virgin olive oil

6 eggs

Kosher or sea salt (optional)

Generous handful of chopped fresh Italian parsley

Labneh, homemade (page 22) or store-bought

Thickly sliced country bread, toasted, or pita bread

In a 12-inch (30.5-cm) skillet, thin the Matboucha with water to the consistency of thick spaghetti sauce. Add the olive oil and set over medium heat. When the sauce is bubbling, reduce the heat to medium-low.

Using the back of a large spoon, make an indentation in the sauce at the 12 o'clock position. Crack an egg into the depression. Repeat with remaining eggs, spacing them evenly in the pan. Cook until the eggs are set to your liking, about 7 minutes for over easy. Cover the pan to hasten cooking, especially if you like your eggs more well-done.

Season the eggs with salt, if desired, and shower the parsley over all. Serve directly from the pan into shallow individual bowls, accompanied by labneh and bread or pita.

THE ISRAELI OMELET

PAREVE

An Israeli omelet is the opposite of a slow-cooked, delicate, practically-poached-in-butter French *omelette*. It is kibbutz breakfast or supper fast food: thin omelets cooked over relatively high heat in olive or vegetable oil until golden, ready to be folded into a pita or roll with Israeli salad, a slab of salty white cheese, and a hit of hot sauce.

For 1 serving, use a 6- or 7-inch (15- or 17-cm) pan for a 1-egg omelet and an 8- or 9-inch (20- or 23-cm) pan for a 2-egg omelet. While the skillet is heating over medium-high heat, use a fork to whisk 1 or 2 eggs with salt and about 1 tablespoon water (the water helps to make the omelet tender). Swirl a bit of oil into the hot pan. It should shimmer and liquefy almost immediately. Pour in the egg(s), which should begin to set immediately. Wait until you have a nice frill of set egg at the edges before lifting an edge to let the uncooked egg run underneath. When the bottom is golden, flip the omelet to finish cooking. The whole process should take a couple of minutes. Just as I said, fast food.

PURE AND SIMPLE BRISKET

MAKES 12 SERVINGS

MEAT

I've been making brisket this way for nearly forty years, ever since I learned a version of this recipe from Fran Loew, when we were nursery-school parents together. The recipe calls for onions, garlic, bay leaves, stock, and, of course, a great piece of well-raised beef. No ketchup, sugar, gingersnaps, flour, or beer mask the savory focus of this iconic dish. You will be amazed at how much flavor the roasting-and-braising technique delivers. I rarely need to add salt or pepper. Although there will be more waste and shrinkage, for a more flavorful result, it is best to use a brisket that includes the fattier "point" that rests like a split-level on the leaner "flat." Like all good party food, brisket is best made at least a day ahead, chilled before slicing, and then reheated to serve.

1 beef brisket, 6 pounds (2.7 kg), about
    8 x 12 x 3 inches (20 x 30.5 x 7.5 cm) thick,
    including at least some of the point
2 large onions, chopped, about 3 cups (480 g)
6 cloves garlic, unpeeled
3 bay leaves
4 cups (960 ml) homemade beef stock (recipe
    follows), or 2 cups (480 ml) canned beef
    broth diluted with 2 cups (480 ml) water,
    heated

Preheat the oven to 475°F (240°C). Pat the meat dry, then place flat side down on a work surface. Trim the excess fat from the brisket, especially around the point, or cap. Do your best to leave a layer of fat no more than ¼ inch (6 mm) thick. This will give you enough fat to flavor the meat but not so much that it overpowers it.

Place the meat, point side down, in a large roasting pan and roast, turning once halfway through the cooking, until thoroughly browned and crisp on both sides, about 1 hour.

Add chopped onions to the pan, scattering them around the brisket. Stir to coat the onions with the drippings and scrape up any brown bits. Return the brisket to the oven and roast until the onions are soft, about 15 minutes.

Remove the pan from the oven and reduce the heat to 350°F (180°C). Add garlic and bay leaves to the pan. The brisket should be point side up. Pour in enough stock to reach about 1 inch (2.5 cm) up the sides of the brisket (about 2 cups/480 ml), and stir to scrape up brown bits. Cover the pan tightly with a lid or heavy-duty foil and return it to the oven. Braise until very tender, about 3 hours. Check the meat every 30 minutes during the cooking time and add stock as needed to keep the simmering juice about 1 inch (2.5 cm) deep and to keep the onions from burning. You may not need all 4 cups (960 ml) of stock, but if you do run out of stock, add water.

Remove the pan from the oven and transfer the brisket to a shallow pan or platter. Pour the pan juices and onions into a glass container. Add a little water to the pan, place over medium heat, and stir, scraping up the brown bits from the bottom. Add these drippings to the container.

Let the meat and juices cool. Ideally, refrigerate them overnight. Lift the congealed fat from the juices and discard. Spread a few spoonfuls of the jellied meat juices and onions over the bottom of an ovenproof rimmed platter or shallow 9 x 13-inch (23 x 30.5-cm) baking dish.

continued »

There are a couple of ways to slice a brisket: Slice through the horizontal layer of fat that separates the point from the flat lower part of the brisket and lift off the point and set it aside. Cut the flat against the grain into slices ¼ inch (6 mm) thick. This is where you'll get your neat slices. Then, do your best to cut slices from the point across its grain. This is the part of the brisket that falls apart from long cooking that everyone loves to pick at or use to soak up juices and mashed potatoes. Or, leave the two parts attached and cut against the grain into slices ¼ inch (6 mm) thick; with each slice topped by long fibers from the point.

Lay the meat slices, overlapping them, on the prepared platter. Scatter a few spoonfuls of the juices and onions over the meat. (The brisket can be prepared up to this point, covered tightly, and refrigerated overnight, with the extra juices refrigerated separately. Or it can be frozen for up to 2 weeks, with the remaining juices frozen separately. Thaw the meat and juices before reheating.

To heat and serve the brisket, preheat the oven to 325°F (165°C). Cover the platter tightly with heavy-duty foil and place in the oven until the brisket is heated through. Warm the extra pan juices and onions separately. Spoon some of them over the warm meat and serve the remainder at the table.

A BASIC BEEF STOCK

MAKES ABOUT 6 CUPS (1.4 L)

MEAT

Use a mix of beef and/or veal bones and collagen-rich beef shank meat, which gives heft to the stock. Roasting meaty bones and vegetables first produces a richer, deeper-flavored stock. This recipe can easily be doubled.

5 pounds (2.3 kg) mixed beef shanks and beef
    and/or veal bones
2 large carrots, quartered
2 ribs celery with leaves, cut into large pieces
1 large onion, quartered
1 cup (240 ml) water
6 large Italian parsley sprigs
2 large thyme sprigs
1 bay leaf
Kosher or sea salt

Preheat the oven to 400°F (200°C). Place the shanks and bones, carrots, celery, and onion in a single layer in a large roasting pan and roast until everything is well browned and fragrant, about 45 minutes.

Transfer the roasted shanks, bones, and vegetables to an 8-quart (8-L) stockpot. Pour the water into the roasting pan, place over medium heat, bring to a simmer, and scrape up any brown bits from the pan bottom. Pour the contents of the roasting pan into the stockpot. Add the parsley, thyme, bay leaf, and water to cover barely (about 8 cups/2 L). Cover the pot, set over medium-high heat, and bring almost to a boil (avoid a rolling boil or the stock will be cloudy). Uncover, reduce the heat to low, and skim off any foam as it rises to the surface. Cover partially and simmer over low heat (you want to see bubbles coming up from the bottom of the pot) for 3 to 4 hours.

Strain the stock through a fine-mesh sieve into a bowl and discard the meat, bones, and vegetables. If you want a clearer stock, strain the stock again through a sieve lined with a paper towel, paper coffee filter, or piece of kitchen muslin. Season to taste with up to 1 tablespoon salt. If using the stock immediately, skim the fat off the surface with a large spoon. Or, let cool completely, then cover and refrigerate until well chilled. Lift off and discard the congealed fat before using. The stock may be refrigerated in an airtight container in the refrigerator for up to 4 days or in the freezer for up to 3 months.

LAMB, BUTTERNUT SQUASH, AND QUINCE TAGINE

MAKES 8 SERVINGS

MEAT

Quince, an autumn fruit related to apples, is thought by some to have been the forbidden fruit in the Garden of Eden and is a favorite Rosh Hashanah ingredient. This savory tagine, inspired by a sweet Bulgarian holiday meat-and-quince stew, is fragrant with *ras el hanout* and topped with a cilantro gremolata. The trick to a delicious tagine, with or without a traditional clay pot, is not to have too much liquid in the pot, so that the aromatic steam infuses deeper flavor into the food. Lamb neck and shoulder are ideal braising meats; opt for one of these over precut "lean" stew meat. The result is much more succulent.

2 quinces, about 1½ pounds (680 g) total

1 heaping tablespoon ras el hanout

Kosher or sea salt

2 tablespoons extra-virgin olive oil

2 pounds (900 g) boneless lamb for stew, such as neck or shoulder, cut into 2-inch (5-cm) cubes

1 large onion, chopped into 1-inch pieces

2 large cloves garlic, minced

2 tablespoons chopped fresh cilantro or Italian parsley

2 pounds (900 g) butternut squash, halved, seeded, peeled, and cut into 2-inch (5-cm) cubes

1 cup (240 ml) water or stock

2 bay leaves

Pomegranate arils (see page 17 for how to seed) for serving (optional)

Couscous or Basic White Rice (page 21) for serving

FOR THE GREMOLATA

1 lemon

¼ cup packed/25 g cilantro or Italian parsley leaves

1 small clove garlic, chopped

Scrub the quinces to remove the fuzz. Using a cleaver or chef's knife, quarter the quinces through the stem end. Resting a quarter on one of its flat surfaces and anchoring it on its skin side with one hand, dig out the core, using a paring or oyster knife. The cut surfaces will start to turn brown, but don't worry. If you've been able to remove all the fuzz, leave the quinces unpeeled, or peel them if you like. Cut the quarters into 2-inch (5-cm) chunks.

Stir together the ras el hanout and 1 teaspoon salt and dredge the lamb pieces in the spice mixture. Heat a wide pot large enough to accommodate all the ingredients over medium-high heat and add 1 tablespoon of the olive oil. Add half the meat and cook, turning once, until fragrant and well browned, about 3 minutes per side. Lower heat as needed to keep the spices from blackening. Transfer the meat to a plate. Repeat with remaining meat and oil.

Lower heat to medium-low and add the onion and a little salt. Cook onion until softened and translucent, 5 to 7 minutes, scraping the pot to incorporate any brown bits. Stir in the garlic and cilantro and cook 1 minute more.

Return meat and any juices to the pot along with the quinces. Stir, cover, and reduce the heat to low. Simmer 20 minutes and check the pot. Thick juices should be forming. Add the squash, water, bay leaves, and a little more salt to the pot and re-cover. Continue to simmer gently until the meat, quinces, and squash are very tender, 40 to 60 minutes longer. (The dish can be prepared up to this point a day ahead, cooled, covered, and refrigerated. Lift off the layer of congealed fat before reheating.)

TO MAKE THE GREMOLATA: Using five-hole zester, remove the zest from the lemon in long strands. Mince together the lemon zest, cilantro, and garlic.

TO SERVE: Reheat stew if necessary. Add a healthy squeeze of lemon juice to the stew and serve over couscous. Top each serving with gremolata and pomegranate arils.

ROASTED AUTUMN FRUIT

MAKES 10 TO 12 SERVINGS

PAREVE

This is my go-to autumn dessert, perfect for all the season's holidays, whether served on its own or as an accompaniment to cakes or ice cream. Roasting fall fruit brings out the spicy notes we associate with desserts this time of year. And it's very forgiving: just about any combination of seasonal fruit will do, and no special techniques, precise measuring, or timing is required. This impressive dish is naturally gluten- and dairy-free. Here's one of my favorite combinations to get you started.

4 pounds (1.8 kg) mixed apples and Bosc or Anjou pears (about 6 apples and 3 or 4 large pears), including some firm-fleshed, such as Pippin, and some melting-flesh apple varieties, such as Golden Delicious

2 Fuyu persimmons

1 to 2 pints figs (about ¾ pound/340 g)

2 cups (200 g) Concord, Autumn Royale, or wine grapes

2 ounces (55 g) dried fruit, such as plums, apricots, or apples, snipped into small pieces

¼ cup (85 g) honey

⅓ cup (75 ml) off-dry red or white wine or a muscat dessert wine, such as Beaumes de Venise

A few thyme sprigs (optional)

Preheat the oven to 400°F (200°C). Peel the apples, pears, and persimmons, if desired. Halve and core them and cut into large wedges or chunks. Cut the figs in half lengthwise. Place all the fruit, including the grapes and the dried fruit, in a large ovenproof pan and use your hands to mix them gently. It's okay if you need to mound the fruit to fit. In a small saucepan, combine the honey and wine, warm over low heat, and then pour evenly over all the fruit. Toss in the thyme sprigs, if desired.

Roast the fruit until it is bubbly and well browned in places, about 45 minutes. Serve warm or at room temperature on its own or with one of the suggestions below.

DELICIOUS WITH

Aunt Sarah's Honey and Apple Cake (page 77)

Semolina and Walnut Oil Cake with Coffee Hawaij (page 243)

Granny's Citrus Sponge Cake (page 201)

Tahini Butter Cookies (page 149)

Carob Molasses Ice Cream (page 151)

POMEGRANATE-ORANGE GELÉE
WITH A **CITRUS SALAD**

MAKES 8 SERVINGS

MEAT

Gelatin desserts deserve a comeback. This easy, from-scratch gelée has a luscious silky texture and jewel-tone appeal. It is a refreshing finish to a rich meal, a beautiful autumn starter, or a between-course palate cleanser. Orange tempers the more assertive flavors of pomegranate; feel free to shift the balance of juices, keeping the total amount of liquid the same. If possible, use freshly squeezed pomegranate juice available in season where the fruit is grown. Gelatin is typically a meat product; for vegetarian and kosher gelatin options, see page 10. Autumn pomegranates symbolize the hope that one's blessings in the new year will be as plentiful as its many kernels (arils).

3 cups (720 ml) pomegranate juice
1 cup (240 ml) strained fresh orange juice
   (from 3 to 4 oranges)
2 packets (¼ ounce/7 g each) unflavored gelatin
2 tablespoons sugar
2 teaspoons orange flower water

In a measuring pitcher, mix together the pomegranate and orange juices. If any pulp rises to the surface, skim it off. Pour 1 cup (240 ml) of the juice blend into a small bowl. Sprinkle in the packets of gelatin and let stand for 5 minutes to soften.

In a medium pot, bring 1½ cups (340 ml) of the remaining juice blend almost to a boil over medium heat. Turn off the heat and stir in the sugar and the gelatin mixture, stirring until completely dissolved. Stir in the remaining juice blend and orange flower water, mixing well. Pour into small jelly glasses. Cover and chill until set, about 4 hours. (The gelée may be made a day ahead.)

CITRUS SALAD

MAKES 8 SERVINGS

PAREVE/VEGAN

The merest hint of orange flower water elevates this versatile fruit salad into something exotic. Take a few moments to learn the handy skill of "supreming" citrus (page 17) for membrane-free, jewel-toned segments.

4 oranges

½ cup (115 g) pomegranate arils (see page 17 on how to seed)

1 tablespoon sugar

1 tablespoon dessert wine, such as Beaumes de Venise or a late-harvest Riesling, optional

½ teaspoon orange flower water

Leaves from handful of mint sprigs, preferably Persian, torn

¼ cup (30 g) salted roasted pistachios, coarsely chopped

Using a five-hole zester, remove the zest from the oranges in long strands, allowing them to fall into a medium bowl. Peel and segment the oranges (see page 17) and add the segments to the bowl. Add the pomegranate arils, sugar, wine, and orange flower water, stir well, and set aside to marinate for up to 1 hour.

Just before serving, add the mint leaves and pistachios to the salad and stir gently. Serve the salad alongside or as a topping for the gelée.

SHOPPING TIP: Choose pomegranates that are heavy for their size and have a fresh-looking rind. Some splitting, thought to signify the fruit is ripe and bursting with juice, is okay, but avoid fruit with cracks that show signs of mold. The fruit will keep in the refrigerator for up to 1 month.

"GREEN" PISTACHIOS

Young or "green" soft-shelled pistachios are a Middle Eastern favorite in early fall. You can slice them, shell and all, into the salad; their translucent and gelatinous nature add an interesting dimension.

EUROPEAN PLUM MERINGUE TORTE

MAKES ONE 10-INCH (25-CM) TORTE, ABOUT 12 SERVINGS

DAIRY

Meringue-topped fruit tortes were *the* thing in Israel in the 1950s and 1960s. During our family trip there in 1961, anyone we visited for afternoon coffee and cake presented this dessert baked with whatever seasonal fruit or jam they had on hand. Eggs, which were less expensive than heavy cream, and could be stored at room temperature (not everyone had a refrigerator back then), were economically divided: yolks went into the batter and whites into the topping. This recipe is based on the one in my aunt Hanna's decades-old baking journal. Although the term *torte* classically refers to nut cakes with little or no flour, the popular definition includes single layer flour-based cakes such as this one. European plum varieties, such as the dusky blue-purple, tawny-fleshed oval Italian or French prunes (see page 29, upper left), are traditionally used in French Jewish and German Jewish autumn holiday desserts. The fruits are meaty, sweet, and good for baking. Japanese varieties (Santa Rosa, Satsuma, and the like) are much juicier and better eaten out of hand. Later in the year, this torte is delicious made with apples or pears. In summer, it is gorgeous with ripe apricots.

FOR THE FILLING

1½ pounds (680 g) ripe European-type plums
    (10 to 25, depending on size)

½ cup (50 g) sugar

2 tablespoons butter

2 tablespoons fresh lemon juice

FOR THE CAKE

¾ cup plus 2 tablespoons (200 g) butter, at
    room temperature, plus more for the pan

3 eggs, separated

2 cups (250 g) unbleached all-purpose flour

1½ teaspoons baking powder

½ teaspoon salt

¼ teaspoon baking soda

⅓ cup (65 g) sugar

1 teaspoon vanilla extract

½ cup (125 g) plain whole-milk yogurt

FOR THE MERINGUE

Reserved egg whites

½ cup (100 g) sugar

½ cup (45 g) sliced almonds

TO MAKE THE FILLING: Pit the plums. Most varieties are not freestone, so to pit them, cut each plum in half through the stem end, shaving alongside the pit, and then cut the meat away from the sides of the pit. Cut the plums into pieces. If very ripe, they may fall apart, but don't worry. You should have 3 to 4 cups (500 to 660 g).

In a wide pot or skillet, cook the plums, sugar, butter, and lemon juice over medium-high heat, stirring occasionally to prevent sticking, and adjusting heat to prevent burning, until the mixture is glossy, thick, and reduced to about half the volume, 10 to 15 minutes. Scrape onto a plate or sheet pan, spreading it out to cool rapidly. (The filling can be made ahead and refrigerated.)

TO MAKE THE CAKE: Preheat the oven to 350°F (180°C). Butter the bottom and sides of a 10-inch (25-cm) springform pan.

Separate the eggs, placing the whites in the sparkling clean bowl of an electric mixer and the yolks in a small bowl. Cover the whites and set aside. Sift together the flour, baking powder, salt, and baking soda.

Using an electric mixer fitted with the paddle attachment on medium speed, or a bowl and a wooden spoon, beat the butter until creamy and light in color. Add the sugar and beat until incorporated. Add the egg yolks, one at a time, beating well after each addition, and beat in the vanilla. Add the flour mixture in three batches alternating with the yogurt, beginning and ending with the flour mixture and mixing just until completely blended. The batter will be stiff.

Spread the batter in the prepared pan. Bake the cake until pale golden and a toothpick inserted into the center comes out barely clean, about 18 minutes. Remove from the oven and place on a wire rack (do not remove cake from pan). Adjust the oven rack to the upper third of the oven and raise the temperature to 375°F (190°C).

TO MAKE THE MERINGUE: Fit the electric mixer with the whisk attachment and beat the egg whites on low speed until foamy. On high speed, gradually add the sugar and beat until stiff peaks form.

TO ASSEMBLE THE CAKE: With the cake still in the pan, spread the plum filling over the top of the cake. Spoon meringue in large dollops over the filling, then spread and swirl it to cover the filling. Sprinkle almonds evenly over the meringue. Return the cake to the oven and bake until the meringue is golden and the almonds are lightly browned, about 15 minutes.

Transfer the cake to a wire rack and let cool completely. Run a thin-bladed knife or spatula around the inside edge of the pan to loosen the cake sides, then unlatch and remove pan ring. If desired, use an offset spatula to loosen the cake from the pan bottom and slide it onto a serving platter. Cut into wedges to serve. The torte can be made up to 6 hours ahead and held at room temperature until serving. Refrigerate any leftovers.

APPLE, PEAR, AND CONCORD GRAPE GALETTE
IN RYE PASTRY WITH GINGER CREAM

MAKES ONE 15-INCH (38-CM) TART, ABOUT 12 SERVINGS

DAIRY

This free-form rustic autumn tart is mellow with the floral aromas of apples and juicy pears. Instead of raisins, use fresh Concord grapes to add a burst of color and flavor. Rye flour adds a dusky, earthy note to the pastry, perfect for autumn and winter baking. If you don't have rye flour, whole wheat flour can be substituted. Use a mix of firm-fleshed and melting-flesh apples and pears for a luscious filling. Caramelized honey, the by-product of heating honeycomb to extract all the honey, adds further complexity and is often available from local honey producers. The Sardinian version, *abbamele*, is also wonderful. Or, use a dark honey, such as chestnut.

FOR THE CRUST

1½ cups (190 g) unbleached all-purpose flour

½ cup (50 g) rye flour

1 tablespoon sugar

½ teaspoon salt

¾ cup (170 g) cold butter, cut into ½-inch (12-mm) pieces

⅓ to ½ cup (75 to 120 ml) ice water

FOR THE FILLING

1 pound (450 g) apples (about 4), a mix of firm-fleshed, such as Spitzenberg, Winesap, and Pink Lady, and melting-flesh, such as Jonagold

1 pound (450 g) pears (2 or 3), such as Bosc or Bartlett

1 lemon

1 cup Concord grapes (about 125 g)

⅓ cup (115 g) caramelized or dark honey, such as chestnut or buckwheat, warmed

3 tablespoons Calvados

¾ cup (40 g) crushed amaretti or panko bread crumbs

4 tablespoons (55 g) butter, melted

2 tablespoons sugar

FOR THE GINGER CREAM

¾ cup (180 ml) heavy cream

½ cup (115 g) crème fraîche

1 tablespoon sugar

3 tablespoons crystallized ginger, minced

TO MAKE THE CRUST: In a large bowl, using a fork, stir together the flours, sugar, and salt. Scatter the butter over the flour mixture and, using your fingertips or a pastry blender, cut in the butter until the mixture resembles coarse sand with some flattened pieces of butter still visible. Using a fork, stir in the ice water, a little at a time, just until the dough sticks together when pressed between your fingertips. Gather the dough into a ball, wrap in plastic wrap, and flatten into a disk about ½ inch (12 mm) thick. Refrigerate for at least 15 minutes and up to 3 days (or freeze up to 3 weeks). Let dough rest at room temperature until soft enough to roll.

Preheat the oven to 425°F (220°C).

continued »

TO MAKE THE FILLING: Peel, quarter, and core the apples and pears. Cut each quarter lengthwise into slices ¼ inch (6 mm) thick, then cut the slices in half crosswise. Place the apple and pear slices in a bowl. Using a Microplane grater, grate the zest from the lemon over the apples and pears, so both the zest and the spray of citrus oils land in the bowl. Cut the lemon in half and give a healthy squeeze over the fruit. Add the grapes, honey, and Calvados and toss together.

On a lightly floured work surface, roll out the dough into a 15-inch (38-cm) circle or an 18 x 12-inch (46-x-30.5-cm) rectangle about ⅛ inch (3 mm) thick. Transfer to an ungreased large, rimless baking sheet (if you don't have a rimless pan, turn a rimmed sheet pan upside down). If you prefer, line the pan with parchment paper. Sprinkle amaretti crumbs over the center of the dough, leaving a 3- to 4-inch (7.5- to 10-cm) border.

Using a slotted spoon, transfer the filling to the dough, mounding it on the crumbs. Reserve the juices. Fold up the border, pleating the edges of the dough to create a round or rectangular pastry, leaving about 4 inches (10 cm) of filling exposed in the center. Spoon the reserved filling juices over the exposed fruit. Brush the crust with the butter, allowing some to drip into the fruit, then sprinkle the galette with the sugar.

Bake for 15 minutes. Reduce the heat to 375°F (190°C) and continue to bake until the crust is golden and the fruit is bubbly and its [edges are browned, about 25 minutes more. Transfer to a wire rack and let cool for 5 minutes. Use a large offset spatula to loosen the galette from the pan, then leave it on the pan for 30 minutes to set up.

TO MAKE THE GINGER CREAM: In a metal bowl, stir together the cream, crème fraîche, and sugar. Cover and chill until close to serving time. Whip with a balloon whisk until the mixture is thick but still pourable, or whip until soft peaks form. Stir in the ginger.

TO SERVE: Slide the galette onto a platter and serve warm or at room temperature. Top each serving with a dollop of the ginger cream. The galette is best served the day it is made. If desired, the galette can be reheated in a 325°F (165°C) oven.

AUNT SARAH'S HONEY AND APPLE CAKE

MAKES 1 BUNDT OR RING CAKE OR 2 LOAF CAKES, 12 TO 16 SERVINGS

PAREVE

This cake, delicately spiced, tender, and moist with grated apples, is the perfect homage to two of the symbolic foods of Rosh Hashanah, honey and apples, which represent wishes for a good and sweet year. But by all means, make this easy dessert more often! Use a dark or caramelized honey for a deeper flavor. This cake is best made a day ahead and is delicious with Roasted Autumn Fruit (page 68) or Peppered Red Wine Fruit Compote (page 112).

1 cup (240 ml) mild oil, such as grapeseed, safflower, or avocado, plus more for the pan(s)

4 cups (500 g) unbleached all-purpose flour

1 teaspoon baking soda

¾ teaspoon salt

½ teaspoon ground cinnamon

⅛ teaspoon ground cloves

1 cup (340 g) caramelized or dark honey, such as chestnut or buckwheat (see headnote of the galette, page 75)

1 cup (200 g) sugar

4 eggs

¾ pound (340 g) tart apples (about 2 large), such as Granny Smith, peeled, halved, cored, and grated on the large holes of a box grater

1 cup (240 ml) hot brewed black coffee

Preheat the oven to 325°F (165°C). Oil a 12-cup/3-liter Bundt pan or two 9-x-5-inch (23-x-12-cm) loaf pans.

In a medium bowl, sift together the flour, baking soda, salt, cinnamon, and cloves. In a large bowl, using a wooden spoon, beat together the honey, oil, sugar, eggs, and grated apples until well mixed. Add the flour mixture in three batches alternating with the coffee, beginning and ending with the flour mixture, stirring after each addition until the batter is smooth.

Pour the batter into the prepared pan(s). Bake until a wooden toothpick inserted into the center of the cake comes out almost clean (with moist crumbs), about 35 minutes for the loaf pans and about 50 minutes for the Bundt pan. Let cool completely in the pan(s) on a wire rack. Unmold, wrap and store overnight at room temperature before serving.

November & December

THE DARK HOURS

As we hurtle toward the shortest days of the year, we crave warming foods and a fire's glow to cheer us through long nights. Hanukkah, the joyous Festival of Lights, couldn't come at a better time.

For many farmers, this is a last chance to get things out of the ground and into storage. Citrus growers, on the other hand, are starting to bring the first of their winter crops to market. We cooks are making the most of late-fall ingredients before winter sets in and, unable to resist, begin dabbling in still-tart mandarins and blood oranges to accent our food.

This chapter offers dishes that make us smile, keep us warm, and celebrate the miracle of light in the midst of darkness.

November & December

GREEN OLIVES WITH ZA'ATAR AND CITRUS

MAKES 2 CUPS (340 G)

PAREVE/VEGAN

In late autumn, new-crop olives abound. They are often fresh-cured with their buttery flavor and meaty texture intact, making them a perfect partner to a marinade of warm olive oil, garlic, citrus peel, and za'atar, the Middle Eastern spice blend of wild hyssop, ground sumac, sesame seeds, and salt. French Lucques or bright green Sicilian Castelveltrano olives are also delicious here. (If your olives are too briny, soak them in water for 15 minutes first to remove some of the saltiness.) Olives are an evergreen option for any mezze table. In summer, use Valencia oranges and Eureka lemons; in winter, navel oranges and Meyer lemons. Be sure to have country bread or pita on hand to sop up the seasoned oil.

¼ cup (60 ml) extra-virgin olive oil

¾ pound (340 g) green olives

2 tablespoons za'atar

1 large clove garlic, sliced

1 dried árbol chile

1 lemon

1 orange

In a medium saucepan, warm the olive oil over medium-low heat until it liquefies and shimmers. Add the olives, reduce the heat to low, and warm through. Remove from the heat, add the za'atar, garlic, and chile, and toss to coat. Using a swivel-blade vegetable peeler, and working over the pan, remove the zest from the lemon and the orange in long, wide strips, getting both the zest and the spray of citrus oils into the pan. Stir to mix, and serve warm or at room temperature. Cover and refrigerate any leftover olives and bring to room temperature or reheat to serve.

SALATA DE ICRE

MAKES ABOUT 1 CUP (240 G), 6 TO 8 SERVINGS

FISH

Think of this Romanian spread as a luscious home-made mayonnaise prepared with fish eggs instead of egg yolks from hens. More delicate than its heartier cousin, *taramosalata* (Greece and Romania were both part of the Ottoman Empire), it is traditionally made with fresh, rather than salt-cured, carp or herring roe. My grandfather Phillip had cause to celebrate if there was an egg sac in the fresh whole fish my grandmother brought home from the store. He'd scrape the crunchy eggs into a deep bowl and slowly whip them with oil to a pale pink briny spread that retained some of the snap of the roe. He'd swirl it like hummus onto a plate and serve it up with slabs of black bread to his four daughters. For his own sandwich, my grandfather always first rubbed a clove of garlic over the shiny bread crust. Customary accompaniments include finely chopped onion and boiled potatoes. In summer, it is delicious with ripe tomatoes and cucumbers, and used in place of mayonnaise, it makes a great deviled egg. In the fall, serve it with toasted challah after Yom Kippur. If you have access to fresh whole fish with its egg sac, by all means use it. Jars of salted fish roe, or *tarama* (not the prepared salad, *taramosalata*), are available year-round at Greek or specialty markets (see Resource Guide, page 298). A short soak in water removes excess saltiness to more closely approximate fresh eggs.

7 tablespoons (100 g) tarama (cured fish roe)
1 lemon
Up to 1 cup (240 ml) mild oil, such as safflower
    or grapeseed

Spoon the tarama into a small bowl, pour in water to cover, and let stand for 15 minutes. Drain through a fine-mesh sieve, rinse under cool running water, and drain thoroughly, 10 to 15 minutes. Remove 1 tablespoon of the roe and reserve.

Spoon the remaining roe into a deep nonreactive bowl and place in a pan, or larger bowl, of hot water to soften the eggs, stirring and mashing them with a wooden spoon. Remove the bowl from the water.

Add a squeeze of lemon juice to the roe, and whisk to combine. Whisking constantly, begin adding the oil, a drop at a time, until you have added about 2 tablespoons oil and the mixture is soupy. Whisk in another squeeze of lemon juice and resume whisking in oil, a drop at a time, waiting until each drop is fully incorporated before adding the next. After you have added about half the oil, the mixture should be a glossy pale pink and start looking fluffy. Add another squeeze of lemon juice and begin adding the oil in a thin, steady stream while whisking constantly, stopping when you have a fluffy mayonnaise-like mixture. Stir in the reserved roe.

To make the spread in a food processor, warm the roe as directed, then transfer it to the work bowl fitted with the plastic S attachment. Add a squeeze of lemon juice and, with the motor running, begin adding the oil through the feed tube, drop by drop, as described above. Continue adding the lemon juice and the oil as described for the hand method—drop by drop until the mixture is starting to look fluffy, then in a thin stream—until the mixture is fluffy and mayonnaise-like. Stir in the reserved roe.

Cover and refrigerate until ready to serve; the spread will keep for up to 3 days. Discard any that sits out at room temperature for more than an hour or two.

KITCHEN NOTE: To store the opened jar of *tarama*, smooth the surface of the contents with a spoon and pour in a little mild vegetable oil to cover and seal the roe. Cover and refrigerate for up to 6 months. Before using, spoon out the uppermost layer of roe that discolored during storage and discard, if you wish. Replace the oil when you are ready to return the remainder to the refrigerator.

בצ"ל ריינ... _____

1 קופ... תחת   50 גרם שמרים

1/2 מרגרינה   כ... כפות חמה

כוס מים   כוס מים פושרים

קמח ביצה + כפית חומץ + מעט פושרים...

ברוקולי - גבעת...   כולסים בתחת...

חביתה ברוקולי

3 ב.צ.ה   1 שמנת   2 כפית קמח

כפים - מרק עף 1/2 כולסם, מעלה

150 גרם עריף לבנה.

בצק בריך ופל... מתוק ולניה

3 כוסות קמח רגיל

2-3 כפית שמן   קמח לפתח

2 " חומץ

1 מרגרינה אותה - ...טול... זאת אותו

כד... ...צרים... לף - ...ם ...רים

בצק בריך מלוח - למרגרינה, רגיל...

...תחת כולס קמח מעט

SAFTA RACHEL'S SESAME SEED BAGELEH

MAKES 36 RINGS

DAIRY

My grandmother's small, crisp, butter-rich rings are nothing like American bagels. Fragrant with yeast and butter, they are a savory nibble, divine with an aperitif or afternoon tea or coffee. They are known as *roscas* in Spanish-speaking countries and *roschette* in Italy. In fact, some version, savory or sweet, shows up in Jewish bakeries all over the world.

4 cups (500 g) unbleached all-purpose flour

1½ teaspoons salt

2 packages (¼ ounce/7 g each) active dry yeast

¼ teaspoon sugar

½ cup (120 ml) warm water (100° to 110°F/38° to 43°C)

¾ cup plus 2 tablespoons (200 g) butter, at room temperature

¼ cup (60 ml) mild oil, such as safflower or grapeseed

¼ cup (40 g) sesame seeds

In a large bowl, sift together the flour and salt. In a small bowl, stir the yeast and sugar into the warm water and set aside for 5 minutes. While the yeast is proofing, use the back of a wooden spoon or a rubber spatula to work the butter into the flour mixture. Make a well in the center of the flour mixture.

When the yeast mixture is ready, pour it into the well along with the oil and stir to blend the mixtures together. Then, using your hands, work the mixture until all the ingredients are thoroughly incorporated and a dough has formed, 3 to 5 minutes. The dough will be slightly wet, but the oil and butter will prevent it from sticking to your hands. Form the dough into a ball in the bowl and cover the bowl with a plate and a couple of towels for insulation. Place the bowl in a warm place and let the dough rise until spongy and doubled in bulk, about 1 hour.

Preheat the oven to 375°F (190°C). Line 2 sheet pans with parchment paper. Put the sesame seeds in a small shallow bowl. Divide the dough into 36 walnut-size pieces. I like to place the pieces to one side of my work surface and cover them with a dish towel to prevent them drying out.

On a lightly floured work surface, using your palms, roll several pieces of the dough into cylinders about 3 inches (7.5 cm) long and ¾ inch (2 cm) in diameter. Dip one side of each cylinder into the sesame seeds. On a clean work surface, roll each cylinder to a length of 6 to 7 inches (15 to 17 cm), form it into a ring, and pinch the ends together to seal. Place the rings, seed side up and close together, on a prepared sheet pan. Repeat with the remaining dough and seeds. Let the bageleh rest for 5 to 10 minutes.

Bake until golden, about 20 minutes. Transfer the bageleh to a wire rack and let cool completely before serving. Store them in an airtight container at room temperature for up to 2 days or in the freezer for up to 1 month. To restore their crispness before serving, refresh them in a 350°F (180°C) oven for 5 to 10 minutes.

HEARTY WINTER SLAW (FACING PAGE), UPPER RIGHT;
AUTUMN SLAW (PAGE 41), LOWER LEFT

HEARTY WINTER SLAW: SHAVED CABBAGE, RADICCHIO, AND CELERY WITH BOSC PEARS

MAKES 6 TO 8 SERVINGS

PAREVE/VEGAN

Here's a lovely winter salad whose colors, textures, and mellow flavors complement seasonal menus. Most of the components can be prepared a day ahead, making this a terrific choice for holiday entertaining. Apples or citrus can be added or substituted for the pears. This salad is a natural with shaved or chunked aged sheep's milk cheeses or Parmigiano-Reggiano.

FOR THE DRESSING

2 teaspoons Dijon mustard

½ teaspoon kosher or sea salt

Freshly ground white pepper

1 Meyer or Eureka lemon

¼ cup (60 ml) walnut oil

Finishing salt, such as Maldon sea salt

FOR THE SALAD

½ head napa cabbage, cored

1 small head radicchio, halved and cored

3 ribs celery with leaves

Large handful of arugula

2 Bosc pears

½ cup (60 g) walnuts, toasted (see page 18) and coarsely chopped

TO MAKE THE DRESSING: In a small bowl, whisk together the mustard, salt, and several grinds of pepper and whisk in 1 tablespoon lemon juice. Whisk in the oil in a thin stream until the dressing is blended. (The dressing can be made 1 day ahead and refrigerated in an airtight container. I like to use a Mason jar for this. Whisk, or shake the jar, to blend the dressing before using.)

TO MAKE THE SALAD: Have a large bowl of ice water ready for crisping the vegetables. Using a sharp knife, a Japanese mandoline, or a food processor fitted with the slicing disk, cut the cabbage and radicchio crosswise into ribbons ¼ to ½ inch (6 to 12 mm) wide and place in the ice water. Using a vegetable peeler, remove the strings from the celery. Pluck off any leaves and add to the bowl. Shave the celery ribs into thin slices and add to the water.

Drain and dry the cabbage, radicchio, and celery. Place in a salad bowl. If the arugula leaves are large, cut them crosswise into ribbons and then add them to the bowl. (The salad can be made up to this point up to 1 day ahead, covered, and refrigerated.)

Up to 1 hour before serving, toss the salad with the dressing. Taste and add more salt, pepper, or lemon if needed. Just before serving, quarter and core the pears and cut lengthwise into thin slices. Add the pears and walnuts to the salad, toss, and top with the finishing salt.

FREEKEH WITH **KALE, BUTTERNUT SQUASH,** AND **SMOKED SALT**

MAKES 6 SERVINGS

PAREVE/VEGAN

Freekeh, fire-roasted green wheat, is a perfect canvas for autumn vegetables. The grain's smoky notes are enhanced with smoked paprika (*pimentón* in Spain) and smoked salt. This dish is great for entertaining, as it can be served at room temperature or made a day ahead and reheated. It is also delicious made with farro or red or black quinoa. The cooking method for freekeh comes from Orie Habshoush, grandson of the founder of a spice, legume, and grain shop near the Levinsky market in Tel Aviv. If you are using whole grain freekeh, allow several hours for soaking. For more about freekeh, see page 227.

1 cup freekeh (155 g), preferably finely cracked

1 small butternut squash, about 1¼ pounds (570 g)

1 small bunch tender kale, such as cavolo nero, about 6 ounces (170 g), or ¼ pound (115 g) loose-leaf baby kale

3 tablespoons extra-virgin olive oil

1 teaspoon smoked paprika

Kosher or sea salt

1 small onion, chopped

2½ cups (600 ml) hot water

Smoked salt for finishing

If using whole or cracked freekeh, soak in water to cover for at least 6 hours or up to overnight, then drain well. If using finely cracked freekeh, skip this step.

Halve the squash and remove and discard the seeds and fibers. Using a vegetable peeler, peel the squash halves, then cut into cubes no larger than 1 inch (2.5 cm). You should have about 3 cups (420 g). If using a bunch of kale, strip the stems from the leaves and discard as directed on page 17, then massage the leaves to tenderize, if you like. If using baby kale, skip this step. Roughly chop the leaves.

In a wide pot, heat 1 tablespoon of the oil over medium-high heat. Add the squash, the smoked paprika, and a little kosher salt and cook, stirring occasionally, until the squash is golden in places and crisp-tender, about 10 minutes. Remove from the pot and set aside.

Add 1 tablespoon oil, the onion, and a bit of salt to the same pot and sauté until the onion is soft and golden, about 10 minutes. Stir in the kale and cook for 2 minutes. Push the kale and onion to the side of the pot. Add the remaining 1 tablespoon oil and the freekeh and cook for 1 minute, stirring to coat the grains with oil. Stir in the water, squash, and about ½ teaspoon kosher salt, cover, reduce the heat to medium-low, and cook until almost all the water is absorbed and the freekeh is tender, about 20 minutes. Uncover the pot and cook until all the water is absorbed, about 5 minutes longer.

Transfer to a serving dish and sprinkle with the smoked salt. Serve warm or at room temperature.

YEMENITE PUMPKIN AND CARROT SOUP

MAKES 8 TO 10 SERVINGS
MEAT OR PAREVE/VEGAN

Traditional Yemenite seasonings—cumin, coriander, and black pepper—give a lift to this vegetable blend. Or use *hawaij*, the Yemenite spice blend for soups and stews. A meaty squash, such as Tahitian works best. Carrots balance the flavors of the squash, especially if yours turns out not to be very sweet. This soup is lovely as is, or dressed up with a swirl of pesto.

½ pound (225 g) carrots (2 large), finely chopped

1 large onion, finely chopped

2 ribs celery with leaves, finely chopped

¼ cup (15 g) chopped fresh Italian parsley, plus more finely chopped for garnish (optional)

Kosher salt

3 tablespoons mild oil, such as avocado, grapeseed, or safflower

3 cups (735 g) roasted squash puree (see page 19), or 1½ pounds (680 g) raw winter squash, such as butternut, Tahitian, or kabocha, peeled and cut into 1-inch (2.5 cm) cubes

½ teaspoon ground coriander

¼ teaspoon freshly ground black pepper

¼ teaspoon ground cumin

7 cups (1.7 L) homemade chicken stock, vegetable stock (page 92), or water

4 cloves garlic, peeled

Parsley or Cilantro Pesto (recipe follows), optional

In a wide pot, sauté the carrots, onion, celery, and ¼ cup parsley with a little salt in the oil over medium heat until the vegetables have softened, 7 to 10 minutes. If using raw squash, add it to the pot along with the coriander, pepper, cumin, and about ½ teaspoon salt and cook, stirring occasionally, until the color brightens and the squash is no longer rock-hard, about 10 minutes. If using squash puree, add it to the pot with the spices and cook, stirring often, for 5 minutes to develop the flavors.

While the vegetables are cooking, bring the stock to a simmer in a saucepan, then adjust the heat to maintain a bare simmer. Add 4 cups (960 ml) of the stock and the garlic cloves to the softened vegetables, reduce the heat to medium-low, and simmer the soup until the vegetables are very tender, 20 to 25 minutes, adding more stock as necessary to keep the soup from becoming too thick.

Remove the soup from the heat and let cool slightly, then puree using a stand blender or an immersion blender, adding the remaining stock as needed until the soup is a pleasing consistency, and adding salt to taste. Reheat to serving temperature.

Ladle soup into warmed bowls and top each with finely chopped parsley and smoked salt or with the pesto.

PARSLEY OR CILANTRO PESTO
PAREVE/VEGAN

Pound with mortar and pestle or process in a food processor fitted with an S blade a couple garlic cloves, a teaspoon of salt, and a cup of cilantro or parsley leaves. Work in ⅓ to ½ cup of extra-virgin olive oil until the pesto is a rough pureé. Drizzle a little on each serving of soup. Any leftover pesto is delicious over roasted or grilled lamb or fish or as a spread on bruschetta. The topping will keep, refrigerated, for 3 days.

HOMEMADE VEGETABLE STOCK

MAKES 7 TO 8 CUPS (1.7 TO 2 L)

PAREVE/VEGAN

Use a variety of vegetables, such as those below, to make a versatile vegan stock. Avoid using strongly flavored vegetables, such as cabbage and broccoli, as they will impact the finished soup. This recipe may easily be doubled or tripled and frozen in convenient two-cup quantities. (Do not double red pepper; its flavors become too pronounced in the stock when used in greater quantity.)

1 large leek, split lengthwise with greens and
    roots intact

3 carrots

1 large or 2 medium onions, about ½ pound
    (225 g) total

2 ribs celery with leaves

2 zucchinis

1 red bell pepper

A few large Swiss chard leaves with stems

½ bunch Italian parsley (about 20 large sprigs)

6 thyme sprigs

2 bay leaves, preferably fresh

1 tablespoon olive or mild oil, such as grapeseed
    or safflower

1 tablespoon kosher or sea salt

A few black peppercorns (optional)

Cut all the vegetables into 1- to 2-inch (2.5- to 5-cm) pieces. Put the vegetables and herbs in an 8-quart (8-L) stockpot with the oil, salt, and peppercorns. Sauté over medium heat until wilted, 10 to 15 minutes. Add water to cover the vegetables barely, cover the pot, and bring to a boil over medium-high heat. Reduce the heat to low, adjust the lid to cover partially, and simmer gently for 45 minutes to 1 hour to develop the flavor.

Strain the stock through a fine-mesh sieve placed over a bowl, pressing on the vegetables with the back of a spoon to extract all their goodness. Discard the vegetables. If the flavor of the stock is weak, return it to the pot and boil it uncovered to reduce it and concentrate the flavor. Use immediately, or let cool completely, cover, and refrigerate for up to 4 days or freeze for up to 3 months.

Hanukkah

FESTIVAL OF LIGHTS

Hanukkah has always been my favorite holiday. My parents were immigrant students when I was a child, so my affection for the holiday doesn't stem from elaborate presents or large parties. Even then, I was drawn to the warmth of the *hanukkiyah* (menorah) as though it were a cozy fireplace in our small apartment.

Hanukkah celebrates the David and Goliath-type rebellion led by Judah and the Maccabees against Syrian–Greek rule and assimilation, the rededication of the Temple in Jerusalem, and the mythical bit of olive oil that miraculously kept the holy Temple lamps lit for eight nights. Clearly not an agricultural holiday (although thought to be a reenactment of Sukkot for the fighters who had missed it), but its place on the calendar puts us in mind of the seasons' cycles. Hanukkah begins on the dark moon closest to the winter solstice, the shortest day and longest, darkest night of the year, when the ancient Hebrews would have most craved light and heat.

The feeling of warmth is still what's most important to me: Hanukkah parties with friends and my now-large family, lots of glowing candles, an actual fireplace, and yes, a pile of presents too. We decorate the dinner table with multicolored dreidls, chocolate *gelt*, tea lights, and persimmon or early tangerine branches. We've accumulated enough *hanukkiyot* over the years—including those my children made in preschool a very long time ago—so that all children present can light their own. We sing traditional songs, and my husband tells the story of Hanukkah.

And, of course, we eat fried foods— latkes (vegetable pancakes), *sufganiyot* (jelly doughnuts), *zengoula* (Iraqi funnel cakes)— to remember the magical eight nights of oil. So that all can experience this more personally (read: so I don't have to cook alone), everyone takes a turn at one of the skillets. In Israel, in addition to parties and winter vacations, Hanukkah torchlight runs are held to commemorate the rebellion and the miraculous oil. To my mind, a long walk or run sounds like the perfect antidote to holiday indulgence.

RECIPE SUGGESTIONS
FOR HANUKKAH

Best Potato Latkes (page 94)

Roasted Smashed Apples and Pears (page 98)

Sweet Potato and Butternut Squash
Mini-Latkes with Labneh and Smoky Harissa
(page 96)

Hearty Winter Slaw: Shaved Cabbage,
Radicchio, and Celery with Bosc Pears
(page 87)

Pure and Simple Brisket (page 65)

Zengoula with Lemon Syrup:
Iraqi Funnel Cakes (page 117)

BEST POTATO LATKES

MAKES 24 LATKES, 6 SERVINGS

PAREVE OR DAIRY

These latkes are thin, crisp, and pan-fried, not deep-fried. My family's traditional recipe is inspired by Sara Kasdan's, from her hilarious 1956 cookbook *Love and Knishes*, which my mother received as a gift nearly sixty years ago. You need a starchy potato for good latkes; the starch helps bind the pancake together. Sierra Gold (a cross between a Yukon Gold and a russet), German Butterball, Kennebec, and King Edward are all wonderful here. This recipe is easily doubled or tripled, and it works well with other wintry vegetables, as you'll discover in the following pages (and with summer squash in season, see page 50). See The Art of Perfect Latkes on page 97 for cooking tips.

2 pounds (900 g) starchy potatoes, peeled

1 small onion

2 heaping tablespoons unbleached all-purpose flour or potato starch

1 teaspoon kosher salt

½ teaspoon baking powder

Freshly ground black pepper

2 eggs, lightly beaten

Mild oil with a medium-high smoke point, such as grapeseed, sunflower, or avocado, for pan-frying

Coarse finishing salt, such as Maldon sea salt

Applesauce or Roasted Smashed Apples and Pears (page 98) and/or sour cream

Using the large holes of a box grater or a food processor fitted with the grating disk, grate the potatoes. You should have about 5 cups (730 grams). Place the potatoes in a sieve to drain. Grate the onion on the large holes of the box grater or fit the processor with the metal S blade and grate. It should look like pulp; mince or discard any large onion pieces.

In a large bowl, stir together potatoes, onion, flour, salt, baking powder, and a few grinds of pepper. Stir in eggs.

Line 2 or 3 sheet pans with paper towels. Place the prepared pans, the latke batter, a large spoon, and a spatula near the stove. Heat 1 or 2 large skillets over medium heat. Generously film the skillet(s) with oil (not more than ¼ inch/6 mm deep). When the oil is shimmering and a tiny bit of batter sizzles on contact, start spooning in the latke batter, making sure to add both solids and liquid. Using the back of the spoon, flatten each spoonful into a circle 3 to 4 inches (7.5 to 10 cm) in diameter. Do not crowd the latkes in the pan. You'll get 4 or 5 latkes in a 12-inch (30.5-cm) skillet.

Cook the latkes, flipping them once, until golden on both sides, 5 to 6 minutes total. Transfer the latkes to a prepared baking sheet. Cook the remaining batter in the same way, stirring the batter before adding more to the pan and adding oil as needed at the edge of the pan.

Arrange the latkes on a warmed platter, sprinkle with finishing salt, and serve with applesauce or sour cream.

CRISP PARSNIP LATKES VARIATION: Sweet, lemony, and spicy parsnips and smashed apples and pears are a fabulous root-and-fruit pairing for latkes. Substitute 2 pounds (900 g) juicy-looking medium to large parsnips for the potatoes and use white pepper in place of black pepper. The grated parsnips won't release liquid that requires draining, but they will discolor slightly after they are peeled.

SWEET POTATO AND BUTTERNUT SQUASH MINI-LATKES WITH LABNEH AND SMOKY HARISSA

MAKES 48 MINI-LATKES, 8 TO 12 APPETIZER SERVINGS;
OR 18 TO 20 LARGE LATKES, 6 SERVINGS

DAIRY

The year Hanukkah and Thanksgiving overlapped into Thanksgivikkuh, I made latkes from everything I could find, including turkey stuffing leftovers. These bright pancakes are sweet, spicy, and salty, and when made mini-size, they are a good appetizer that wakes up the taste buds. Sweet potatoes tend to burn easily because of their high sugar content, but that problem is remedied by including less-sweet butternut squash, which also makes more tender pancakes. See the Art of Perfect Latkes (facing page) for cooking tips.

½ pound (225 g) sweet potatoes, peeled or
   scrubbed
½ pound (225 g) butternut squash, peeled
1 small onion
2 eggs, beaten to blend
2 heaping tablespoons unbleached all-purpose
   flour or potato starch
1 teaspoon kosher salt
¼ teaspoon baking powder
A few drops Tabasco
Mild oil with a medium-high smoke point, such as
   grapeseed, sunflower, or avocado, for pan-frying
Labneh, homemade (page 22) or store-bought
Smoky Harissa (page 33)
Smoked salt or other finishing salt

Using the large holes of a box grater or a food processor fitted with a grating disk, grate the potatoes and squash into a large bowl. You should have about 4 cups (400 g) total. Grate the onion into the bowl the same way. You should have about ⅓ cup (50 g) pulp; mince or discard any large onion pieces. Stir in the eggs, flour, salt, baking powder, and Tabasco.

Line 2 or 3 baking sheets with paper towels. Have the prepared pans, the latke batter, a large spoon, and a spatula near the stove. Heat 1 or 2 large skillets over medium heat. Generously film the pan(s) with vegetable oil (not more than ¼ inch/6 mm deep). When the oil is shimmering in the pan (a tiny bit of batter dropped into it should sizzle on contact), start spooning in the latke batter by the level tablespoon, making sure to add both solids and liquid. Flatten each spoonful with the back of the spoon into a circle 2 to 3 inches (5 to 7.5 cm) in diameter. Do not crowd the latkes in the pan. You'll get 6 to 8 mini-latkes in a 12-inch (30.5-cm) skillet. If making large latkes, use twice as much batter for each latke and cook only 4 or 5 latkes in the pan(s) at a time.

Cook the latkes, flipping them once, until golden on both sides, about 5 minutes total. Transfer the latkes to a prepared baking sheet. Cook the remaining batter in the same way, always stirring the batter before adding more to the pan and adding oil as needed to the edge of the pan. The latkes can be made a few hours ahead and reheated in a single layer on baking sheets in a 350°F (180°C) oven.

To serve, arrange latkes in a single layer on a platter and top each latke with a dollop of labneh, a dab of harissa, and a little finishing salt. Or, pile latkes on a platter and accompany with bowls of self-serve condiments.

THE ART OF PERFECT LATKES

1. You can peel potatoes up to 2 hours before you grate them and keep them immersed in a bowl of water to prevent them from discoloring.

2. Although food processors now make short work of preparing latkes for a crowd, I find that the large-hole side of an old-fashioned box grater still produces the best pancakes.

3. Prepare the latke batter just before you are ready to begin cooking. Grated potatoes will start to discolor immediately, turning orange and then gray. As long as you begin cooking the latkes within 30 minutes or so of making the batter, the color will return to normal when the potatoes hit the heat. Don't even think about making latke batter the night before. You will end up with charcoal-gray latkes!

4. Heat the skillet(s) over medium heat, not high.

5. Keep the oil to a depth of no more than ¼ inch (6 mm) and make sure it remains hot enough so that the latke batter sizzles on contact. This will prevent the latkes from soaking up the oil. You will need to add oil to the pan from time to time. Tilt the pan a bit to give the oil a chance to heat quickly before allowing it to flow under the latkes.

6. From time to time, remove the little brown bits that accumulate in the pan as you cook the latkes. These burn easily and will impart an acrid taste to the cooking oil and the latkes. If the pan gets too hot and the oil starts to smoke, turn off the heat and allow the oil to cool enough to pour it out of the pan. Then wipe out the pan and start all over again with fresh oil.

7. Stir the batter frequently, as the starch will sink to the bottom of the bowl, especially with potato latkes. Be sure to include both vegetable and some of the starchy, eggy liquid when spooning out the batter for each latke.

8. Keep your latkes thin! Thick latkes are a recipe for disaster: raw inside and burnt outside. One generous tablespoonful is enough to make a 3- to 4-inch (7.5- to 10-cm) pancake. Place the spoonful in the hot pan and immediately flatten it into a pancake with the back of the spoon.

9. If you are cooking latkes for a crowd, preheat the oven to 300°F (150°C). When you fill a paper towel–lined sheet pan with a layer of cooked latkes, slip the pan uncovered into the oven to keep the latkes warm while you cook the remaining batter.

10. Latkes taste best when cooked *à la minute*, so make cooking part of your Hanukkah party, and enlist guests to take a turn at the stove.

11. If you must, you can cook the latkes a few hours ahead and let them cool on the baking sheets. Just before serving, reheat them in a single layer in a 350°F (180°C) until they are piping hot.

ROASTED SMASHED APPLES AND PEARS

MAKES ABOUT 3 CUPS (750 G)

PAREVE/VEGAN

Roasting apples and pears in their skins produces concentrated fruit-forward flavors that don't need any added sweeteners or seasonings to shine. All you'll need here is a sheet pan or shallow baking dish, a knife, a fork, and a piece of foil. If you must gild the lily, add spices sparingly so that you don't mask the flavor of the fruit. Use any of the interesting tart apple varieties available at farmers' markets, such as Spitzenberg, Winesap, Northern Spy, or Cox's Orange Pippin. If you like your fruit sweet, include Golden Delicious or Golden Russet apples in the mix. Use Bartlett, D'Anjou, or Bosc pears. This dish can be made using all apples or all pears.

3 pounds (1.4 kg) medium-size apples and pears
    (8 or 9 total)
A few sprigs thyme (optional)
2 to 3 tablespoons water, fresh lemon juice,
    Calvados, pear brandy or eau-de-vie, hard cider,
    or dessert wine
Ground cinnamon or nutmeg (optional)

Preheat the oven to 375°F (190°C). Halve the pears and apples through the stem end, then core them and place the halves, cut side down, on 1 or more sheet pans, spacing them 1 to 2 inches (2.5 to 5 cm) apart. If using the thyme, scatter it among the apples and pears. Cover the pan(s) tightly with aluminum foil.

Bake the apples and pears until tender when pierced with a knife tip, 30 to 40 minutes. When they are cool enough to handle, slip the fruits from the skins and back into the pan(s), scraping any pulp from the skins. Discard the skins and thyme stems.

Mash the apples and pears with a fork, stirring in enough water to help scrape up any brown bits from the pan bottom and lighten the texture of the fruit. Stir in the cinnamon to taste, if using. Scrape the mixture into a bowl and serve warm or at room temperature, or cover and refrigerate up to a day ahead and serve cold.

ROASTED BRUSSELS SPROUTS WITH WALNUTS, POMEGRANATE MOLASSES, AND SHANKLISH

MAKES 6 TO 8 SERVINGS

DAIRY OR PAREVE/VEGAN

On a visit to Kalustyan's, the Middle Eastern food emporium in Manhattan, I discovered fresh *shanklish*—thick *labneh* seasoned with za'atar and Aleppo pepper—made by The White Moustache, a small-batch yogurt producer in Brooklyn. I devoured it for breakfast and again as an afternoon snack with pita. The next day, I ordered glazed Brussels sprouts and walnuts at the upscale Lebanese restaurant ilili (also in New York City). And that is how this recipe came to be. I like to dip the warm Brussels sprouts into the cool *shanklish*, but you can also thin the topping with a little olive oil to make it more like a dressing. Pomegranate molasses is the Middle Eastern equivalent of a balsamic reduction. For a pareve/vegan version of this recipe, omit the *shanklish*.

2 pounds (900 g) small-to-medium Brussels sprouts, halved lengthwise

2 tablespoons extra-virgin olive oil

Kosher or sea salt and freshly ground black pepper

4 tablespoons (60 ml) pomegranate molasses

1 cup (100 g) walnut halves, toasted (see page 18)

1 cup (225 g) Shanklish (recipe follows)

Position a rack in the upper third of the oven and preheat the oven to 400°F (200°C).

Boil the Brussels sprouts in salted water or steam them over salted water until crisp-tender, about 3 minutes. Drain and dry thoroughly on paper towels or dish towels. (This step can be done a day ahead; store covered in the refrigerator.) On a large baking sheet, toss the sprouts with the olive oil, season them with salt and pepper, and spread them evenly over the baking sheet.

Roast the Brussels sprouts, shaking the pan halfway through the cooking, until they are tender, browned in places, and any loose leaves are crisped, about 35 minutes. Remove the pan from the oven, drizzle 2 tablespoons of the molasses over the sprouts, toss, and return the sprouts to the oven for about 5 minutes to glaze.

Remove from the oven and scrape the Brussels sprouts and any juices onto a serving platter. Scatter the walnuts over and around the sprouts, season with additional salt, and drizzle with the remaining 2 tablespoons molasses. Top with a large dollop or two of Shanklish and serve the remaining sauce in a bowl alongside.

SHANKLISH

MAKES 2 CUPS (450 G)

DAIRY

2 cups (450 g) labneh, homemade (page 22) or store-bought

1 tablespoon za'atar

Leaves from 6 thyme sprigs, chopped or crushed

½ to 1 teaspoon Aleppo pepper

½ to 1 teaspoon kosher salt

In a bowl, combine the labneh, za'atar, thyme, ½ teaspoon Aleppo pepper, and ½ teaspoon salt and stir to mix. Let stand for at least 30 minutes before serving. Taste and adjust with more Aleppo pepper and salt if needed. The shanklish will keep refrigerated for up to 3 days.

WINTER GREENS SAUTÉ

MAKES 6 TO 8 SERVINGS

PAREVE/VEGAN

Consider this a master recipe for any number of the quick-cooking winter greens that are abundant this time of year. Swiss chard, beet tops, spinach, escarole, radicchio, and dandelion greens all show their best in a simple sauté and lend themselves to a variety of flavorings. Take a page from both Italian and Catalan food traditions and add sweet raisins and hot red pepper. Or, play up the meaty aspects, by using a little chicken stock in the cooking and topping the dish with a generous shower of *gribenes* (page 24).

1 large bunch Swiss chard or other quick-cooking greens, such as spinach, escarole, radicchio, beet greens, or dandelion greens

1 small onion, chopped

Kosher or sea salt

1 to 2 tablespoons extra-virgin olive oil

3 cloves garlic, sliced

Generous pinch of red pepper flakes

½ cup (75 g) raisins

1 to 2 teaspoons ground sumac, optional

FOUR SMART THINGS TO DO WITH WINTER GREENS SAUTÉ

1. Chop it finely, add olive oil, pepper, salt, and sumac and serve at room temperature on bruschetta with or without a schmear of ricotta cheese as an appetizer.

2. Stir it into a pot of risotto.

3. Toss it with pasta and top with toasted bread crumbs and/or grated Parmigiano-Reggiano.

4. Stir it into cooked white beans.

Strip the stems from the chard as directed on page 17 and trim off and discard any tough ends. Chop the stems as you would celery and cut the leaves into wide strips.

In a large skillet, sauté the onion and chard stems with a bit of salt and 1 tablespoon of the olive oil over medium heat until softened, 5 to 7 minutes. Add the garlic and red pepper flakes and cook for a minute or two. Add the chard leaves, a little more salt, and more oil if needed to prevent sticking and cook until wilted, about 2 minutes. If the pan will not accommodate all the leaves at once, add them in batches, waiting for each batch to wilt slightly before adding more. Add the raisins and cover the pan to help steam the chard and plump the raisins. Cook until the chard is tender, 5 to 10 minutes, adding a bit of water, if necessary, to keep the chard from sticking. If you'd like to add a tart note, add the sumac to taste. Serve warm or room temperature.

MEAT VARIATION: Use schmaltz instead of olive oil and chicken stock in place of water. Omit the raisins and red pepper flakes. Toss in about ½ cup (60 g) gribenes just before serving.

SHOPPING TIP: When shopping for greens, look for glossy, unblemished leaves and succulent stems. Avoid limp or yellowed leaves. Store greens in a loose plastic bag in the crisper drawer of the refrigerator. It is best to use them within three to four days, but freshly harvested bunches may keep a week or longer. Swiss chard is a mild-flavored cousin of beets. It comes in white- and multicolor-stemmed "rainbow" versions, and its celery-like stems are edible, adding textural contrast to a dish.

TOASTED ISRAELI COUSCOUS
IN **WINTER SQUASH CASES**

MAKES 8 SERVINGS

PAREVE OR MEAT

Redolent with cinnamon and orange, this aromatic marriage of Moroccan and autumn flavors makes a festive vegetarian or meat main dish or side. Scooping bits of tender pumpkin with each forkful of couscous is reminiscent of the traditional dish. Use small Sweet Dumpling, butternut, delicata, or acorn squashes. Mini-pumpkins are adorable, but they don't have enough meat. So if you want to use them, you will need an extra squash or two for the filling. Pearls of toasted Israeli couscous, *ptitim* in Hebrew, add great texture. Traditional couscous, Sardinian *fregola*, or quinoa is good here, too.

4 or 5 small butternut, acorn, Sweet Dumpling, or delicata squash, 10 to 12 ounces (280 to 340 g) each, or 9 or 10 single-serving-size orange or white pumpkins

Extra-virgin olive oil

Kosher or sea salt and freshly ground black pepper

1 onion, finely chopped

1 teaspoon ground cinnamon

1 orange

1 cup (150 g) Israeli couscous

½ cup (60 g) dried cranberries or (70 g) black currants

2 to 3 cups (240 to 360 ml) chicken or vegetable stock (page 44 or 92)

Smoky Harissa (page 33), optional

Preheat the oven to 425°F (220°C). Cut 4 squashes in half lengthwise and scoop out and discard the seeds and strings. Scoop out the flesh, leaving a shell ¼ inch (6 mm) thick. Chop the flesh into ¼- to ½-inch (6- to 12-mm) pieces. You should have 1½ to 2 cups (210 to 280 g). Peel and chop the flesh from an extra small squash if necessary to make up the difference. If using mini-pumpkins, cut the tops off of 8 pumpkins just where each pumpkin gets wide, then hollow them out as directed for the small squash. Peel and chop the flesh from an extra pumpkin or two as needed to make up the flesh amount. Reserve the caps.

Brush the cut cavity and cut surface of each squash with olive oil and season with salt and pepper. Place the squash cut side down on a sheet pan and roast until the cut surfaces are nicely browned and the squash are beginning to get tender, 15 to 20 minutes. Remove from the oven, turn cut side up, and let cool. (The squash can be roasted up to 1 day ahead, covered, and refrigerated. Bring to room temperature before proceeding.) Reduce the oven temperature to 375°F (190°C).

In a wide pot, sauté the onion in 2 tablespoons olive oil over medium heat until softened and translucent, 5 to 7 minutes. Add the squash pieces and cinnamon and season with salt and pepper. Turn the heat to medium-high and cook, stirring occasionally, until the squash brightens in color and starts to soften, about 7 minutes. While the squash is cooking, remove the zest from the orange, using a Microplane grater and working over the pot to capture both the zest and the spray of citrus oils.

Reduce the heat to medium. Push the squash mixture to the side of the pot or transfer it to a plate. Add a teaspoon or two of oil if the pot seems dry and then add the couscous. Cook, stirring frequently, until the couscous is lightly browned, about 2 minutes. Return the squash mixture to the pan and stir well.

Add the cranberries and 2 cups (480 ml) of the stock to the pot, stir well to scrape up any brown bits from the bottom of the pot, cover, and bring to a simmer. Reduce the heat as needed to maintain a gentle simmer and cook for 10 minutes. Uncover and continue cooking until the couscous is tender and the pearls have enlarged, about 10 minutes more, adding the remaining stock as needed to keep the mixture moist and loose. Taste and season as needed.

Fill the squash cases with the couscous mixture, mounding the filling. Leave them on the sheet pan or transfer them to an attractive shallow baking pan. If using pumpkins, perch a cap on each one. (The squash can be prepared up to this point 1 day ahead, covered, and refrigerated. Bring to room temperature before continuing.) Bake until squash cases are blistered and tender, exposed filling is browned, and the dish is wonderfully fragrant, about 40 minutes. Accompany with harissa.

BRAISED BEEF WITH SEMOLINA DUMPLINGS

MAKES 8 TO 10 SERVINGS

MEAT

This hearty winter braise is inspired by two of the most beloved dishes my grandmother (*safta* in Hebrew) Rachel used to make: *kubbe*, miniature meat-filled semolina dumplings simmered in a vegetable or meat stew, and long-cooked green beans variously known as loubia or fasoulia. Here herb-flecked semolina dumplings capture the flavor and nubbly texture of my *safta*'s original recipe without all the work. The stew flavors the dumplings, which in turn thicken the juices into a rich gravy. In late fall, use snap, romano, or Chinese long beans or okra, along with carrots and late-season sauce tomatoes. In winter, substitute blanched cauliflower (*karnabit*) for the beans, and use canned or sun-dried tomatoes. Use a cut of meat that has some fat and connective tissue, such as chuck roast or short ribs, which becomes succulent with long cooking. This is especially important with leaner grass-fed beef. My Iraqi grandmother would have served this over rice, but you can add potatoes or let the dumplings be the only starch.

1 bunch good-size carrots (6 to 8),
     about 1¼ pounds (570 g)
3 pounds (1.4 kg) chuck roast, trimmed and cut
     into 1- to 2-inch (2.5- to 5-cm) pieces
Kosher or sea salt and freshly ground black pepper
2 tablespoons olive oil
1 large onion, finely chopped
2 ribs celery, finely chopped
1 tablespoon chopped fresh cilantro or Italian
     parsley, plus more for garnish
1 teaspoon hot or sweet paprika, or a mix
2 large cloves garlic, minced
3 Roma tomatoes, grated, and 1 tablespoon
     minced sun-dried tomato or tomato paste, or
     1 can (8 ounces/225 g) tomato sauce

About 2 cups (480 ml) homemade beef stock
     (page 66), or 1 cup (240 ml) canned beef
     broth diluted with 1 cup (240 ml) water
1 pound romano bean or snap beans, preferably
     Blue Lake
Semolina dumplings (recipe follows)
Basic White Rice (page 21) or thick slices of
     country bread for serving, optional

Finely chop 1 of the carrots. Heat a large, wide pot over medium-high heat. Season the beef with salt and pepper. Working in batches to avoid crowding, add the beef to the pot and brown well on all sides, 5 to 10 minutes for each batch. Transfer the meat to a plate and drain off all but 2 tablespoons of the fat from the pot. If there is not enough fat in the pot, add olive oil as needed.

Reduce the heat to medium-low and add the onion, chopped carrot, celery, and cilantro and season with ½ teaspoon salt and the paprika. Stir to scrape up any brown bits from the pot bottom and cook, stirring occasionally, until the vegetables are tender, about 10 minutes. Stir in the garlic, wait a moment, and then add the grated and sun-dried tomatoes and 1 cup (240 ml) of the stock. Raise the heat to high and bring to a boil. Cook until the tomatoes have lost their raw look and are slightly thickened, about 5 minutes. Return the meat to the pot and reduce the heat to low. The liquid in the pot should come about halfway up the sides of the meat. If necessary, spoon out some of the liquid and reserve.

Cover and braise the meat until tender, 1 to 2 hours, checking from time to time to be sure there is sufficient liquid and that the juices are simmering rather than boiling. Add the reserved juices or stock as necessary to maintain the original level.

While the stew is cooking, prepare the dumpling dough

continued »

and the remaining carrots and beans. Peel the carrots and cut crosswise into 2-inch (5-cm) pieces (cut in half lengthwise first if the carrots are very fat). Trim the stem end from the beans and either fillet them first or simply cut crosswise into 1-inch (2.5-cm) pieces.

When the meat is tender, add the carrots and beans to the pot and continue cooking until the meat and vegetables are very tender, about 1 hour more. (The dish can be made to this point up to 1 day ahead, cooled, covered, and refrigerated. Remove any fat that hardens on the surface before continuing.) Use a large spoon to skim off any fat from the surface. Add the dumplings to the pot during the last 30 minutes of cooking.

Serve the stew in shallow bowls over rice or with thick slabs of bread on the side, if desired, to soak up the juices. Garnish the stew with cilantro.

PAREVE/VEGAN VARIATION: Substitute equal amounts of winter squash and waxy or all-purpose potatoes, cut into 2-inch (5-cm) chunks, for the beef, and use vegetable stock in place of the beef stock. The stew will take 1 hour to cook instead of 2 hours.

SEMOLINA DUMPLINGS

MAKES 30 TO 35 DUMPLINGS

PAREVE/VEGAN

½ onion, finely chopped

5 tablespoons (75 ml) mild oil, such as grapeseed or safflower

½ bunch cilantro or Italian parsley, finely chopped (about ¼ cup/15 g)

1 cup (220 g) coarse semolina (in a pinch, regular Cream of Wheat (210 g) can be substituted)

1 teaspoon kosher or sea salt

Freshly ground black pepper

⅛ to ¼ teaspoon hot paprika, or ¼ teaspoon sweet paprika

⅔ cup (165 ml) water

In a small skillet, cook the onion in 1 tablespoon of the oil over medium-low heat until soft and pale golden, 7 to 10 minutes. Stir in the cilantro, remove from the heat, and let cool. You'll have about ⅔ cup (95 g).

In a medium bowl, use a fork to stir together the semolina, salt, several grinds of pepper, and the paprika. Stir in the onion mixture and the remaining 4 tablespoons (60 ml) oil, then beat in the water. You should have a loose mixture with the consistency of cottage cheese. Cover and refrigerate for at least 30 minutes or up to overnight. The semolina will absorb the liquid and swell to become a smooth, very soft dough.

Pinch off small pieces of the dough and roll them into marble-size balls no larger than 1 inch (2.5 cm) in diameter. As you shape them, place them in a single layer on a plate or tray. The oil in the dough will keep it from sticking to your hands.

To cook the dumplings, drop them into the simmering stew, cover the pot, and simmer over low heat until they are cooked through, about 30 minutes. (The stew and dumplings can be cooled, covered, and refrigerated and then reheated the next day.)

THE GIFT OF SHABBAT

Pausing for a day of rest is truly a gift, a time to restore and re-center after a hectic week. For my family, the Sabbath has an added layer of meaning.

On the last day of her life, my ninety-four-year-old grandmother, Rachel, prepared the Sabbath meal, as she did every Friday, in her apartment in Bat Yam, Israel. She dropped miniature meat-filled *kubbe* into a simmering okra stew. Filleted snap beans yielded their tiny peas to the beef stew bubbling on the back burner.

My grandmother turned the flame low to keep the food warm and went to lie down in the bedroom. When my aunt Hanna arrived at three in the afternoon, as she did every Friday to share an early Shabbat with her mother before going home to her own family, my grandmother did not awaken.

Later that afternoon, when the necessary details had been taken care of, Hanna and her sister Daliah and their children and grandchildren sat down to honor and partake of Rachel's last gift: chicken soup with egg drop noodles, *kubbe bamia* (dumplings and okra), *loubia* (green beans with beef), white rice, and a cabbage.

Twenty years later, the power of that moment still echoes for us in the simple act of preparing a Friday-night dinner.

ROAST CHICKEN WITH TANGERINES, GREEN OLIVES, AND SILAN

MAKES 6 TO 8 SERVINGS

MEAT

What a great way to celebrate the arrival of early winter citrus and the season's holidays: tender roast chicken burnished with a sweet-hot rub of *silan*, or date syrup, and harissa, and perfumed with tangerines that are caramelized from their time in the oven. If you don't like it hot, feel free to reduce the amount of harissa or substitute sweet smoked paprika. This is delicious served with freekeh, rice, or Simcha's Rice with Almonds and Raisins (page 188). If you're making this dish for a crowd, you can use the same weight in chicken parts (thighs and drumsticks work best). Use lightly brined olives, such as bright green Sicilian Castelveltranos, that marry well with the other flavors of the dish; avoid overly brined or sour varieties. This recipe will take you straight through the spring.

1 chicken, 4 pounds (1.8 kg)

Extra-virgin olive oil

2 tablespoons silan (date syrup, see page 12)

2 to 3 teaspoons harissa spice mix, harissa
    paste, or ½ teaspoon each cayenne pepper,
    smoked paprika, coriander, and cumin

Kosher or sea salt

¾ pound (340 g) shallots (about 4 large or
    8 small)

6 tangerines or other sweet mandarins

1 cup (175 g) lightly brined green olives, such as
    Castelveltrano

1 to 2 cups (240 to 480 ml) white wine, stock, or
    water

Preheat the oven to 400°F (200°C). Pat the chicken dry. Whisk together 4 tablespoons (60 ml) olive oil, the silan, harissa to taste, and 1 teaspoon salt. Peel shallots and cut into quarters if large or halves if small. Cut unpeeled tangerines into quarters or sixths and poke out visible seeds.

Scatter shallots and tangerines in the bottom of a large roasting pan and toss with a little olive oil and salt. Rub chicken inside and out with the harissa-silan mixture. Toss a few tangerine and shallot pieces into the cavity of the chicken. Place chicken, breast side up, in the pan and tie the legs together loosely with twine, if desired.

Roast 30 minutes, baste with juices that have collected in the pan, and add the olives. Continue roasting, adding wine to the pan as needed to prevent the juices from burning and basting the bird once or twice more during the cooking, until the skin is a rich brown and the chicken is cooked all the way through, about 30 minutes longer.

Transfer chicken, shallots, olives, and tangerines to a platter and tent loosely with foil. Place roasting pan on the stove top over medium heat, pour in 1 cup of wine, and stir to deglaze the pan, scraping up any brown bits. Cook until heated through, reduced, thickened, and glossy, about 2 minutes. To defat the juices, pour them into a fat separator or skim off the fat with a large spoon.

Carve the chicken and serve with the shallots, olives, tangerines, and the warm pan juices.

SHOPPING TIP: The word "tangerine" originally referred to a native of Tangier and has no botanical meaning. This type of citrus has many varieties, all technically mandarins. Some, such as early-ripening Satsumas, are commonly sold as "tangerines." Since these are what you are most likely to find this time of year and since this dish has a North African quality, it seems appropriate to name it after the Moroccan seaport.

PEPPERED RED WINE FRUIT COMPOTE

MAKES 4 TO 5 CUPS (1 TO 1.3 KG) COMPOTE, 10 TO 12 SERVINGS

PAREVE

This dried-fruit compote is perfect in winter and early spring, when fresh fruit is scarce. It is versatile on its own, as a sauce for cool-weather cakes, and even as a sundae topping. (See some of my favorite pairings, below.) Black peppercorns complement the red wine and add warmth, rather than heat, to the juices and are a nice change from the usual cinnamon stick.

1 bottle (750 ml) dry red wine, such as a
    Zinfandel, Pinot Noir, or Côtes du Rhône
3 tablespoons honey
6 to 8 black peppercorns
1¼ pounds (570 g) mixed dried fruits, such as
    pitted prunes or other plum varieties, apricots,
    peaches, cherries, and/or raisins, in any
    combination
2 to 3 cups (480 to 720 ml) water

In a deep pot large enough to hold all the ingredients, combine the wine, honey, and peppercorns and bring to a boil over medium-high heat. Cook uncovered until the mixture has reduced by one-third, 10 to 15 minutes.

Meanwhile, cut any large pieces of dried fruit into halves or quarters. When the wine mixture has reduced, add the fruit, cover the pot, and turn down the heat to low. Simmer until the fruit is plump and much of the wine has been absorbed, 15 to 20 minutes. Check the pot occasionally; if the mixture appears dry, add a little water.

Add 2 cups (480 ml) of the water to the pot, re-cover, raise the heat to return the juices to a simmer, and continue cooking until the fruit is very tender and the juices are syrupy. Remove from the heat, uncover, and let the mixture stand for at least 15 minutes to allow the juices to continue to thicken.

Serve the compote warm or at room temperature. (The compote can be made a day or two ahead, covered, and refrigerated. The fruit will continue to absorb the juices, so you will need to add more water or a fruit juice when reheating.)

DELICIOUS WITH

Aunt Sarah's Honey and Apple Cake (page 77)

Cozonac: A Simple Yeast Cake (page 113)

Semolina and Walnut Oil Cake
with Coffee Hawaij (page 243)

Carob Molasses Ice Cream (page 151)
and Rustic Almond-Orange Macaroons
(page 152) for Tu B'Shevat

Roasted Smashed Apples and Pears (page 98) for
an intriguing dairy- and gluten-free "sundae"

COZONAC: A SIMPLE SWEET YEAST CAKE

MAKES ONE 10-INCH (25-CM) RING, 12 TO 16 SERVINGS

DAIRY

Lemon scented and versatile, my grandmother's Romanian yeast-and-butter cake is delicious toasted for breakfast and beautiful with any of the seasonal fruit condiments in this book. The dough can be rolled babka-like with many types of fillings, such as the decadent halvah variation at the end of this recipe.

2 packages (¼ ounce/7 g each) active dry yeast

½ cup (100 g) plus 1 tablespoon sugar

½ cup (120 ml) warm water (100° to 110°F/38° to 43°C)

3 cups (375 g) unbleached all-purpose flour

1 tablespoon packed finely-grated lemon zest (from 2 lemons)

5 tablespoons (70 grams) butter, at room temperature, plus more for the pan

2 egg yolks

½ cup (120 ml) whole milk or heavy cream

1 tablespoon vanilla extract

½ teaspoon salt

1 egg, beaten

In a small bowl, stir together the yeast, 1 tablespoon of the sugar, and the warm water. Let stand in a warm place until the mixture bubbles, about 10 minutes.

In the bowl of en electric mixer fitted with the paddle attachment, stir together the flour, the remaining ½ cup (100 g) sugar, and the lemon zest. On medium speed, beat in the butter, egg yolks, milk, and yeast mixture, followed by the vanilla and then the salt, beating until all the ingredients are thoroughly blended, about 4 minutes total. The dough will be soft and sticky. Sprinkle the dough with a little flour, cover the bowl with a towel, and place in a warm, draft-free place until doubled in size, about 1½ hours.

Preheat the oven to 350°F (180°C). Butter a 10- x 4-inch (25- x 10-cm) tube pan (with or without a removable bottom). Scrape the dough into the pan and ease it into a ring, working the dough from the middle, rather than pulling the ends, to keep the thickness even. Brush the top of the dough with the egg.

Bake the cake until golden brown, lightly puffed, and a toothpick inserted near the center comes out clean, 30 to 35 minutes. Let cool in the pan on a wire rack for 10 minutes. Run a thin-bladed knife or spatula around the outer edge of the cake and around the central tube to loosen the cake. If the cake has a removable bottom, lift the cake out of the pan by its tube and run the knife between the cake and the bottom of the pan. Lift the cake off and set it upright on a wire rack to cool. (If the pan does not have a removable bottom, invert the pan to release the cake and set it upright on the rack.)

Serve the cake at room temperature. The cake will keep well wrapped in plastic wrap at room temperature for up to 4 days or in the freezer for up to 1 month.

HALVAH-AND-MORE VARIATION: After the dough rises, scrape it onto a lightly floured work surface, then gently roll and pat it into a rectangle about 8 x 12 x ¾ inch (20 x 30.5 x 2 cm). Brush the top all over with 1 to 2 tablespoons melted butter. Top evenly with ½ pound (225 g) halvah, crumbled, leaving a narrow border at the long side farthest from you. Top the halvah evenly with 1 cup (115 g) chopped almonds and ½ cup (85 g) chopped semisweet chocolate. Starting at the long side closest to you, roll up the dough into a log. Place the log, seam side down, in the prepared tube pan and bake as directed.

APPLES IN NIGHTGOWNS

MAKES 8 SERVINGS

DAIRY

My parents wed at the height of apple season, and my maternal grandmother Mina made these festive, yet cozy apples in pastry as the star dessert for the small reception. (She also made my mother's cream-white wool wedding suit, à la Jean Patou, as she used to say, and cream lace blouse with pearl shank buttons and ruffled jabot.) The rich *Muerbeteig* dough (German shortcrust pastry) reveals my *saftik's* (grandma's) great love of butter. Use tart-sweet apple varieties that are tender but still hold their shape when baked, such as Spitzenberg, Honeycrisp, Pink Pearl, Golden Russet, Winesap, or Pink Lady

FOR THE DOUGH

3¼ cups (405 g) unbleached all-purpose flour

¼ cup (50 g) granulated sugar

Scant 1 teaspoon salt

Fine zest of 1 lemon

1½ cups (340 g) butter, cut into small pieces

3 egg yolks

1 tablespoon Cognac, brandy, or Calvados

FOR THE APPLES

½ cup (75 g) raisins

½ cup (60 g) walnuts or pecans

Zest of 1 lemon

3 tablespoons granulated sugar

2 tablespoons Cognac, brandy, or Calvados

8 small tart-sweet apples, about 2 pounds (900 g) total, 4 ounces/115 g each

FOR FINISHING AND SERVING

1 egg yolk

1 tablespoon heavy cream

Coarse or sanding sugar for dusting

Heavy or softly whipped cream for serving (optional)

TO MAKE THE DOUGH: In a large bowl, using a fork, stir together the flour, granulated sugar, salt, and lemon zest. Scatter the butter over the flour mixture and, using a pastry blender or your fingertips, cut in the butter until the mixture resembles coarse crumbs. In a small bowl, whisk together the egg yolks and Cognac until blended and stir the mixture into the flour-butter mixture until a buttery dough comes together. Gather the dough into a ball and press together. Cut the dough in half, place each half on a sheet of plastic wrap, and loosely bring the ends of the wrap over to cover. Press the dough with the heel of your hand into a disk ½ inch (12 mm) thick. Chill the dough for at least 30 minutes or up to 2 days.

Remove the dough from the refrigerator and, if necessary, let rest until soft enough to roll. Have a parchment paper-lined sheet pan handy. Place half the dough between 2 lightly floured sheets of parchment paper and roll out the dough into a long rectangle ¼ inch (6 mm) thick. Cut the rectangle into four 4-inch (10-cm) squares and reserve the scraps. Roll out each square into a 6-inch (15-cm) square ⅛ inch (3 mm) thick. Using a large offset spatula, transfer the squares onto the prepared pan in a single layer and cover with a sheet of parchment. Repeat with the remaining dough, creating a second layer of squares on the parchment. Reroll the scraps, cut into decorative leaf shapes, scoring them with the tip of a small knife to indicate veins, and add them to the pan. Place the dough in refrigerator while you prepare the apples. (This step can be done ahead, wrapped in plastic wrap, and refrigerated for up to 2 days or frozen for up to 5 days.)

TO PREPARE THE APPLES: On a cutting board, chop together the raisins, nuts, and lemon zest. Transfer to a small bowl and stir in the granulated sugar and Cognac.

continued »

Using an apple corer or vegetable drill (see page 20), and starting at the stem end, hollow out the apples almost to the bottom, boring a cavity about 1 inch (2.5 cm) in diameter. Pack about 1 tablespoon of the raisin-nut mixture into each apple, then mound a bit extra on top.

TO ASSEMBLE THE PASTRIES: Remove the dough from the refrigerator. Have a parchment-lined sheet pan ready. Place an apple in the center of a dough square and, when the dough is warm enough to be pliable without cracking, fold it up the sides of the apple, pushing upward with your fingertips gently from the bottom until the apple is completely encased in dough. Press together any cracks. Press a leaf or two onto the top, then place the apple on the prepared pan. Repeat with remaining apples.

In a small bowl, whisk together the egg yolk and cream until blended and brush evenly over the apples. Sprinkle the apples generously with the coarse sugar. Refrigerate until the pastry has firmed, 15 to 30 minutes. (The pastries can instead be refrigerated overnight; wait until just before baking to brush with the egg wash and sprinkle with the sugar.) Meanwhile, preheat the oven to 425°F (220°C).

Bake the pastries for 15 minutes. Reduce the oven temperature to 350°F (180°C) and continue baking until the dough is deep golden and glazed and the apples are fragrant and tender when pierced with a toothpick, about 20 minutes longer. Remove the pastries from the oven and let cool for 5 minutes before loosening them from the parchment with an offset spatula. Let cool for at least another 10 minutes to allow the pastry to set.

Serve the pastries warm or at room temperature with a pour of cream, if desired.

SILAN AND TAHINI ICE CREAM SUNDAES

MAKES 8 SERVINGS

DAIRY

This is one of those miraculous desserts that can be pulled together in an instant and have you looking like a genius. Its warm, spicy flavors are the essence of Middle Eastern sweets and a perfect fit for this time of year. *Silan*, or date syrup, is a Middle Eastern equivalent of maple syrup, sorghum, or molasses. Use a good-quality brand that tastes like dates: sweet and spicy with hints of citrus.

1 quart (1 L) vanilla ice cream

½ to ¾ cup (120 to 180 g) top-quality raw, toasted, or unhulled tahini

½ to ¾ cup (170 to 255 g) silan (date syrup)

½ cup (50 g) pecans, toasted (see page 18) and chopped

¼ cup (30 g) crumbled halvah (optional)

Scoop the ice cream into 8 bowls, dividing it evenly. Top each serving with a generous drizzle each of tahini and silan. Sprinkle generously with the pecans and top with halvah.

A CLEVER BREAKFAST IDEA: For a new take on PB&J, spread tahini on toast (unhulled tastes especially warm and nutty), drizzle with silan, and top with sliced bananas.

ZENGOULA WITH LEMON SYRUP:
IRAQI FUNNEL CAKES

MAKES 8 SERVINGS

PAREVE

Also known as *jalabi*, these crisp fritters, or funnel cakes, were adopted by Iraqi Jews centuries ago as the perfect fried food to celebrate the miracle of Hanukkah. Traditionally soaked in sugar syrup, they are infinitely more wonderful when infused with a tangy lemon syrup (in spring or summer, dip them in Rose Geranium Syrup, page 242). It takes only a few minutes to whisk together the forgiving batter the night before you want to serve *zengoula*, and the pastries can be fried early in the day you want to serve them. Or, make the frying a Hanukkah party activity. My cousin Elan Garonzik has vivid memories of our grandmother turning out perfect coils, which is how they're sold at Arab bakeries like Moutran in Nazareth and Jaffa. That takes a bit of practice. Free-form Rorschach-like shapes—sea horses, dolphins, geese—that magically appear as they bubble up in the hot oil are just as delicious. You will need to begin this recipe at least six hours before you want to serve the zengoula.

continued »

FOR THE DOUGH

1⅛ teaspoons (½ package) active dry yeast
1¼ cups (300 ml) warm water (100° to 110°F/38°
   to 43°C)
1 cup (125 g) unbleached all-purpose flour
¾ cup (95 g) cornstarch
Scant ½ teaspoon salt

FOR THE SYRUP

2 to 3 lemons
½ cup (120 ml) water
1 cup (200 g) sugar
2 quarts mild oil with a medium-high smoke point,
   such as grapeseed, sunflower, or avocado, for
   deep-frying

TO MAKE THE DOUGH: In a small bowl, stir together the yeast and ¼ cup (60 ml) of the warm water and let stand in a warm place until the mixture bubbles, about 10 minutes.

In a medium bowl, using a fork, stir together the flour, cornstarch, and salt. Stir in ½ cup (120 ml) of the warm water and the yeast mixture. Then slowly stir in enough of the remaining ½ cup (120 ml) warm water until the dough is lump-free and the consistency of thick pancake batter. You should have 1½ to 2 cups (360 to 480 ml) batter.

Cover the bowl with plastic wrap and refrigerate until doubled in bulk, at least 6 hours or up to 24 hours. The dough will be loose and spongy and have a yeasty aroma.

TO MAKE THE LEMON SYRUP: Using a five-hole zester, remove the zest from 1 of the lemons in long strands. Halve and squeeze enough lemons to yield ⅓ cup (75 ml) juice. In a small pot, stir together the lemon juice and zest, water, and sugar over medium heat. Bring to a boil and cook, stirring frequently, until the sugar is completely dissolved and clear, about 1 minute. Pour into a pie pan and let cool. (The syrup can be made 1 day ahead, covered, and refrigerated.)

TO MAKE THE FRITTERS: Scrape the dough into a 1-gallon (4-L) resealable plastic bag or large pastry bag fitted with a ¼-inch (6-mm) plain pastry tip and set the bag in a bowl for support. Let the dough stand for about 15 minutes before frying. Line a large plate with paper towels. Place the prepared plate, tongs, a small spider or slotted spoon, the syrup, and a tray to hold the finished fritters near the stove.

Pour the oil to a depth of 3½ inches (8.5 cm) into a 4- or 5-quart (4- or 5-L) pot, wok, or electric fryer and heat to 375°F (190°C). If using a plastic bag for the dough, snip ¼ inch (6 mm) off of one of the bottom corners, cutting on the diagonal, to create a piping tip. Roll the top of the pastry bag closed to move the batter toward the opening. Don't worry about air pockets.

Pipe a bit of the batter into the hot oil. The oil should bubble around the batter immediately. If it does not, continue heating the oil and try again. Pipe the dough into the hot oil, creating 3- to 4-inch (7.5- to 10-cm) coils or squiggles, letting gravity help push the batter out. Be careful not to crowd the pan. Fry the dough, turning once at the halfway point, until bubbled, golden, and crisp, 4 to 5 minutes total. Use a spider or slotted spoon to fish the fritters out of the oil, drain them briefly on the towel-lined plate, and then drop them into the syrup for a moment or two, turning them to coat evenly. Lift them out of the syrup and transfer them to the tray in a in a single layer to cool. Repeat with remaining batter, skimming any loose bits of dough from the hot oil between batches to prevent burning. Scrape any batter that escaped into the bowl back into the pastry bag to make more pastries.

The cooled pastries can be piled on a platter. Pour any remaining syrup over the top. The fritters taste best served the same day they are made, although they will hold their crispness overnight. Store loosely covered at room temperature.

KITCHEN NOTE: A couple of 2-inch (5-cm) chunks of raw carrot added to the frying oil act as magnets, attracting all those little brown bits that might otherwise burn and impart an acrid taste to the oil. It's an old-fashioned trick that works!

January & February

GLIMMER OF RENEWAL

January and February may offer the year's grayest moments in the Northern Hemisphere, but we've passed the winter solstice, and days are getting longer. It's a fragile time; roots must find nourishment, yet buds are beginning to swell.

A glimmer of renewal appears with the first fruit of the year to blossom: the almond. The flowering almond tree is the symbol of Tu b'Shvat, the birthday of trees, and no wonder. When the winter sun rises high enough in the sky to warm the air, bees awaken and orchards comes alive with the sounds and sweet smells of pollination. There's a perfect moment in the life of an almond orchard in bloom: the branches are still laden with snowy blossoms but enough have dropped their petals to create a snow-like carpet, a true hovering between winter and spring.

In the heart of winter, we reach deep into our pantries for roots, grains, legumes, dried fruits, and nuts that we brighten with fresh citrus and the vegetables that are sweetest after the frost. These are the foods of Tu b'Shvat and the foods that inspire the recipes in this chapter.

January & February

QUICK-PICKLED BABY TURNIPS AND BEETS

MAKES 1 QUART (1 L)

PAREVE/VEGAN

Here's my farmers' market version of the ubiquitous pickled turnip condiment found at falafel and hummus shops. Use pearly white, small Japanese turnips, their tops, and a few young red beets that dye everything in the jar deep magenta. Chioggia (candy-striped) beets will impart a paler pink tint. If you have large turnips, peel and blanch them, as you do the beets in this recipe, and slice them. This is my favorite cool-weather pickled accompaniment to chopped chicken or duck livers (page 35) and is always part of an array of sours on a mezze table. In spring, pickle red or multicolor Easter Egg radishes. Save the leftover beet and turnip tops for Winter Greens Sauté (page 102).

¾ pound (340 g) small red or candy-striped
    beets (more if tops attached)
1½ pounds (680 g) small Japanese turnips
    (more if tops attached)
4 large cloves garlic, sliced
4 dried red chiles, such as árbol chiles
1 teaspoon coriander seeds
1 teaspoon cumin seeds
1 cup (240 ml) cider vinegar
1½ cups (350 ml) water
3 tablespoons kosher salt
1 tablespoon sugar

If the leafy tops are attached, cut them off the beets, leaving a bit of stem attached. Scrub beets well and cook them in salted boiling water for 5 minutes. Drain, rinse under cool running water, and when cool enough to handle, rub off skins as best you can. Cut off the taproots and discard. Cut beets in half through the stem end, place cut side down, and cut into slices ¼ inch (6 mm) thick.

If the leafy tops are attached, cut them off the turnips, leaving a bit of stem attached. If you like, select a few of the prettiest greens, rinse, and pat dry. Scrub the turnips well. If the turnips are 1 inch (2.5 cm) or so in diameter, cut them in half through the stem end. If they are a little larger, quarter them. If the leaves are larger than 3 inches (7.5 cm), cut them in half lengthwise.

Pack beets and turnips into an impeccably clean 1-quart (1-L) jar or two 1-pint (500-ml) jars along with the garlic and chiles, including some chile seeds in the jar as desired for added heat. If adding turnip leaves, slide them vertically into the jar, using a bamboo skewer to help.

Put the coriander and cumin seeds in a plastic bag, and crack them using the flat side of a large knife. In a medium pot, combine the vinegar, water, salt, sugar, coriander, and cumin and bring to a boil over high heat. Cook for 3 minutes, then pour the hot brine over turnips and beets. You may have more brine than you need, but make sure that all the coriander and cumin seeds get into the jar(s).

Cap jar(s) tightly and let stand in a sunny spot for the day. Refrigerate vegetables for at least 12 hours before serving. They will keep several weeks in the refrigerator.

KITCHEN NOTE: The term *quick* (also known as fresh-pack) refers to pickles ready in a matter of hours rather than the week required for *refrigerator* pickles or the 3 required for true *fermented* pickles and sauerkraut. Because of their short curing time, quick pickles aren't considered self-sealing or shelf-stable over a long period unless they are properly canned, that is sealed, in a water bath process.

Tu b'Shvat
THE BIRTHDAY OF TREES

Tu b'Shvat, also known as the New Year for Trees and Israel's Arbor Day, offers some of the Bible's most significant sustainability practices to today's farmer, shopper, and cook. The holiday began as a way to calculate the age of trees in order to tax the prior year's harvest and predict the yield of the coming one. The passages in Leviticus are specific: no fruit is to be harvested during the first three years of a tree's life, a fruit offering of thanks is to be given in the fourth, and not until the fifth year are we to reap the benefits. Today's careful farmer will tell you this is sound advice for the health of our orchards, for it allows the tree's energy to go first to establishing strong roots. Resist the temptation to hurry the process, and you will be rewarded with more bountiful crops.

The Bible called it the tree of life with good reason. "Trees are necessary for our survival," says Andy Lipkis, founder of TreePeople, the Los Angeles–based organization dedicated to restoring damaged urban ecosystems through reforestation. "Trees are vital to protecting the land, air quality, and our water supply." Andy planted his first tree on Tu b'Shvat as a youngster and credits that moment as the inspiration for his life's work.

In Israel, Tu b'Shvat, the fifteenth of the lunar month Shvat, is celebrated with picnics and school outings to plant trees. Holiday foods honor the fruits of the earth, tree, and vine, drawing from the medieval custom of eating fifteen fruits and reading fifteen psalms to mark the occasion. These include the seven biblical species—wheat, barley, figs, olives, dates, pomegranates, grapes— as well as carob, citrus, (dried) stone fruits, cinnamon, walnuts, almonds, and more recently, New World avocados.

A Tu b'Shvat Seder, established by seventeenth-century Kabbalists to give the holiday and its foods mystical significance, is enjoying a renaissance among secular Jews as a way to connect spiritual meaning to real-world actions and an appreciation for the year's cycle. This Seder's four cups of wine trace the seasons, moving from winter white to autumn red (the spring and summer pinks are achieved by mixing together white and red wines . . . not by pouring a rosé). One could call Tu b'Shvat Judaism's first vegetarian holiday.

RECIPE SUGGESTIONS FOR TU B'SHVAT

Quick Blood Orange Marmalade
with Ras el Hanout (page 127)

Green Olives with Za'atar and Citrus (page 82)

Citrus and Avocado Salad with Spicy Greens
(page 132)

Roasted Roots and Their Greens
with Wheat Berries and Horseradish Cream
(page 141)

Carob Molasses Ice Cream (page 151)

Spiced Date and Walnut Oatmeal Cake
(page 153)

Blood Orange and Olive Oil Polenta
Upside-Down Cake (page 154)

Rustic Almond-Orange Macaroons (page 152)

Peppered Red Wine Fruit Compote (page 112)

QUICK BLOOD ORANGE MARMALADE
WITH **RAS EL HANOUT**

MAKES ABOUT ½ CUP (160 G)

PAREVE

The Moroccan spice blend *ras el hanout* adds winter spice, heat, and floral notes to this savory marmalade—a lovely accent with a winter cheese tray or a platter of smoked meats, sausages, or *salame*. It is also a delicious condiment alongside a simple roast chicken or duck or with a winter main-dish salad: toss arugula or other winter salad greens with olive oil, lemon juice, and salt. Add slices of smoked chicken or duck breast and top with a dollop of the marmalade.

4 blood oranges
¼ cup (85 g) honey
¾ teaspoon ras el hanout
½ teaspoon crushed white pepper

Use a vegetable peeler to remove the zest in wide strips from 3 of the oranges. Chop the zest into ⅛-inch (3-mm) pieces and place in a medium saucepan. Peel and segment all the oranges as directed on page 17, then coarsely chop and add them, along with their juices, to the pot. Squeeze the juice from the orange membranes into the pot and discard the membranes. Stir in the honey, ras el hanout, and pepper.

Bring the orange mixture to a rolling boil over medium-high heat. Cook, uncovered, until the mixture is thick, glossy, and reduced to about ½ cup (160 g), about 15 minutes. Remove from the heat and let cool. The marmalade will thicken as it cools.

Taste and adjust the seasoning with additional pepper or ras el hanout if needed. The marmalade will keep in an airtight container in the refrigerator for 3 to 5 days. Bring to room temperature before serving.

SHOPPING TIP: You can't judge the color of the flesh of a blood orange by its peel. Many varieties barely show a blush, yet reveal an almost ruby-black interior. Juiciness is more important than color. Look for fruit that is heavy for its size with fairly smooth, tight skin. Blood-orange flesh ranges in color from barely red dappled to almost black and has a berrylike quality to its flavor that increases as the season progresses.

CARROT, DATE, AND PRESERVED KUMQUAT SALAD

8 SERVINGS

PAREVE/VEGAN

Cooked vegetable salads are perfect for winter: they're substantial, comforting, and just the right treatment for what's in season. Here, lightly steamed or boiled carrot coins are accented with dates and salty-sweet-tart preserved kumquats (store-bought preserved lemons or fresh citrus also work well). A chewy date variety, such as Deglet Noor, is best for this dish, and the salad improves when made a few hours ahead.

2 pounds (900 g) carrots, peeled and sliced ⅛ inch (3 mm) thick

½ pound (225 g) pitted dates (about ⅔ pound/300 g unpitted), quartered lengthwise

⅔ cup (4 ounces/110 g) Quick-Preserved Kumquats (recipe follows)

2 to 3 tablespoons extra-virgin olive oil

Aleppo pepper or red pepper flakes

Kosher or sea salt

1 lemon, if needed

Handful of fresh cilantro leaves (from about 12 sprigs)

Cook the carrots in (or steam over) salted boiling water until their color brightens and they are crisp-tender, 2 to 3 minutes. Drain and shock in a bath of ice and cold water to stop the cooking and preserve the color. Drain well and pat dry. (This step can be done 1 to 2 days ahead; cover and refrigerate until ready to use.)

Place the carrots and dates in a large bowl. Cut the kumquat halves into quarters or thinner slivers if you prefer. Add them to the bowl along with 2 tablespoons of the olive oil and the Aleppo pepper to taste. Toss well, adding a little more oil if needed to coat evenly and lightly, and let stand for a few minutes. Taste for seasoning and add salt, additional Aleppo pepper, and/or lemon juice if needed. (The salad can be made to this point up to 3 hours ahead, covered, and set aside at room temperature.) Just before serving, tear the cilantro leaves into large pieces, add to the bowl, and toss well. Mound the salad on a pretty platter to serve.

QUICK-PRESERVED KUMQUATS

MAKES 1 PINT (500 ML)

PAREVE/VEGAN

Kumquats, with their sweet, edible skin and tart flesh, make an interesting and quick alternative to traditional Moroccan preserved lemons. Use them to add color and a unique flavor to winter salads, sides, and poultry dishes.

¾ pound (340 g) oval (Nagami variety) kumquats (about 2½ cups)

1 tablespoon kosher salt

Remove stems from kumquats, then cut each kumquat in half through the stem end. Use the tip of a knife to poke out visible seeds. Mix together kumquats and salt, massaging the salt into the fruit. Pack fruit and juice into a sparkling clean 1-pint (500-ml) jar or other glass container, pushing down on the kumquats to make them fit.

Cover with a nonreactive lid and set in a sunny spot for the day, giving the jar a shake from time to time. The kumquats will be usable after 2 hours but will improve as they sit. They will keep in the refrigerator for up to 1 week.

APPLE, FENNEL, AND WATERMELON RADISH SALAD

MAKES 6 SERVINGS

PAREVE/VEGAN

Large watermelon radishes reveal bright magenta centers ringed with lime-green "rinds" when shaved crosswise into thin slices. An inexpensive Japanese mandoline slicer (see page 20) will help you quickly shave the radish, apple, and fennel, so that you get all the interesting flavors of this salad in each bite. Or, use a knife to slice the ingredients as thinly as you can. The mild, floral qualities of Meyer lemon are the perfect complement, but a more common Eureka lemon will do.

1 large or 2 golf-ball-size watermelon radishes,
    or 5 or 6 small red or pink radishes
2 medium-size fennel bulbs, preferably with tops
2 tart-sweet apples, such as Pink Lady
Handful of winter salad greens, such as wild
    arugula or winter mesclun mix
⅓ cup (40 g) walnuts, toasted (see page 18)
2 tablespoons walnut oil
Juice of ½ lemon, preferably Meyer
Kosher or sea salt and freshly ground black or
    white pepper

If the leafy tops are still attached to the radishes, cut them off, leaving about 1 inch (2.5 cm) of the stem attached. Save any tender radish leaves to add to the salad. If using watermelon radishes, lightly peel the tough outer layer to expose the lime green ring. Cut the radishes into halves or quarters. Using a Japanese mandoline, and holding the stem end of each piece to protect your fingers, shave the radish pieces crosswise into paper-thin slices. I like to rest the mandoline right in the bowl I am using for the salad. If you are using small red or pink radishes, do not peel or quarter them before shaving.

Cut away the fennel stalks, leaving 1 to 2 inches (2.5 to 5 cm) of the stem attached. Save some of the feathery tops for the salad or save them for seasoning fish. Discard the tough outer layers from each bulb, then cut the bulb in half from the stalk to the core end. Holding the stem end to protect your fingers, shave the fennel halves crosswise on the mandoline into paper-thin slices. Quarter and core the apples, then shave each quarter into the bowl.

Add the salad greens, radish leaves, fennel fronds, and walnuts to the bowl. Drizzle with the walnut oil and lemon juice, season with salt and pepper, and toss well. (The salad can be made up to 1 hour ahead; add the walnuts just before serving and toss again.)

CITRUS AND AVOCADO SALAD WITH SPICY GREENS

MAKES 8 SERVINGS

PAREVE/VEGAN

This symphony of winter citrus and avocados pays homage to my home state of California *and* my roots in Israel, both key producers of these crops. The orange and lemon in this salad balance the grapefruit's base notes. Sweeter pummelo-grapefruit crosses, such as Oro Blanco or Pomelit, are delicious here. For something different, use a thick-skinned pummelo (also spelled pomelo and pommelo), grapefruit's ancient relative that has crunchy juice vesicles that you can scatter onto the salad. Pummelos are found at some winter farmers' markets and at Asian groceries, especially around Lunar New Year. Arugula and water- and upland cresses, which are at their best this time of year, add a peppery contrast. This salad is too beautiful to toss in a bowl. Layer the elements on a platter or on individual plates to brighten the grayest winter day.

1 large orange

2 grapefruits, pummelos, or Oro Blancos (pummelo-grapefruit cross)

2 large handfuls of wild arugula, watercress, pepper cress, or a mix (about 2 ounces/55 g)

½ bunch green onions (about 4) or 8 tiny spring onions, thinly sliced crosswise

2 ripe avocados

¼ cup (40 g) oil-cured black olives

Juice of ½ lemon

¾ teaspoon kosher or sea salt

Freshly ground black pepper

2 tablespoons extra-virgin olive oil

Using a five-hole zester, remove the zest in long curls from the orange and reserve. Peel and segment the orange and grapefruits as directed on page 17. Drink the juice from the membranes or save it for another use.

Tear the arugula and cress and scatter over a serving platter or divide among individual salad plates. Top with half the onions. Halve, pit, and peel the avocados, then thinly slice each half lengthwise and arrange the slices over the greens along with the citrus segments. Oil-cured olives should be soft enough to tear into pieces to pit them. Scatter the olive pieces, the remaining onions, and the orange zest over the salad.

In a small bowl, whisk together the lemon juice, salt, and several grinds of pepper, then whisk in the oil. Pour the dressing over the salad to serve.

SHOPPING TIP: When you want avocado slices that hold their shape even when the avocado is fully ripe, look for Fuerte or Pinkerton varieties. The green, rough-skinned Pinkerton is a cross between the ubiquitous Hass and the smooth-skinned Fuerte. The latter was the most important commercial variety before being replaced in the 1970s by the Hass, which was discovered in Southern California in 1926.

SIMPLE FARRO SOUP WITH CHICKPEAS AND ESCAROLE

MAKES 6 TO 8 SERVINGS

PAREVE/VEGAN

"Since ancient times, grains have been magnificent at capturing sunlight and water," says farmer John de Rosier, who small-farms wheat, "the great fertility collector of the powerful cycle—grain, animals, manure, vegetables." Indeed, wheat is one of the Bible's seven species, giving gravitas to this simple but satisfying water-based soup. Farro, an ancient wheat, is one of my favorite pairings with chickpeas and bitter greens, but wheat berries, spelt, quinoa, buckwheat (groats), barley, and brown rice are also good choices. The soup is hearty enough for a light main dish.

1 onion, chopped

Kosher or sea salt and freshly ground black pepper

3 tablespoons extra-virgin olive oil, plus more for finishing

2 cloves garlic, minced

1 head escarole, about ¾ pound (340 g), roughly chopped, or other quick-cooking green such as Swiss chard (see Kitchen Note)

2 cups (390 g) cooked farro (from ¾ cup/150 g uncooked; see page 18)

1½ cups (250 g) cooked chickpeas, plus their cooking liquid; or 1 can (16 ounces/450 g), drained

6 to 8 cups (1.4 to 2 L) water or vegetable stock (page 92)

In a wide pot large enough to hold all the ingredients, sauté the onion with a little salt in the olive oil over medium heat until softened and translucent, 5 to 7 minutes. Lower the heat as needed to prevent browning. Stir in the garlic, then add the escarole and cook until wilted, 3 to 5 minutes.

Add the farro, chickpeas, 4 cups (960 ml) of the water, about 1 teaspoon salt (use less if using salted stock), and a few grinds of pepper. Bring to a gentle boil, cover partially, and reduce the heat to keep the soup at a simmer. Cook until the escarole is tender and the flavors of the soup have blended, 10 to 15 minutes. If the soup is too thick, add the remaining liquid as needed and simmer briefly. (The soup can be made up to this point a day ahead, cooled, covered, and refrigerated, and then reheated, adding additional water as needed to thin.)

Taste and adjust the seasoning. Ladle into warmed bowls and top each serving with a drizzle of olive oil.

PAREVE AND DAIRY VARIATIONS: Add a poached egg to each serving; top with Parmigiano-Reggiano cheese.

KITCHEN NOTE: If using Swiss chard, strip the leaves from the stems as directed on page 17. Chop the stems as you would celery and add them to the pot with the onion.

CABBAGE, RICE, AND GREEN GARLIC PORRIDGE WITH MEATBALLS

MAKES 8 SERVINGS

MEAT

This soup began as a riff on classic stuffed cabbage, but soon expanded to the broader concept of rice-and-cabbage comfort foods, such as Chinese congee and Japanese *zosui*. Starchy short- or medium-grain rice yields a savory porridge that Italians, and my Iraqi father, love. Cabbage tastes sweetest in winter; try an heirloom variety, such as conical Wakefield Jersey, or use a Savoy type. Green garlic, also called spring garlic, adds mild flavor and color to this dish, but you can substitute regular cured garlic cloves from fully formed bulbs with papery skins. If you like your stuffed cabbage sweet and sour, add a little brown sugar. In summer or fall, use meaty Roma tomatoes. For a gluten-free version, substitute ½ cup (80 g) cooked rice for the bread crumbs.

6 to 7 cups (about 1 pound/425 g) thinly sliced
    cabbage
1 bunch green garlic, or 3 cloves garlic
1 onion, chopped
Kosher or sea salt and freshly ground black or
    white pepper
2 tablespoons mild oil, such as grapeseed,
    avocado, or sunflower
½ cup (55 g) dried bread crumbs
1 egg, lightly beaten
¾ pound (340 g) moderately lean ground beef
    or ground turkey, preferably dark meat
¾ cup (145 g) short- or medium-grain white rice
6 cups (1.4 L) homemade chicken (page 44),
    vegetable (page 92), or beef stock (page 66),
    or 3 cups (720 ml) canned broth diluted with
    3 cups/480 ml water)
1 can (16 ounces/450 g) diced tomatoes
Juice of 1 lemon
Light or dark brown sugar (optional)
Generous handful of fresh Italian parsley, chopped

Cook cabbage in salted boiling water for 2 minutes to remove any hidden sharpness. Drain well and lightly squeeze out excess moisture. Cut green garlic crosswise into thin slices, including about 5 inches (13 cm) of the tender green tops. If using regular garlic cloves, mince them.

In a wide pot large enough to hold all the ingredients, cook the onion and green garlic with a little salt in the oil over medium heat until softened, 5 to 7 minutes. Lower the heat as needed to prevent browning. If using regular garlic, add it after you have sautéed the onions. Turn off the heat, measure out ½ cup (100 g) of the mixture, chop finely, place in a medium bowl, and stir in the bread crumbs. Leave the remaining onion mixture in the pot.

TO MAKE THE MEATBALLS: Stir the egg, 1 teaspoon salt, and a few grinds of pepper into the cooled onion mixture. Add the meat and use a fork to mix the ingredients together completely, but with a light hand. Overworking yields tough meatballs. Have a tray or baking sheet and a small bowl of cold water handy. Form 40 small meatballs each about 1 inch (2.5 cm) in diameter, dipping your hands into the water from time to time to keep the meat from sticking to them. Place the meatballs on the baking sheet as you work. (The meatballs can be made up to this point 1 day ahead and refrigerated, covered.)

Turn the heat under remaining onion mixture to medium. Add the cabbage, rice, 3 cups (720 ml) of the stock, and the tomatoes and their juices to the pot. Season with salt and pepper. Bring to a simmer, cover, and lower the heat to maintain the simmer. Cook until the rice and cabbage are tender, about 20 minutes.

Add the remaining stock and bring the soup back to a simmer. Drop in the meatballs, and simmer until the meatballs are cooked through, about 10 minutes. During

continued »

the cooking time, gently spoon the soup over the meatballs as soon as they hold their shape when nudged with a spoon.

When the meatballs are done, add the lemon juice to taste, then season with salt and pepper and add a little brown sugar if you like. If the soup seems too thick, add water to thin. Ladle into warmed bowls and shower each serving with a generous amount of parsley.

PAREVE/VEGAN AND DAIRY VARIATIONS: Omit the meatballs and use vegetable stock; top with grated Parmigiano-Reggiano cheese.

SHOPPING TIP: Green garlic is the mild-tasting immature plant harvested as a thinning technique before its bulb has formed. Farmers bring them to farmers' markets in late winter and early spring. You can quickly distinguish green garlic from a green onion by its flat, rather than tubular, greens (see page 123, upper left). Green garlic is at its most delicious when young, finger thick, and wholly edible. As the season progresses, the plants develop their familiar bulb shape and their tops become tougher and yellowed, but they are still juicier, milder, and fresher tasting than cured heads of mature garlic.

SCHMALTZ-ROASTED POTATOES

MAKES 8 SERVINGS

MEAT OR PAREVE/VEGAN

Parboiling is the secret to perfect roasted potatoes. This extra step also keeps the potatoes from sticking to the pan. And for better crisping, don't crowd the pan. For a pareve/vegan version, substitute olive oil for the schmaltz.

3 pounds (1.4 kg) starchy or all-purpose potatoes, such as Yukon Gold, russet, or German Butterball
4 to 5 tablespoons (55 to 75 g) schmaltz (page 24), or 3 to 4 tablespoons (45 to 60 ml) olive oil
Kosher or sea salt
Paprika of your choice (see page 14)
Several sprigs thyme or rosemary (optional)

Preheat the oven to 400°F (200°C). Bring a large pot of generously salted water to a boil. Peel the potatoes, if you like, then cut them into 1-inch (2.5-cm) cubes. Add the potatoes to the boiling water and cover the pot. Once the water returns to a boil, cook the potatoes for 3 minutes. Drain well and return them to the pot. Turn the heat to medium-high until any excess moisture has evaporated, 30 to 60 seconds. (This step can be done a few hours ahead and the potatoes kept at room temperature.)

Meanwhile, warm a large sheet pan or roasting pan in the hot oven for 5 minutes. Add the schmaltz and leave to melt. When the fat has liquefied, add the potatoes and the herb (if using), season liberally with salt and paprika, and toss to coat. Spread the potatoes in roughly a single layer and roast for 15 minutes. Give the pan a shake or use a spatula to turn them. Continue to roast until the potatoes are completely tender, nicely browned, and crisped in places, 20 to 30 minutes longer. If the potatoes begin to darken too much, reduce the heat to 375°F (190°C) to prevent burning. Serve hot with additional salt, if desired.

BUCKWHEAT, BOW TIES, AND BRUSSELS SPROUTS

MAKES 8 TO 10 SERVINGS

PAREVE

Kasha varnishkes, the traditional eastern European dish of buckwheat groats (kasha) and bow-tie pasta, is updated here with winter-sweet Brussels sprouts (purple varieties are gorgeous) and walnut oil to play up the nutlike qualities (be sure to use a delicious oil). An ancient relative of sorrel and rhubarb, fast-growing buckwheat is ideal in cold climates, where the growing season is short. The grain-like, gluten-free seeds have an earthy flavor and aroma that is enhanced by toasting. Kasha, Russian for buckwheat cereal or porridge, is perfect for soaking up the savory juices of Oven-Braised Romanian Chicken (page 189) or Pure and Simple Brisket (page 65). Try a meat variation with schmaltz and *gribenes*, or turn it into a decadent vegetarian dish with browned butter and sour cream.

¾ pound (340 g) Brussels sprouts

1 cup (92 g) egg bow-tie or farfalle pasta

1 cup (165 g) buckwheat groats (kasha),
    picked over

1 egg, lightly beaten

2 cups (480 ml) water or stock

1 medium onion, chopped

Kosher or sea salt and freshly ground black or
    white pepper

2 tablespoons mild oil, such as grapeseed,
    safflower, or avocado

3 tablespoons walnut oil

Finishing salt, such as fleur de sel or smoked salt

Cut off and discard the stem ends of the Brussels sprouts. Break apart the sprouts into leaves; don't worry about being too precise. (If sprouts are very tight, boil them in salted boiling water for 3 minutes, then break apart.) Cook the pasta in boiling salted water. Drain and set aside.

In a bowl, combine the groats and egg and stir together with a fork to coat all the grains, breaking up any clumps. Add the groats to a wide pot and cook over medium-high heat to seal, dry, and toast them, stirring constantly, until nutty brown and aromatic, about 2 minutes. Add the water and 1 teaspoon salt (less if using salted stock). Bring to a boil, reduce heat to low, cover, and cook until groats are tender, about 15 minutes.

Meanwhile, in a large skillet fitted with a lid, sauté the onion with a little kosher salt in the grapeseed oil over medium-low heat until tender and golden, 7 to 10 minutes. Add the Brussels sprouts, a little kosher salt, and several grinds of pepper and cook, covered, until the leaves are tender but retain color, 5 to 10 minutes.

Add the noodles and the Brussels sprouts mixture to the cooked groats and, using a fork, gently stir together all the ingredients. Taste and adjust the seasoning with kosher salt and pepper. Stir in the walnut oil, sprinkle with fleur de sel, and serve.

DAIRY VARIATION: Replace the walnut oil with 4 tablespoons (60 ml) brown butter and top each serving with a dollop of sour cream.

MEAT VARIATION: Cook the onions and Brussels sprouts in schmaltz instead of oil. Replace the walnut oil with 3 tablespoons schmaltz and ¼ cup (25 g) gribenes (page 24).

ROASTED FENNEL AND ONIONS WITH PRESERVED
KUMQUATS (FACING PAGE), LEFT;
CURRIED ROASTED CAULIFLOWER (PAGE 142), RIGHT

ROASTED FENNEL AND ONIONS WITH PRESERVED KUMQUATS

MAKES 6 TO 8 SERVINGS

PAREVE/VEGAN

It's hard to believe that the iconic Italian ingredient fennel was considered strictly a Jewish food well into the nineteenth century. Only in the early twentieth century did Pellegrino Artusi, renowned Tuscan codifier of Italian cooking, sing its praises to the broader population. Fennel is at its most tender in winter and spring, and its delicate licorice notes pair well with citrus. I like the kick from preserved kumquats or lemons, but fresh kumquats or oranges are also delicious. Parboiling the fennel and onions first yields a more tender result.

6 fennel bulbs (about 2½ pounds/1.2 kg without tops)
2 red onions
⅔ cup (85 g) Quick-Preserved Kumquats (page 129)
2 to 3 tablespoons extra-virgin olive oil
Freshly ground black pepper
Kosher or sea salt (optional)

Preheat the oven to 400°F (200°C). Cut away the fennel stalks from the bulbs. Pluck some of the nicest fronds and reserve. Save the remaining stalks and fronds for another use. Discard the tough outer layers from each bulb, then cut each bulb into quarters or sixths from the stalk to the core end. Cut each onion into 8 wedges.

Cook the fennel in boiling salted water for 5 minutes. Lift out with a slotted spoon or spider and drain well on a dish towel or paper towels. Add the onions to the boiling water, cook for 5 minutes, and drain in the same manner. Or, if you prefer, steam the fennel and onions over salted boiling water for 10 minutes. This step can be done a day ahead and the fennel and onions refrigerated.

Cut the kumquat halves in half lengthwise. On a large sheet pan, toss together the fennel, onions, and kumquats with enough of the olive oil to coat evenly. Season with pepper and toss again. Roast, stirring the mixture once halfway through the cooking, until the fennel and onions are tender and are browned in places, about 35 minutes. Taste and season with additional pepper and with salt, if desired. Serve warm or at room temperature.

ROASTED ROOTS AND THEIR GREENS WITH WHEAT BERRIES AND HORSERADISH CREAM

MAKES 8 TO 10 SERVINGS

DAIRY OR PAREVE/VEGAN

This warming vegetarian stew includes many of the symbolic foods of Tu b'Shvat, the holiday that celebrates the birth of trees and the fruit of the earth. It is also delicious made with farro, spelt, barley, or quinoa. Take advantage of all the available beautiful colors of carrots and beets. Red beets will tint the dish magenta. If this bothers you, add them to the stew just before you are ready to serve. For a vegan or pareve version, omit the crème fraîche or yogurt.

4 cups (620 g) cooked wheat berries
     (from 2 cups/360 g raw; see page 18)
6 tablespoons (90 ml) extra virgin olive oil
2 teaspoons ground cumin
2 teaspoons ground coriander
Kosher or sea salt and freshly ground black pepper
2 to 3 bunches beets with greens attached,
     1½ pounds (680 g) total
1 bunch small turnips with greens attached,
     about 1 pound (450 g)
10 medium carrots, about 1 pound (450 g)
2 onions
2 cloves garlic, finely chopped
½ cup (75 g) raisins
1 bay leaf
1 to 2 cups (240 to 480 ml) homemade vegetable
     stock (page 92), or 1 cup canned diluted with
     1 cup water
1 to 2 tablespoons sherry vinegar

FOR THE HORSERADISH CREAM

½ cup (100 g) crème fraîche or plain Greek yogurt
3 to 4 tablespoons (30 to 60 g) prepared horseradish
1 lemon
Kosher salt

Cook the wheat berries, if necessary, while you prepare the vegetables. Preheat the oven to 400°F (200°C).

Put 4 tablespoons (60 ml) of the olive oil in a small pot or microwavable dish. Stir in the cumin, coriander, 1 teaspoon salt, and a few grinds of pepper. Place over low heat until the oil shimmers (about 30 seconds in a microwave). Remove from the heat and let stand.

Cut the leafy tops off the beets and turnips, leaving 1 inch (2.5 cm) of stem attached, and reserve the tops. Set the turnips aside. Scrub the beets well. If they are 2 inches (5 cm) in diameter or smaller, leave them whole. Cut larger beets into halves or quarters. Place the beets in a shallow baking pan. Drizzle with about 1 tablespoon of the oil mixture, toss to coat evenly, and turn any cut beets cut side down. Cover the pan with foil and roast until almost tender, about 30 minutes. Remove the foil and continue roasting until tender and browned in places, about 10 minutes more. If using both red and yellow beets, roast each color in a separate pan to preserve their color.

Cut the turnips into halves or quarters, depending on their size. Cut the carrots crosswise into 2- to 3-inch (5- to 7.5-cm) pieces. If carrots are very fat, cut them in half lengthwise first. Cut each onion into 8 wedges. Place the turnips, carrots, and onions in a roughly single layer in a large shallow baking pan (or use 2 pans), drizzle with the remaining oil mixture, and toss to coat evenly. Roast uncovered until nicely browned, 30 to 40 minutes. Remove from the oven and reserve.

TO MAKE THE HORSERADISH CREAM: In a small bowl, whisk together the crème fraîche and horseradish. Add a squeeze of lemon juice and a pinch of salt and stir well. Cover and refrigerate until serving.

continued »

Cut away and discard the excess stems from the beet and turnip greens, then cut the greens crosswise into strips 1 inch (2.5 cm) wide.

In a wide pot large enough to hold all the ingredients, heat the remaining 2 tablespoons of olive oil over medium heat. Stir in the garlic, wait 30 seconds, and then add the greens and raisins. Cook until the greens are wilted, 2 to 3 minutes (you may have to add the greens in batches). Add the wheat berries, all the roasted vegetables, the bay leaf, and 1 cup (240 ml) of the stock and season with salt and pepper. Cover and simmer over medium-low heat to blend the flavors, about 10 minutes, adding the remaining stock as needed to keep the mixture moist.

Stir in the vinegar to taste. Ladle into bowls and top each serving with a little of the horseradish cream.

CURRIED ROASTED CAULIFLOWER

MAKES 6 SERVINGS

DAIRY OR PAREVE/VEGAN

Cauliflower lends itself to multiple Jewish Diaspora flavor profiles, in this case, Indian. Purchase a curry blend from a spice store or make your own using the formula below. The secret to luscious roasted cauliflower is to blanch the florets in boiling salted water first. This extra step accomplishes three things: it gets rid of any off odors common to brassicas like cauliflower and cabbage; it plumps the florets, so they will be more tender after roasting; and it shortens the roasting time to allow for good browning without burning. Recipe is shown on page 138.

1 to 2 heads cauliflower, about 3 pounds (1.4 kg) total, broken into small florets
2 tablespoons ghee (clarified butter) or extra-virgin olive oil, plus more for finishing
Kosher or sea salt
2 teaspoons curry blend, homemade (see opposite) or store-bought
½ cup (75 g) raisins
2 cloves garlic, sliced
Handful of fresh cilantro leaves, chopped
Aleppo pepper or red pepper flakes (optional)

Preheat the oven to 425°F (220°C). Cook the cauliflower in boiling salted water for 2 to 3 minutes. Drain and rinse well under cool running water to cool. Spread the florets on a kitchen towel to dry. (This step can be done up to 2 days ahead; cover and refrigerate.)

Transfer the florets to a baking sheet that will accommodate them in a single layer (or use 2 pans). Drizzle the ghee over the florets and toss to coat evenly. Season with salt and the curry blend and toss again, then spread the florets in a single layer. Roast the florets, giving the pan a shake about halfway through the cooking, until they are tender, browned, and crisped in places, about 30 minutes, adding the raisins and garlic to the pan during the last 5 minutes of cooking. The florets will shrink quite a bit.

Toss the florets with a little more ghee and the cilantro and season with salt and with Aleppo pepper, if using. Serve warm or at room temperature.

A SIMPLE CURRY BLEND: Stir together 1 teaspoon each ground turmeric and cumin, ½ teaspoon each ground coriander and ginger, and ⅛ to ¼ teaspoon Aleppo pepper or red pepper flakes.

KITCHRI: RED LENTILS AND RICE WITH GOLDEN GARLIC PUREE

MAKES 8 SERVINGS

DAIRY

I like to think this is the red lentil stew Jacob served to Esau to seduce him into selling his birthright. Every Iraqi Jewish family has a version of this vegetarian comfort food. This is mine. Red lentils melt during cooking to coat tomato-tinted rice, and the dish is perfumed with garlic gently cooked to sweetness. If possible, use tiny red lentils, which are similar in size to French green lentils and have a creamier texture than the larger disk-shaped ones. I use ghee (clarified butter) in this dish to add a nutty undertone (Ancient Organics is an exceptional brand). For a pareve/vegan version, use a healthful oil and skip the *labneh*. In summer, use fresh Roma or other meaty tomatoes in place of tomato paste. Sometimes I think the best reason to make *kitchri* is to turn the leftovers into crisp croquettes for a kind of Middle Eastern *arancini*.

1 onion, chopped

Kosher or sea salt and freshly ground black or white pepper

5 to 6 tablespoons (75 to 90 ml) avocado, grapeseed, or olive oil or (70 to 85 g) butter or ghee

5 tablespoons (80 g) tomato paste, or ½ pound (225 g) Roma or other sauce tomatoes, halved, seeded, and grated on the large holes of a box grater

4 or 5 cups (960 ml or 1.2 L) boiling water

2 cups (370 g) long-grain white or basmati rice

1 cup (200 g) tiny red lentils, picked over

10 cloves garlic

Labneh, homemade (page 22) or store-bought, or Greek yogurt for serving

In a wide pot large enough to hold all the ingredients, sauté the onion with a little salt in 2 tablespoons of the cooking fat over medium-low heat until the onion is golden, 7 to 10 minutes. Dissolve the tomato paste and 1 to 2 teaspoons salt in the boiling water; if using fresh tomatoes, reduce the water to 4 cups (960 ml). The mixture should taste salty. Season to taste with pepper.

When onion is golden, add the rice and lentils, raise the heat to medium, and cook, stirring, to coat the grains, about 1 minute. Stir in the tomato liquid, cover, and bring to a boil over medium heat. Reduce heat to very low and cook until rice is tender, lentils have melted, and liquid has been absorbed, 15 to 20 minutes. Check now and again to make sure rice is not sticking to the pot. Taste the dish; if it needs salt, dissolve salt in a little hot water and add to the pot. When the rice-lentil mixture is done, place pot on a damp dish towel to steam and loosen the rice.

To make the garlic puree, push garlic cloves through a garlic press or mash with the flat side of a large knife. You should have 1½ to 2 tablespoons. In a small pot, heat remaining fat over medium-low heat. Add garlic and cook, stirring constantly, until pale golden, about 2 minutes. Remove from heat and continue stirring until mixture stops bubbling, about 1 minute.

Stir the garlic puree into the lentil-rice mixture. Serve in bowls and top each serving with a dollop of labneh.

KITCHRI CROQUETTES: For each croquette, pat ⅓ cup (85 g) cold kitchri into a thin disk. Place a little labneh or feta cheese in the center and fold disk into a half-moon to encase the filling, pressing edges to seal. Coat with bread crumbs if you want extra-crisp croquettes, and season with salt. (You can prepare croquettes up to this point a few hours ahead and refrigerate.) Pan-fry in oil or ghee over medium to medium-high heat until golden brown on both sides, 2 to 3 minutes total.

BLISTERED CHICORIES WITH TUNA AND SALSA VERDE

MAKES 6 TO 8 SERVINGS

FISH

The robust flavors here are classic Roman Jewish. Like other brassicas (cauliflower, broccoli, and the like), chicories, such as Chioggia radicchio (round), Treviso radicchio (torpedo shaped), and Belgian endive, taste milder in winter and spring. Blistering them in a skillet or on a grill further sweetens them and adds a smoky note. Serve the dish warm or let it marinate and serve at room temperature. You'll have more *salsa verde* than you need, but it is a versatile condiment to have on hand and will keep in the refrigerator for up to a week.

1½ pounds (680 g) Chioggia (round) or Treviso (torpedo shaped) radicchio or Belgian endive
1¼ pounds (570 g) tuna fillet
Extra-virgin olive oil
Kosher or sea salt and freshly ground black pepper

FOR THE SALSA VERDE

½ cup (120 ml) extra-virgin olive oil
5 oil-packed flat anchovy fillets
½ cup (30 g) packed chopped fresh Italian parsley
3 cloves garlic, minced (about 1 tablespoon)
2 tablespoons capers in brine, coarsely chopped
2 tablespoons red wine vinegar or fresh lemon juice
Freshly ground black pepper
1 dried árbol or similar small chile, or big pinch of red pepper flakes (optional)

Cut the chicories lengthwise into slabs ¾ inch (2 cm) thick, leaving the root stem attached. (If using especially thin Treviso or endives, cut lengthwise into halves or quarters.) Soak in ice water to cover for 15 minutes.

Cut the fish fillet into medallions ½ inch (12 mm) thick. If using a small albacore loin, cut on the diagonal for larger medallions. You should have 12 to 14 slices.

TO MAKE THE SALSA VERDE: In a small pot, heat the olive oil over medium-low heat until it thins and shimmers. Remove from the heat, add the anchovies, and mash them with a fork until they dissolve. Stir in the parsley, garlic, capers, vinegar, a few grinds of pepper, and the chile, if using. The salsa may be made up to several days ahead and refrigerated. Bring to room temperature to use.

TO COOK THE DISH: Heat a grill to medium-high or a grill pan or cast-iron skillet over medium-high heat. Have a serving platter nearby. Drain the chicories, pat dry, brush with olive oil, and season with salt and pepper. Working in batches if needed to avoid crowding, place the chicories on the hot grill or pan, fanning out the leaves a bit and pressing down on them so that more surface area makes contact with the hot surface. Cook the chicories, turning them once, until blackened in spots and blistered in others, 2 to 3 minutes on each side. Transfer the chicories to a platter and spoon some of the salsa verde over them.

Brush the tuna pieces on both sides with olive oil and season with salt and pepper. Grill, turning once, until light golden with a pink center, about 2 minutes on each side (the fish will continue to cook off the heat). Transfer the tuna pieces to the platter, arranging them on top of the chicories, and spoon some salsa over the fish. The dish can be served right away or it can be set aside for up to 1 hour and served at room temperature. Any leftovers make a wonderful marinated fish and chicory salad.

DUCK WITH WHITE BEANS AND GRIBENES

MAKES 6 SERVINGS

MEAT

This make-ahead dish evokes thoughts of cassoulet and *cholent*, the Ashkenazic all-night Shabbat stew, but with less fat and more sophistication. The beans become luscious and creamy, the duck burnished and falling-off-the-bone tender. Duck requires a first roasting to render its fat, but the extra step is worth the effort, plus it yields a jar of delicious cooking fat. The recipe's fairly simple steps are best done a day or two in advance, because this dish is tastier when it is reheated. Cooking time varies depending on the tenderness and size of the duck legs but will take longer than chicken does. Home-cooked beans hold up better than canned during this longer cooking time.

6 whole duck legs, about 1 pound (450 g) each, chilled

Kosher or sea salt and freshly ground black pepper

Handful of thyme sprigs (about 12)

1 large onion

½ pound (225 g) carrots (2 to 3 large)

2 ribs celery and their leaves

3 large cloves garlic

½ cup (120 ml) Cognac

6 cups (1 kg) drained al dente–cooked cannellini beans, plus 2 cups (480 ml) of their cooking liquid, stock, or water (from 1 pound/450 g dried; see page 18)

3 bay leaves

1 orange

About 2 cups (480 ml) water or chicken stock

Finishing salt, such as fleur de sel

Pat the duck legs dry. Use kitchen scissors to cut all visible fat and excess skin from the underside of the thigh end of each leg. Put the trimmings on a shallow plate and place in the freezer until partially frozen, 30 to 45 minutes. Rub the duck legs with salt, pepper, and the leaves from several of the thyme sprigs. Let the legs rest for at least 30 minutes while you organize the remaining ingredients. (Or, cover and refrigerate the seasoned duck legs and the trimmings overnight.)

Chop the onion, carrots, and celery into ¼- to ½-inch (6- to 12-mm) pieces and peel the garlic cloves. (This step can be done a day ahead and the ingredients refrigerated.)

Use scissors to cut the chilled fat and skin into ¼- to ½-inch (6- to 12-mm) pieces and use them to make schmaltz and gribenes as directed on pages 24–25. Save the schmaltz for another purpose. (This step can be done a day ahead and the ingredients refrigerated.)

Preheat the oven to 400°F (200°C). Place the duck legs, skin side up, in a single layer in a flameproof roasting pan large enough to accommodate all the ingredients and fitted with a lid. Roast the duck legs, uncovered, until they are nicely browned, the meat is easily pierced with a knife, and a lot of fat has rendered out, about 1 hour. Transfer the duck legs to a platter or tray. Pour off all but 1 tablespoon of the fat from the pan and reserve for another use (you may have up to 2 cups/480 ml fat).

Add the onion, carrots, celery, and garlic cloves to the roasting pan, season with salt and pepper, and stir well, scraping up any brown bits. Return the pan to the oven and roast the vegetables, uncovered, until they are softened, about 20 minutes.

Remove the pan from the oven and place on the stove top. Reduce the oven temperature to 325°F (165°C). Put the duck legs, skin side up, back in the pan and add any juices that have collected on the platter. Warm the

continued »

Cognac, pour it over the contents of the pan, and ignite with a long match or a fire lighter. Stir until the flames die out, about 1 minute, then transfer the duck to a platter. Add the beans and their cooking liquid to the pan along with the remaining thyme, and the bay leaves. Use a vegetable peeler to remove 2 long ribbons of orange peel from the orange and add to the pan. Season with salt and pepper and stir. Lay the duck legs on the beans. Cover the pan and cook until the beans and duck are very tender, about 1½ hours, adding water as needed to keep the beans looking soupy. (The dish can be made up to 1 to 2 hours ahead, partially covered, and kept at room temperature, or it can be made up to 1 day ahead, covered, and refrigerated. Remove the thyme sprigs before reheating.)

The duck skin will be russet brown. To crisp it further, just before serving, place the duck legs under a hot broiler until the skin is crackling and browned to your liking. Serve the duck and beans in shallow bowls, topped with a showering of gribenes and a little finishing salt.

CHICKEN VARIATION: Use whole chicken legs in place of the duck legs, skip the first roasting, and reduce the oven time for the chicken to 45 minutes. Because of the shortened roasting time, good-quality canned beans may be substituted for dried.

KITCHEN NOTE: When a recipe, such as this one, has multiple steps, it is especially helpful to cluster the tasks into groups that can be done around the same time. Begin with those that take longest yet require the least attention. This is one of the simplest ways to shorten preparation time and maximize efficiency. You'll see that the recipe is organized into three multitasking components that can be adjusted to suit your schedule. Here, I've also assumed that you haven't precooked the beans and have added them to the game plan:

- Put the beans to soak (not necessary with current-season beans); trim and season the duck legs and partially freeze the trimmings; chop the vegetables; and prepare the trimmings for gribenes. This group of tasks can be done a day or even two ahead.
- Roast the duck legs to render the fat; cook the beans; make the gribenes while duck is in the oven and beans are on stove. These steps can be done a day ahead or in the morning and refrigerated.
- Assemble the final dish and bake.

TAHINI BUTTER COOKIES

MAKES ABOUT 24 COOKIES

DAIRY

These easy, one-bowl cookies from my aunt Hanna taste like a cross between halvah and old-fashioned peanut butter cookies. They are especially beautiful dipped in a mix of black and white sesame seeds. Tahini varies in consistency from brand to brand; if yours is more pourable than peanut butter, the cookie dough will feel tacky but will be fine. Just be sure to stir any jar or can of tahini very well before measuring. You can use either toasted or raw tahini here (see page 10 for more on tahini).

½ cup (115 g) butter, at room temperature

⅓ cup (65 g) sugar

½ teaspoon salt

½ cup (120 g) tahini

1 teaspoon vanilla extract

1¼ cups (160 g) all-purpose flour

2 tablespoons black or white sesame seeds, or
   1 tablespoon of each

Position racks in middle and upper third of the oven. Preheat the oven to 350°F (180°C). Have ready 2 large sheet pans.

In a bowl, using a wooden spoon, cream the butter until smooth and fluffy. Beat in the sugar and salt until thoroughly incorporated, then beat in the tahini and stir in the vanilla. Add the flour in three batches, mixing after each addition just until blended.

To shape the cookies, scoop up nuggets of the dough (a generous ½ ounce/15 g) and roll between your palms into walnut-size balls (about 1¼ inches/3 cm in diameter). As the balls are formed, place them on the ungreased baking sheet(s), spacing them 2 inches (5 cm) apart.

Pour the sesame seeds into a small bowl. Dip the top half of each ball into the sesame seeds and return the ball to the pan, seed side up. Press the center of each cookie with the back of a small spoon to flatten into a roughly 2-inch (5-cm) round. Don't worry if the cookies aren't perfectly even or if a crack or two forms on the edges.

Bake the cookies, switching the pans top to bottom and back to front halfway through the baking to ensure they bake evenly, until lightly golden and fragrant, about 15 minutes. Be careful not to overbake. Let the cookies cool on the pan(s) on a wire rack for 5 minutes, then transfer them to the rack to cool completely. Store in an airtight tin at room temperature.

CAROB MOLASSES ICE CREAM

MAKES 1 TO 1½ QUARTS (1 TO 1.5 L)

DAIRY

Poor misunderstood carob: it's so much more than ersatz chocolate. With notes of caramel, molasses, fruit, and toast, as well as chocolate, carob deserves to star on its own in this ice cream that evokes thoughts of malt and stout. Carob trees are abundant in the eastern Mediterranean, California, and anywhere, actually, where citrus grows well. The tree's long dark pods are harvested in fall, roasted, and processed into many evergreen food products: powdered coffee and chocolate substitutes, food thickeners, and the carob molasses used here, which is available at Middle Eastern markets. From biblical times until now, the drought-resistant carob, also known as locust bean and St. John's bread, has been used as a subsistence food during famine. It is one of the symbolic foods of Tu b'Shvat, making this ice cream a perfect finish to a holiday meal. (Save the egg whites for the Rustic Almond-Orange Macaroons, page 152.)

4 egg yolks
2 cups (480 ml) heavy cream
1 cup (240 ml) whole milk
¼ cup (50 g) sugar
⅛ teaspoon salt
½ cup (160 g) carob molasses, warmed

Set a mesh sieve over a 2-quart (2-L) bowl. Rest the bowl in a larger bowl filled with a good handful of ice and a little water, and place near the stove. In a medium bowl, lightly whisk together the yolks.

In a medium saucepan, combine cream, milk, sugar, and salt over medium heat and bring to a rolling boil. Turn off the heat. Take 1 cup (240 ml) of the hot cream mixture and stream it slowly into the yolks, whisking constantly. Slowly whisk egg-cream mixture back into the saucepan. Turn heat to low and cook, stirring frequently with a wooden spoon, until the mixture is thick enough to coat the back of the spoon and stays parted like the Red Sea when you run your finger across the spoon, 2 to 4 minutes. Be careful not to overcook, as the mixture will curdle. Pour through the prepared sieve to remove any bits of cooked egg.

Stir the custard a few times to cool it down a bit and then stir in the carob molasses. Strain through the sieve again. When cool, cover with plastic wrap, pressing it directly onto the surface of the custard, and refrigerate for several hours or up to overnight.

Freeze in an ice cream maker following manufacturer's instructions. Transfer to a chilled container, cover tightly, and freeze, preferably for several hours, before serving. This ice cream is creamy enough that you should have no trouble scooping it straight from the freezer.

DELICIOUS WITH:

Semolina and Walnut Oil Cake
with Coffee Hawaij (page 243)

Spiced Date and Walnut Oatmeal Cake
(page 153)

Rustic Almond-Orange Macaroons (page 152)

Peppered Red Wine Fruit Compote (page 112)

RUSTIC ALMOND-ORANGE MACAROONS

MAKES ABOUT 3 DOZEN 2-INCH (5-CM) COOKIES

PAREVE

Macaroons derive from marzipan, a smooth paste of blanched almonds and sugar that, when mixed with egg white and baked, turn into chewy little gems. I call these "rustic" because I use skin-on (natural) almonds, which impart a richer flavor and color, and because you are more likely to find well-grown, small-farmed almonds in this unprocessed way. My aunt Hanna told me that her mother, my Iraqi grandmother, used to make *massapan* for Tu b'Sh'vat. It was a lot of work, she said, so Hanna herself, who loves to bake, never bothered with it. *Massapan?* A quick visit to Claudia Roden's *Book of Jewish Food* revealed *massapan* to be marzipan, or almond paste, perfect indeed for the holiday whose symbol is the almond blossom. Marzipan is a centuries-old crossroads sweet brought to Spain by the Arabs and adopted by Spanish Jews before their expulsion in 1492. Marzipan also has a long tradition in central and northern Europe and Scandinavia. I'm sure my *safta* blanched the almonds herself and ground them by hand with sugar. Today, I'm glad we have food processors that take us from almond to macaroon in one step. These gluten-free macaroons are also perfect for Passover.

1 cup (7 ounces/200 g) sugar

2 oranges

1 cup plus 2 tablespoons (7 ounces/200 g) almonds

1 teaspoon orange flower water

½ teaspoon almond extract

⅛ teaspoon salt

2 egg whites, beaten to blend

Ground cinnamon or cardamom or garam
    masala for dusting (optional)

Line 2 sheet pans with parchment paper. Place ¼ cup (50 g) of the sugar in the work bowl of a food processor fitted with metal S blade. Using a Microplane grater or a five-hole zester, and working over the bowl of the processor, remove the zest from 1 of the oranges, catching the zest and the spray of citrus oils in the bowl. Pulse until the sugar is tinted pale orange and looks a little damp from the citrus oil. Add the remaining ¾ cup (150 g) sugar and the almonds to the work bowl and process until the almonds are very finely ground, the mixture has started to pack together, and the volume in the bowl has reduced by about half, 2 to 3 minutes.

Scrape down the sides of the work bowl, add the flower water, almond extract, and salt, and pulse to blend. With motor running, slowly pour the egg whites through the feed tube. At first, the mixture will form a ball. Continue processing until a tan, sticky dough forms, 15 to 30 seconds. Using the five-hole zester, and working over the processor, remove the zest from the second orange, catching both the zest and the spray of citrus oils in the processor. Pulse briefly to distribute evenly.

Drop the dough by generous teaspoons onto the prepared pans, spacing them about 2 inches (5 cm) apart. Dust the cookies with the spice, if using. Let stand for 30 minutes before baking. The cookies will spread a bit and dry. Adjust oven racks to middle and upper third. Preheat oven to 300°F (150°C).

Bake the cookies, switching the pans top to bottom and front to back halfway through baking to ensure even baking, until they are puffed and pale beige and beginning to color a little around the edges, about 25 minutes. Let cookies cool completely on the pans on wire racks before peeling them from the paper. Store cookies in an airtight container at room temperature for up to 1 week.

SPICED DATE AND WALNUT OATMEAL CAKE

12 TO 16 SERVINGS

DAIRY

Moist, dense, and one-bowl-easy, this is a great snacking cake. Since dates, walnuts, citrus, and cinnamon are all traditional for Tu b'Shvat, the cake is also a perfect ending to a vegetarian holiday meal, especially with a scoop of Carob Molasses Ice Cream (page 151). I've used dates here, but feel free to substitute the equivalent amount of mixed dried fruits, such as apricots, figs, prunes, and/or plums, all of which are also traditional foods for the winter holiday.

½ cup (115 g) butter, at room temperature, plus more for the pan

2 cups (250 g) unbleached all-purpose flour, plus more for the pan

1 cup (80 g) old-fashioned rolled oats

1¾ cups (420 ml) boiling water

1 pound (450 g) pitted dates (1¼ pounds/570 g with pits)

1 cup (200 g) granulated sugar

1 cup (220 g) firmly packed light brown sugar

2 eggs, beaten to blend

2 oranges, plus 1 orange for garnish (optional)

1 teaspoon salt

1 teaspoon baking soda

1 teaspoon ground cinnamon

1 teaspoon ground ginger

1 cup (120 g) walnut pieces

Preheat oven to 350°F (180°C). Butter a 9-x-13-inch (23-x-33-cm) pan, dust with flour, and tap out the excess.

Put the oats in a large heatproof bowl, pour the boiling water over the top, and let stand for 10 minutes.

Meanwhile, cut the dates in half lengthwise, then cut each half in half crosswise.

Stir the butter into the hot oat mixture until melted and thoroughly blended. Stir in the sugars until well mixed. Add the eggs and stir until well blended. Using a Microplane grater, and working over the bowl, remove the zest from the 2 oranges, capturing both the zest and the spray of citrus oils in the bowl. Reserve the oranges for another use.

Stir in the flour, salt, baking soda, cinnamon, and ginger just until thoroughly combined. Stir in half the date pieces. Pour the batter into the prepared pan. Scatter the walnuts and the remaining date pieces evenly over the top.

Bake until a toothpick inserted into the center of the cake comes out clean, about 35 minutes. Let the cake cool completely in the pan on a wire rack. Cut into squares to serve. If desired, using a five-hole zester, remove the zest from an additional orange and garnish the cake with the long, fragrant curls of zest.

This cake tastes even better when made a day before serving. It can be wrapped in plastic wrap and stored at room temperature for a couple of days. Refrigerate or freeze any leftover cake.

BLOOD ORANGE AND OLIVE OIL POLENTA UPSIDE-DOWN CAKE

MAKES ONE 10-BY-2-INCH (25-BY-5-CM) CAKE; 12 SERVINGS

MEAT

Syrup-soaked cakes, usually made with semolina and called *tishpishti* or *namoura*, are popular throughout the Middle East. With its stained-glass effect from the variegated colors of blood oranges, this upside-down cake, which gets its nubbly texture from sunny cornmeal, is drenched in a sophisticated ruby-red blood-orange syrup. Use fine-grind cornmeal or polenta; stone-ground meal doesn't get tender enough in baking. Note that the syrup is thickened with gelatin, which is typically a meat product; for vegetarian and kosher gelatin options, see page 10.

FOR THE CAKE

4 blood oranges

⅔ cup (145 g) packed light brown sugar

1 cup (125 g) unbleached all-purpose flour

⅔ cup (105 g) cornmeal (not stone-ground)

1 teaspoon baking powder

¾ teaspoon salt

⅔ cup (165 ml) extra-virgin olive oil, plus more
    for the pan

¾ cup (150 g) granulated sugar

3 eggs

FOR THE SYRUP

½ packet (⅛ ounce/3.5 g) unflavored gelatin

3 tablespoons granulated sugar

2 tablespoons Cointreau

1 tablespoon fresh lemon juice

Preheat oven to 350°F (180°C). Using a Microplane grater, grate zest from 2 of the blood oranges and reserve. Juice the 2 oranges and reserve. Cut both ends off of each of the remaining 2 oranges, then cut each orange crosswise into rounds ⅛ to 1/16 inch (3 to 2 mm) thick. Cut all but one of the slices in half and discard any center pith.

Sprinkle brown sugar evenly over the bottom of a flameproof and ovenproof 10-inch (25-cm) skillet (a well-seasoned cast-iron skillet is perfect) and sprinkle with 2 tablespoons of the orange juice. Heat skillet over medium-low heat until most of the sugar is bubbling. Remove from the heat.

Starting at the outer edge of the pan, lay the halved orange slices in the melted sugar with the "scalloped" edge of each slice touching the edge of the pan. Fit as many orange slices as you can into the circle, pinching their corners as you set them into the hot sugar (use a knife point or tongs to adjust the fruit as needed). Some slices will have a "prettier" side; make sure those are placed face down in the sugar. Arrange the remaining halved orange slices in concentric circles toward the center, finishing with the reserved whole slice in the center.

In a medium bowl, sift together the flour, cornmeal, baking powder, and salt. In an electric mixer fitted with the paddle attachment, beat together the oil and granulated sugar on medium speed until thickened and golden. Add the eggs, one at a time, beating well after each addition until mixture is thick and creamy gold, 3 to 5 minutes total. Beat in the zest and 1 tablespoon of the juice. On low speed, add the flour mixture in three batches, beating after each addition just until blended.

Pour batter evenly over the orange slices and gently smooth the top. Bake the cake until golden brown, the top springs back to the touch, and a toothpick inserted into the center comes out clean, about 25 minutes. Let cool in

the pan on a wire rack for 5 minutes. Run a thin-bladed knife around the inside edge of the pan to loosen the cake sides. Invert a serving plate over the cake, invert the pan and plate together, and lift off the pan. If any fruit sticks to the pan, loosen it with a spatula and place it on the cake. While the cake is hot, use a fork or bamboo skewer to make holes in it without going all the way through.

While the cake is baking, make the soaking syrup. Fill a medium bowl one-third full with ice and a little water and nestle a smaller bowl, preferably metal, in the ice bath. Pour ¼ cup (60 ml) of the remaining orange juice into a small pot, sprinkle the gelatin on top, and let soften for 5 minutes. Stir granulated sugar, Cointreau, and lemon juice into the remaining orange juice, then stir the mixture into the

softened gelatin. Bring to a simmer over medium heat and stir to dissolve sugar and gelatin, about 1 minute. Do not allow to boil. Pour syrup into the waiting bowl and stir from time to time until it thickens to the consistency of maple syrup, about 15 minutes. Spoon or brush some of the syrup over the cake. Allow it to soak in, then spoon or brush on more. Repeat until you have used all the syrup.

Allow the cake to cool completely before slicing, then cut into wedges with a serrated offset knife to serve.

KITCHEN NOTE: To cut picture-perfect cake slices, use kitchen scissors to snip through the oranges first, then follow that line with your knife to cut the cake. I learned this trick from food stylist Karen Gillingham.

March & April

NEW GROWTH

Early spring brings new growth. Bright green shoots emerge from the earth, and trees are in leaf. Herbs and alliums are among the first edibles to arrive. It's no coincidence that so many of them are incorporated into the ritual foods of Passover, and have been since the time of the actual Exodus.

But before Passover comes Purim, a rowdy spring-fever *Carneval* of a holiday. Whatever other symbolic meanings it may have, Purim is surely a welcome release in cold climates when people ache to shed heavy winter coats.

This chapter rejoices in the season's new growth—green garlic, young leeks, spring onions, and herbs—and the height of sweet citrus. Both elements bring a fresh and meaningful approach to early-spring holiday foods. During this transition from cold weather to warm, it's time to enjoy lighter versions of hearty fare.

March & April

GREEN FAVA BEAN AND ENGLISH PEA "HUMMUS" WITH PITA TRIANGLES WITH ZA'ATAR

MAKES ABOUT 2 CUPS (500 G), 6 TO 8 SERVINGS; 64 PITA TRIANGLES

PAREVE/VEGAN

This bright green spread is not technically hummus, which is Arabic for "chickpea," but it captures the freshness of the season with a nod to the lemon-and-garlic zing of the classic. Young, emerald-green fava beans are tender and mildly bittersweet (in contrast to mature, brown, and more aggressively flavored dried favas). The addition of sweet English peas has a mellowing effect. If you want this spread to taste a little sweeter, add more peas, but keep the total weight (volume) of the ingredients the same. Serve with the Pita Triangles with Za'atar here or with fresh, soft pita. In a pinch, you can use frozen peas and favas (a.k.a. broad beans), but this dish is infinitely better with fresh beans.

3 pounds (1.4 kg) young fava beans in the pod
½ pound (225 g) English peas in the pod
    (½ cup/75 g shelled)
1 to 2 cloves garlic
Juice of 1 lemon (about ¼ cup/60 ml)
Kosher or sea salt and freshly ground white pepper
¼ cup (60 ml) extra-virgin olive oil, plus more
    for serving
Finishing salt, such as Maldon sea salt
Aleppo pepper, red pepper flakes, or sweet paprika
1 tablespoon finely chopped fresh Italian parsley

FOR THE PITA TRIANGLES

4 white or whole wheat pita breads, 5 to 6 inches
    (13 to 15 cm) in diameter
Extra-virgin olive oil
1 to 2 tablespoons za'atar
Finishing salt, such as Maldon sea salt or fleur de sel

Shell the fava beans and cook them in boiling salted water until the skins are loose and the beans are tender but still bright green, about 3 minutes. Drain, and when cool enough to handle, slip the skins off the beans and discard. You should have about 1½ cups (255 g) beans.

Shell peas and cook in boiling salted water until tender but still bright green, 3 to 5 minutes for young peas, longer for larger, starchy peas. Drain and reserve peas and cooking liquid separately.

Fit a food processor with the metal S blade. With the motor running, drop garlic cloves through the feed tube to mince. Add beans, peas, half the lemon juice, 2 tablespoons reserved cooking liquid, ¾ teaspoon salt, and a few grinds of white pepper. Process to a coarse paste. With the motor running, add olive oil in a thin stream, processing until the mixture is smooth. Add remaining lemon juice and season with salt and white pepper. (The spread can be made 1 to 2 days ahead and refrigerated. Bring to room temperature before serving.)

Smear the spread onto a dinner-size plate, using the back of a spoon to swirl it. Drizzle with olive oil, season with finishing salt and Aleppo pepper, and shower with parsley.

TO MAKE THE PITA TRIANGLES: Preheat oven to 300°F (150°C). Use kitchen scissors to split each pita into 2 rounds. Stack 2 or 3 rounds and cut into 8 triangles. Place close together, rough side up, on large baking sheets. Brush tops with olive oil, season generously with za'atar and a little salt, and bake until crisp and browned, 10 to 15 minutes. Because pitas vary in thickness, start checking for doneness at 10 minutes, and keep in mind that they will continue to crisp as they cool. Let chips cool completely before placing them in a serving basket. (They can be made 1 day ahead and stored in an airtight container.)

SAVORY PERSIAN HERB AND CHEESE HAMANTASCHEN

MAKES 2 DOZEN 3-INCH (7.5-CM) PASTRIES

DAIRY

Hamantaschen, the traditional triangular Ashkenazic Purim pastries, are typically a sweet treat. I've taken a savory approach here, using spring herbs, a Persian favorite, to honor Esther and Mordechai's heritage, as well as the season. With their flaky dough, these Haman's hats (or pockets or ears) are reminiscent of *bourekas*, the small hand pies popular in Israel and the eastern Mediterranean. You can make snack-size hamantaschen or large ones for a vegetarian main dish (see the variation at the end of the recipe).

FOR THE PASTRY

1½ cups (190 g) unbleached all-purpose flour

½ cup (60 g) whole wheat flour

½ teaspoon salt

¾ cup (170 g) cold butter, cut into ½-inch (12-mm) pieces

½ cup (120 ml) ice water

FOR THE FILLING

1 bunch each Persian or regular mint, leek or garlic chives, pepper cress, green onions, and tarragon

¾ cup (170 g) labneh, homemade (page 22) or store-bought

6 ounces (170 g) feta cheese, crumbled

1 egg, lightly beaten

1 egg, lightly beaten, for egg wash

TO MAKE THE PASTRY: In a large bowl, stir together the flours and salt with a fork. Scatter the butter over the flour mixture and, using your fingertips or a pastry blender, cut in the butter until the mixture resembles coarse sand with some flattened pieces of butter still visible. Stir in the ice water, a little at a time, until the dough just sticks together when pressed between your fingertips. Gather the dough into a ball, wrap in plastic wrap, and flatten into a thick rectangle. Refrigerate for at least 15 minutes. (The dough can be made up to 3 days ahead and refrigerated; let it rest at room temperature until soft enough to roll out, about 15 minutes.)

TO MAKE THE FILLING: Finely chop enough of each of the herbs in any combination preferred to total 1¼ cups (75 g) lightly packed. In a medium bowl, use a fork to mash together the labneh and feta. Stir in the egg, then stir in the chopped herbs.

TO ASSEMBLE THE PASTRIES: Preheat the oven to 425°F (220°C). Have ready 2 sheet pans. If you like, line them with parchment paper.

Divide the dough in half and rewrap and refrigerate half of it. On a lightly floured work surface, roll out the other half into a rectangle or circle $^{1}/_{16}$ to $^{1}/_{8}$ inch (2 to 3 mm) thick. Cut out 12 circles each 3½ inches (9 cm) in diameter, rerolling any scraps as needed.

Mound 1 tablespoon of filling in the center of each dough circle. Fold the sides of the dough up over the filling to form a triangle, leaving a nickel-size bit of filling exposed. Pinch the three corners of the triangle very firmly to seal. Arrange the pastries on a sheet pan, spacing them about 1 inch (2.5 cm) apart. Refrigerate the first

continued »

batch while you make more with the remaining half of the dough and filling. Top off the pastries with any leftover filling. Brush the pastries with the egg wash.

Bake the pastries for 12 minutes; the bottoms will be light golden. Reduce heat to 375°F (190°C) and continue to bake until the crust is a rich gold and the filling is puffed and browned in places, 10 to 12 minutes longer. Using an offset spatula, transfer the pastries to a wire rack and let cool for 5 to 10 minutes before serving. Refrigerate leftover hamantaschen; they can be reheated in a 350°F (180°C).

MAIN DISH VARIATION: To make 6 large hamantaschen, cut three 6-inch (15-cm) circles from each piece of dough. Use about ⅓ cup (70 g) of filling for each dough circle and fold as directed. As you complete shaping each hamantasch, use a wide offset spatula to move it onto the baking sheet. Bake at 425°F (220°C) for 15 minutes and at 375°F (190°C) for about 25 minutes.

KITCHEN NOTE: Unbaked hamantaschen can be frozen, well wrapped, for up to 1 week. Brush frozen pastries with egg wash just before baking, and increase oven times to 15 and 18 minutes, respectively.

Purim

SPRING FEVER

As laid out in the Book of Esther, the holiday of Purim was intended to be a raucous, drunken revelry to celebrate Esther's clever rebuff of the plan by the king's right-hand man, Haman, to exterminate the Jews of Babylon during the Persian reign in the sixth century BCE. The tale of palace intrigue and foiled genocide attempt is also a story of feminine wiles and heroics. As decreed in the Bible, Purim is also a time when the story of Esther is told, money is given to the poor, and gifts of food are sent to friends. Coming as it does in late winter, like Carneval and Mardi Gras, the holiday is pure spring fever, historically a mishmash of Chaucerian- and Shakespearean-style cruel jokes and double entendres, effigy burning, costumes, and masks. Even the festival's name connotes recklessness; the word *purim* means "lots," which is what Haman cast to determine the best date for the massacre, which set the stage for his own undoing.

Today's Purim customs are pretty much the same—minus the cruelty and effigy burning. The "whole megillah" (scroll) is read and sometimes acted out, and there are costume parties for the kids, contributions made to those in need, and plenty of baking and frying of sweets that poke fun at Haman's hat, pockets, or ears.

Sephardic Jews traditionally fry pastry twists known variously as *fazuelas, orecci di Aman,* and *orecchie di Ammon*. Ashkenazic Jews bake hamantaschen, triangular filled yeast- or cookie-dough treats, called *oznei haman* (Haman's ears) in Hebrew. Poppy seeds (*mohn*) are often used as a filling to symbolize coins for the poor. Legumes, especially fava beans, chickpeas, and lentils, are included in savory dishes to commemorate the tradition that Esther was a vegetarian in order to keep kosher in the Diaspora as the Jewish wife of a Persian king.

RECIPE SUGGESTIONS FOR PURIM

Savory Persian Herb and Cheese Hamantaschen (page 163)

Green Fava Bean and English Pea "Hummus" with Pita Triangles with Za'atar (page 161)

Simple Farro Soup with Chickpeas and Escarole (page 134)

Kitchri: Red Lentils and Rice with Golden Garlic Puree (page 143)

Buckwheat, Bow Ties, and Brussels Sprouts (page 137)

Zengoula with Lemon Syrup (page 117)

Poppy Seed Shortbread Cookies (page 290)

Passover

A STORY TOLD THROUGH FOOD

In the Book of Exodus, Moses conveys the escape plan from Egypt to the Israelites, and it includes a recipe for their preflight meal. Standing dressed, sandals on, staffs in hand, and ready to flee, the Hebrews are to fire-roast the sacrificial lamb and eat it with unleavened bread and bitter herbs.

The grab-and-go lamb sandwich epitomizes the speed and stealth of the Israelites' departure and is the opposite of the festival they are to have a week later to mark the successful getaway. From the earliest Seders modeled after Greek and Roman philosophers' banquets, Jews are told to recline, dine leisurely, and retell the events of the Exodus, the birth of the Jewish nation. In ancient times, Jews in the Diaspora couldn't be sure of the holiday's starting date, so to be safe, they celebrated two first days and Seders, which is why Passover is observed for eight days outside Israel and for seven in Israel. Many Jews in the Diaspora continue the two-Seder tradition.

Today, as for two millennia, we tell the story of Passover through the foods on the Seder plate: the roasted shank bone for lamb-on-the-run; a roasted egg and spring herbs for renewal; *charoset* for the mortar the Hebrew slaves used to build Egyptian structures; *maror* (bitter herbs) for enslavement; and matzah, unleavened bread. The leisurely meal that follows the telling is an opportunity to incorporate many of the symbolic ingredients woven into the holiday story.

Passover, one of three agriculturally linked festivals prescribed in the Bible (Shavuot and Sukkot are the others), occurs during the first month of the Jewish calendar, a new year for the growing season. The holiday may be a fusion of nomadic shepherds' thanksgiving for good flocks and (later) farmers' preparation for the spring harvest, which may have included clearing out any fermented grains, a forerunner of the practice of removing all leavened foods from the home.

What constitutes Passover-appropriate food varies by region and degree of observance. Observant Jews do not eat any wheat other than that specially grown and inspected for the holiday and turned into carefully scrutinized matzah products to ensure that no fermentation or rising has occurred and that they are never in contact with any of the "forbidden" grains—barley, rye, spelt, oats, or corn. Consequently, observant Jews drink no grain-based alcohol or beer on Passover. Sephardic Jews include rice and legumes during Passover, but Ashkenazic Jews do not (a prohibition that includes peas and peanuts).

Speaking of matzah, some view it truly as the bread of affliction, a weeklong deprivation of bread products. Others, like me, welcome the return of matzah to the table as cause for celebration, both of a brave people who dared and succeeded and for the week of spring holiday foods about to be enjoyed.

MOM'S SORT-OF-ASHKENAZIC CHAROSET

MAKES 3 CUPS (800 G), ABOUT 12 SERVINGS

PAREVE

Charoset, the fruit-and-nut mixture that symbolizes the mortar the Hebrew slaves used in Egypt, has many versions, depending on whose Jewish cuisine you're talking about. When my Romanian Israeli mother began preparing Seders in California, her adopted homeland, she turned, as she often did, to Sara Kasdan's irreverent cookbook *Love and Knishes*, the original inspiration for this apple-based Ashkenazic *charoset*. My mother uses Manischewitz Concord grape wine, but I prefer to use an off-dry red wine and increase the amount of honey and dates to taste. You'll be using storage apples at this time of year, and many of us in the Diaspora don't have access to local bananas. Be sure to use a banana that is not too ripe and perfumed; its main purpose here is as a "binding" agent. *Charoset* isn't the prettiest dish, but it should be delicious, and this one surely is. My mother doubles the amounts given here to ensure plenty of leftovers for the family to enjoy on matzah the next day with morning coffee. (This recipe is shown in the photo on page 168.)

3 sweet apples, such as Red Delicious or Fuji

3 or 4 pitted dates

½ small banana, slightly underripe

¾ cup (90 g) chopped walnuts, or more if needed

2 tablespoons honey

¼ cup (60 ml) off-dry or other red wine, or more if needed

Peel, halve, and core the apples, then grate on large holes of a box grater or in a food processor fitted with the grating disk. Put the apples in a bowl large enough to hold all the ingredients. Fit processor with the metal S blade and process the dates and banana to a paste. Add the apples to the processor and pulse a few times to blend. Scrape the mixture back into the bowl and stir in the nuts, honey, and wine.

You should have a tan/mauve, chunky mixture. If the charoset is too wet, add more nuts; if it is too dry, add wine. This charoset is best made a day ahead to allow flavors to blend and mellow. Store refrigerated.

SAFTA RACHEL'S IRAQI CHAROSET

MAKES ABOUT 1 CUP (330 G), ABOUT 12 SERVINGS

PAREVE/VEGAN

And now for something completely different. My grandmother's Iraqi *charoset* couldn't be simpler to make. As my cousin Elan says, "It's a little bit of heaven." And, I would add, it's also terrific on morning matzah or toast any time of the year. *Silan* (date syrup) is thought to be what the Bible refers to as "honey." It resembles sorghum or molasses in color and viscosity but with complex fruit notes. You can make your own, as my grandmother did, or buy a good-quality brand that contains only dates and water. (This recipe is shown on page 166.)

¾ cup (75 g) pecans, toasted (see page 18)
¾ cup (255 g) silan (date syrup)

Chop the nuts into about ¼-inch (6-mm) pieces, chopping some almost to "dust." Put the silan in a small bowl and stir in the nuts and dust. You should have a thick honey-like spread. It can be made 1 day ahead and stored, covered, at room temperature.

MAIMOUNA

At the end of Passover, North African Jews celebrate Maimouna, a memorial to Maimon ben Yosef, the father of the Rambam (the twelfth-century Sephardic scholar Moshe ben Maimon, also known as Maimonides). Historically, the observance was important to Jews living in Muslim countries. Due to the huge Moroccan influx into Israel beginning in the mid-twentieth century, Maimouna has become a nationally popular occasion for picnics and a return to leavened products. Traditional foods symbolize birth and fertility and include milk, figs, wheat, and pancakes made with butter and honey. Cheese and Honey Filo Pie (page 237) is a perfect Maimouna treat.

MY FAMILY'S GEFILTE FISH

MAKES ABOUT EIGHTEEN 3-INCH (7.5-CM) OVAL PATTIES, 8 TO 12 SERVINGS

FISH

When done well, some traditional foods need no updating. Alas, too few of us have ever tasted real homemade gefilte fish that are featherlight country-style quenelles, not the dense patties that come out of a jar. *Gefilte* means "filled" or "stuffed," and my Romanian grandmother Mina used to begin with a live carp swimming in the bathtub, which she killed, gutted, and filleted, preserving the integrity of the head and skin. The bones went into the pot for a court bouillon, and she ground the raw fillets with onions, carrots, and eggs, stuffing the mixture back into the skin and poaching the fish "whole" in the bouillon. Mina carved it tableside, with the head going to the guest of honor. And she didn't make it just for Passover; she often prepared gefilte fish for Friday night or other festive dinners.

Today, most of us don't buy our fish live, and making quenelles is usually enough of a project, albeit a worthwhile one. Many fishmongers will fillet and grind the fish for you and give you the head and bones for the stock. Carp is a dark, oily fish. A mix of pike and whitefish yields a more delicate result. If you like carp, use 1 pound (450 g) each of carp and pike. Gefilte fish can be made up to 2 days ahead, and this recipe is easy to double for a large crowd. Adorn the fish patties with spring lettuce, red or purple carrots, and Easter Egg radishes and serve with Bat-Sheva's Horseradish (recipe is on page 174).

2 large onions

2 tablespoons grapeseed or other mild oil

2 large carrots

1 small celery root, about ½ pound (225 g), or the heart of 1 bunch celery

1 parsley root

1 pound (450 g) whole pike, flesh ground, bones and head reserved

1 pound (450 g) whole whitefish, flesh ground, bones and head reserved

5 cups (1.2 L) water

2 eggs

1½ teaspoons kosher or sea salt

2 tablespoons matzah meal or fresh bread crumbs

Freshly ground white pepper

Butter lettuce, steamed or boiled carrot coins, sliced radishes, and horseradish sauce, homemade (recipe follows) or store-bought, for serving

TO MAKE THE STOCK: Cut the onions in half and then cut the halves crosswise into thin slices. In a large, wide pot, cook the onions in the oil over medium-low to low heat until translucent and tender, 15 to 20 minutes. Remove from the heat. Measure out half of the onions and set aside.

Cut the carrots into coins and add to the onions in the pot. Peel the celery root, cut into thin slices, and add to the pot, burying the slices under the onions to keep them from discoloring. If using the celery heart, chops stalks and leaves. Peel the parsley root and add to the pot. Add the fish bones and heads and the water, cover, and bring to a boil over medium-high heat. Reduce the heat to medium-low, shift the lid to cover partially, and simmer for 30 minutes.

TO PREPARE THE FISH: While the stock is simmering, transfer the reserved onions to a food processor fitted with the metal S blade and process until finely ground. In a large bowl, whisk the eggs to blend, then whisk in 1½ teaspoons salt and a few grinds of white pepper until well mixed. Add the ground onions, ground fish, and matzah meal and mix thoroughly but with a light hand. I find it helpful to start with a fork and then finish the job with my fingertips, as if making pastry dough. Wear gloves if you like.

Have a bowl of ice water and a sheet pan nearby. Wet your hands in the ice water to make the fish easier to handle and to prevent the fish from sticking to your fingers. Use a serving spoon to scoop up about ⅓ cup (2 to 3 ounces/55 to 85 g) of the fish mixture into one hand and flip the mixture back and forth between your hands until you have an oval patty about 3 inches (7.5 cm) long. Place the patty on the sheet pan and repeat with the remaining fish mixture. You should have about 18 patties.

Put a medium pot of water on the stove top and bring to a boil. Using a slotted spoon, gently lower the patties into the large pot of simmering stock. Ladle enough boiling water over the patties to cover them. Cover the pot and simmer until the patties are opaque, firm enough to hold together well, and cooked through, about 40 minutes. Turn off the heat and allow the patties to cool in the stock.

When the stock and patties are cool, use a slotted spoon to transfer the patties to a shallow baking dish, arranging them in a single layer and removing and discarding any stray bones that may have attached themselves. Strain the stock through a fine-mesh sieve, discard the solids, and then pour the stock over patties. Cover and refrigerate until ready to serve. (The gefilte fish can be made up to 2 days ahead.)

To serve, nestle 1 or 2 patties in or near a butter lettuce leaf on a salad plate and include a little of the gelled stock, if you like. Garnish with steamed or boiled carrot coins and sliced radishes.

SOURCING FOR THE SEDER
FROM THE FARMERS' MARKET OR GARDEN

Passover is an opportunity to connect the cycle of growing seasons with holiday rituals. Buy market eggs whose yolks are deep golden or orange and flavorful and whose shells come in a variety of colors, from cream to tawny and pale green to pale blue. Don't peel the hard-boiled eggs for the Seder plate ahead of time. They'll stay fresher, and you and your guests can better appreciate their beauty and wholeness. Instead of limp parsley that no one wants to eat, assemble an array of the freshest tender herbs you can find. Include young radishes with their tops, slender chives and garlic chives, Italian parsley, tiny spring onions whose bulbs are no bigger than your pinkie nail, young dill sprigs, and mild Persian mint. Use multicolored carrots and plump spring lettuce leaves to garnish gefilte fish. Seek out flowering or fruiting branches from your local growers or use small pots of fragrant herbs as table decorations (and then plant them in your garden or window box).

BAT-SHEVA'S HORSERADISH

MAKES 1½ TO 2 CUPS (11 TO 15 OUNCES/310 TO 430 G)

PAREVE/VEGAN

Those who know eighty-four-year-old Bat-Sheva Itzhar, a great cook and daughter of one of the founding families of Nahalal, Israel's first moshav, consider her horseradish sauce to be without equal. There are two secrets to "painless" production and delicious results: Partially freeze the root before processing to break down its fibers and to soften the harshness of the volatile oils that are released when its cell walls are broken. And use a meat grinder rather than a food processor for the best texture and for a less violent release of the oils.

Pungency varies from root to root, but the flavor of any root is always strongest when it is first cut. A pre-trimmed root, such as those found at the supermarket, is typically less powerfully flavored than a whole one just pulled from the ground. Vinegar stabilizes the volatile oils; you can control the degree of sharpness to some extent by when and how much vinegar you add to the horseradish. Add it immediately after the root is processed to tame the heat, or wait several minutes for a stronger condiment. Prepared horseradish will mellow over time.

If you prefer your horseradish white, omit the beets. This recipe can be easily multiplied. The difference between this horseradish and store-bought is like night and day. If purchasing ready-made sauce, buy the kind you find in the refrigerator case that contains no fillers.

½ pound (225 g) horseradish root, peeled and cut into small chunks slim enough to fit into the feed tube of your meat grinder or food processor

2 to 4 ounces (55 to 115 g) red beet, peeled and cut into chunks to fit your feed tube (optional)

6 to 8 tablespoons (90 to 120 ml) white or cider vinegar

1 lemon

½ to 1 teaspoon salt

½ to 1 teaspoon sugar

Wrap the horseradish in plastic wrap and freeze for 2 hours. To make the sauce with a meat grinder, fit the grinder with the fine blade, then push the horseradish and beet (if using) through the grinder into a bowl. For a more sharply flavored condiment, let the ground mixture stand for 5 to 10 minutes. Stir in 6 tablespoons (90 ml) of the vinegar, a good squeeze of lemon juice, and ½ teaspoon each of the sugar and salt. Taste and adjust the seasoning with more vinegar, lemon, salt, and sugar if needed. If the mixture looks too stiff, stir in a little water.

To make the sauce with a food processor, freeze the horseradish as directed for the grinder method. Fit the processor with the grating disk and grate the horseradish and beet. Replace the grating disk with the metal S blade and add the vinegar, lemon, salt, and sugar to the work bowl. Process until you have a rough puree, adding a little water as needed (the mixture is likely to be drier when made in a food processor than with a meat grinder). Taste and adjust seasonings.

Cover the sauce tightly and refrigerate for at least 2 hours or up to overnight to allow the flavors to meld. Just before serving, taste again and adjust the seasoning as desired.

THREE SMART THINGS TO DO WITH LEFTOVER SEDER INGREDIENTS

1. Make a Passover *salsa verde* with leftover herbs.

2. Make the spring salads in this chapter and use more herbs.

3. Steam carrots, radishes (yes, radishes!), and asparagus. Serve with *salsa verde* and sieved or quartered hard-boiled eggs.

SPRING SALAD WITH RADISHES, PEAS, AVOCADO, EGGS, AND CREAMY LEMON-SHALLOT DRESSING

MAKES 6 TO 8 SERVINGS

PAREVE

This salad showcases spring ingredients at their most beautiful and delicate. Use early-season radishes when they are at their juiciest, and add their peppery young leaves to the bowl. This eggless, no-cream creamy dressing is a family favorite and one that you will turn to again and again. The recipe multiplies easily, so keep a jar on hand in the fridge. This is another day-after-Seder recipe to repurpose hard-boiled eggs and herbs. If you follow Ashkenazic kashrut and don't eat legumes during Passover, omit the peas and use more of the other ingredients.

FOR THE DRESSING

1 shallot (about 1 ounce/30 g), quartered, or
    1 spring onion, white part only, coarsely
    chopped
3 tablespoons fresh lemon juice
2 teaspoons Dijon mustard
Kosher or sea salt and freshly ground black pepper
½ cup (120 ml) grapeseed or avocado oil

FOR THE SALAD

½ pound (225 g) sugar snap peas, stringed and
    cut into ½-inch (12-mm) pieces, or
1 cup (145 g) shelled English peas
    (about 1 pound/450 g in the pod)
1 small bunch red Easter Egg or French radishes
    with nice green tops attached (about 8 radishes)
1 large head butter lettuce, large leaves torn
¼ cup (3 g) fresh dill sprigs
¼ cup (12 g) snipped fresh chives
1 avocado, halved, pitted, peeled, and cut into cubes
2 hard-boiled eggs
Finishing salt, such as Maldon sea salt

TO MAKE THE DRESSING: In a blender, combine the shallot, lemon juice, mustard, 1 teaspoon salt, and a few grinds of pepper and process until smooth. With the motor running, add the oil in a slow, steady stream and process until the mixture emulsifies. Any leftover dressing will keep in a tightly covered container in the refrigerator for up to 5 days. Stir or shake to reblend.

TO MAKE THE SALAD: Cook the peas in salted boiling water until the color brightens, about 2 minutes. Drain and shock in a bath of ice and cold water to stop the cooking and preserve the color. Drain well, pat dry, and place in a salad bowl.

Pluck off all the prettiest leaves and tender stems from the radish bunch. Rinse and dry them and add them to the bowl. Thinly slice the radishes and add to the bowl. Add the lettuce, dill, and chives and toss with just enough of the dressing to coat the ingredients lightly. Add the avocado and gently toss again.

Mound the salad on a serving platter, in a shallow bowl, or divide among individual salad plates. Press the eggs through a sieve held over the salad, then sprinkle with finishing salt.

MY FAVORITE PASSOVER SNACK OR QUICK LUNCH: Smash ripe avocado onto a sheet of matzah, squeeze a generous amount of lemon juice over the avocado, and season with salt and pepper. It's been a favorite treat since I was a child.

HERB SALAD WITH FETA CHEESE, HALVAH, AND GREEN ALMONDS

MAKES 6 SERVINGS

DAIRY

The Persian tradition of a *sabzi* platter—aromatic herbs, radishes, alliums, salty feta, and sweet halvah—is equally delicious in salad form and a great way to use up all those extra herbs you bought for your Seder. Another seasonal Persian favorite—green, or immature, almonds—adds an unusual tart note. When very young, the entire almond fruit is edible, from its green, peach-like fuzzy outer layer to the clear, jelly-like nascent nut inside. As it matures, the still tender nutmeat whitens and the outer layer becomes too hard to eat. Look for them at farmers' markets in almond-growing areas and also at Persian groceries. Green almonds are lovely both raw and pickled. If you don't have green almonds, make this beautiful early-spring salad anyway.

1 small head butter lettuce, large leaves torn

½ to 1 bunch regular chives or leek chives, snipped

½ bunch mint, preferably Persian, torn

Leaves of a few sprigs of tarragon

4 to 6 radishes, thinly sliced

¼ to ½ cup (1 to 2 ounces/30 to 55 g) green almonds

1 to 2 tablespoons walnut oil

Juice of ½ lemon

Finishing salt, such as Maldon sea salt or sel gris, or kosher salt and freshly ground black pepper

3 ounces (85 g) feta cheese, preferably French, broken into ½- to 1-inch (12-mm to 2.5-cm) chunks or sliced

3 ounces (85 g) halvah, broken into ½- to 1-inch (12-mm to 2.5-cm) chunks or sliced

In a salad bowl, combine the lettuce, chives, mint, tarragon, and radishes. Just before serving, thinly slice the almonds crosswise and add to the salad. Drizzle the oil and lemon juice over the salad, season with salt and pepper, and toss to coat evenly.

Mound the salad on a serving platter or divide among individual salad plates. Top with large feta and halvah crumbles or serve with slabs of each on the side.

A HANDFUL OF PERSIAN HERBS

Aromatic herbs are one of the foundations of Persian cooking. Here's a short list of some favorites with their Farsi transliterations.

Cilantro	*gishneh*
Dill	*shevet*
Fenugreek	*shambalileh*
Green garlic	*seer*
Leek chives	*tareh*
Lemon basil	*rahan*
Mint	*na'na*
Parsley	*jafari*
Pepper cress	*shaheh*
Radishes	*tarobcheh*
Tarragon	*tarkhun*

MY FAMILY'S MATZAH BALL SOUP

MAKES 16 MEDIUM-SIZE MATZAH BALLS, ABOUT 8 SERVINGS

MEAT

The women in my family are known for the suppleness of their *knaidlach*, though only my Yiddish-speaking in-laws referred to matzah balls that way. But it's a tradition that spans only three generations—my mother, me, and my daughters—since there was a break in our food chain when my parents immigrated to the United States. When my mother wanted to learn how to make matzah balls, she followed the recipe on the back of the box of Manischewitz matzah meal. Like the pumpkin pie recipe on the Libby's can, the century-old matzah production company accurately captures the traditional essentials: straightforward, perfect texture, and buoyancy. The original recipe called for schmaltz; today it asks for oil. Honestly, oil doesn't work as well; you need a fat that congeals, so save the delicious stuff that hardens on your homemade soup for this purpose. I've noted the other key tweaks below, all of which will save you from "matzah ball-anxiety." With thanks to "Mani" for getting us started all those years ago, here's how the women in my family do it.

4 eggs

1 cup (130 g) matzah meal

2 teaspoons kosher or sea salt

¼ cup (55 g) schmaltz (page 24) or rendered
    chicken fat from the soup, melted

2 quarts (2 L) plus ¼ cup (60 ml) chicken soup
    (page 44)

In a medium bowl, whisk the eggs to blend completely. Stir in the matzah meal, salt, schmaltz, and ¼ cup (60 ml) of the stock. Cover and refrigerate until the mixture is firm, at least several hours or overnight.

Fill a wide pot with water and bring to a boil over high heat. Place a small bowl of cold water and a plate or sheet pan nearby. Scoop up a walnut-size nugget of the chilled matzah mixture, roll it gently but thoroughly between your palms into a ball, and place on the plate. Repeat with the remaining mixture, dipping your hands in the cold water from time to time to keep the dough from sticking to them and to ensure a prettier finish.

Salt the boiling water and reduce the heat to keep the water at a gentle, rather than rolling, boil. Drop the matzah balls into the water. (You may have to massage the flattened surface where the ball rested on the plate to have perfectly formed rounds, but that will take only a second.) The matzah balls will sink when you first drop them in, but then they will float back up as they cook.

Cover the pot and simmer over low to medium-low heat until the color of the matzah balls has lightened and they are cooked through, 30 to 40 minutes. Stir the pot once about ten minutes into the cooking time to release any matzah balls that are sticking to the bottom. Be sure to keep the water at a simmer. A rolling boil will cook the outside of the matzah ball before the core is cooked through, causing the matzah ball to disintegrate.

To test for doneness, cut a matzah ball in half. It should have an almost uniformly pale color throughout (a *slightly* darker center is okay, as they will continue to cook in the soup later), and it should be tender, yet with a pleasant resistance to the bite.

While the matzah balls are cooking, bring the 2 quarts (2 L) soup to a simmer. Using a slotted spoon, lift matzah balls from the cooking water and gently drop them into the soup. Simmer, uncovered, for at least 10 minutes to infuse the matzah balls with the flavor of the soup.

If you are making this dish a day ahead, remove the matzah balls from the cooking water with the slotted spoon and place them in a shallow container. Heat just enough soup to cover the hot matzah balls and pour it over them. Refrigerate, uncovered, until completely cool before covering. To serve, reheat the chilled matzah balls and the remaining chilled soup together. You can freeze the chicken soup, but for best texture, you should not freeze the matzah balls.

KITCHEN NOTES: For perfect matzah balls:

- Use a fat that hardens.
- Chill batter for several hours or overnight.
- Roll the matzah mixture into balls no larger than walnut size; they expand as they cook.
- As you shape the balls, dip your hands in cold water to keep the mixture from sticking and to ensure a prettier finish.
- Shape all the matzah balls before you begin cooking, so they will finish cooking at the same time.
- Do not let the cooking water come to a vigorous boil or the balls will cook unevenly.

RAPINI AND RICE SOUP

MAKES 8 SERVINGS

MEAT

Rapini, also called broccoli raab, broccoli rabe, *cime di rapa*, and *broccoli di rapa*, is a cool-weather Italian favorite harvested in spring or fall and often paired with rice in an Italian soup for Passover. It has a pleasant, slightly bitter flavor, tender stems (check that they don't look fibrous), small florets, and ruffled leaves that distinguish it from sweeter Chinese broccoli, which has large, leathery leaves, and from sprouting, or "baby," broccoli (also known as broccolini), which has small, oblong leaves. If rapini isn't available, you may substitute baby or sprouting broccoli.

2 bunches rapini, about 1 pound (450 g) total

1 onion, chopped

Kosher or sea salt and freshly ground black pepper

1 to 2 tablespoons extra-virgin olive oil

¾ cup (145 g) medium-grain rice for risotto, such as Arborio, Carnaroli, or Vialone Nano

6 to 8 cups (1.4 to 2 L) chicken soup (page 44) or beef stock (page 66) or 3 to 4 cups canned diluted with 3 to 4 cups water

3 hard-boiled egg yolks, sieved (optional)

Trim away the tough portion—about 1 inch (2.5 cm)—of the rapini stalks and discard. Cut the rapini stalks crosswise into small pieces. In a wide pot, sauté the onion with a little salt in the olive oil over medium heat until soft and translucent, 5 to 7 minutes. Stir in the rapini and cook until the color deepens, 2 to 3 minutes. Stir in the rice and cook until the rice whitens, 1 to 2 minutes.

Add 6 cups (1.4 L) of the soup and bring to a boil. Reduce the heat to a simmer, cover, and cook until the rice and rapini are tender and the soup is thick from the rice starch, about 20 minutes. Add the remaining 2 cups (480 ml) of chicken soup as needed if the soup is too porridge-like. Season with salt and pepper.

Ladle into warmed individual bowls and top each serving with the egg yolk, if desired.

PAREVE/VEGAN OR DAIRY VARIATION: Substitute vegetable stock (page 92) for the chicken soup or beef stock and serve with grated Parmigiano-Reggiano cheese, if desired.

VELVET CELERY ROOT AND POTATO SOUP
WITH SPRING ONIONS

MAKES 6 TO 8 SERVINGS

DAIRY

Early spring in cold climates can be a challenge for a cook: how do you turn winter's roots into lighter fare when not much else has shown up in the market? Celery root—a.k.a. celeriac—is just the ticket. We often don't realize how flavorful celery is, but its subtleties shine in this elegant water-based soup made from the root. Celery root discolors quickly, so peel it just before you use it. I prefer this method over soaking it in acidulated water, which overpowers its delicate flavors. Choose juicy-looking roots. If yours is overly mature or dry, you may need to strain the soup to remove celeriac fibers. For a pareve/vegan version, substitute a healthful oil for the butter and omit the cream. See page 219 for a photo of Velvet Celery Root and Potato Soup.

2 pounds (900 g) celery roots (about 2 large)

1 onion, chopped

3 tablespoons butter

½ pound (225 g) waxy or all-purpose potatoes, such as Red Rose, White Rose, French Fingerling, or Yukon Gold, peeled and cut into 1-inch (2.5-cm) cubes

Kosher or sea salt and freshly ground white pepper

6 cups (1.4 L) water

¼ cup (60 g) crème fraîche

1 to 2 bunches small spring or green onions

Finishing salt, such as Maldon sea salt or fleur de sel

Peel the celery root, cut into quarters, and then cut each quarter into thin slices. In a wide pot, cook the onion in 2 tablespoons of the butter with a little salt over medium-low heat until translucent and softened, 5 to 7 minutes. Stir in the celery root and potatoes and season with ½ teaspoon salt and a few grinds of pepper. Cover and cook until partially tender but not browned, about 10 minutes.

Add 2 cups (480 ml) of the water, cover again, raise the heat to medium, and bring to a gentle boil. Reduce the heat to keep the soup at a simmer and cook until the vegetables are fairly tender, 10 to 12 minutes. Add 2 more cups (480 ml) water and ½ teaspoon salt, cover partially, and continue to simmer until the vegetables are very tender, about 15 minutes more.

While the soup is cooking, trim the spring onions and cut crosswise into small pieces, including most of the green. You should have about 2 cups (200 g). In a medium skillet, sauté the spring onions with a little salt and pepper in the remaining 1 tablespoon butter until tender, 3 to 5 minutes, lowering the heat as needed to keep them from burning. Remove from the heat and keep warm.

When the soup is ready, let cool slightly, then puree with an immersion blender or stand blender. You should have about 5 cups (1.2 L) thick puree, almost the consistency of loose mashed potatoes. Reheat the soup, thinning with the remaining 2 cups (480 ml) water as needed to achieve the consistency of heavy cream. Check the soup for bits of hard fibrous matter. If there are some, pass the soup through a tamis or fine-mesh sieve to remove them. The extra effort will be well worth the result.

Stir in the crème fraîche and season with salt and pepper. Top each serving with 1 tablespoon or so of the spring onion and a little finishing salt. (The soup can be made up to a day ahead.)

Green onions, scallions, spring onions, bunching onions—what's a shopper to do? The white-shanked, greens-topped thin alliums that most Americans call green onions are known as scallions in parts of the Midwest and Northeast. These days, we also see "spring onions" at farmers' markets, which are red or white bulbing onions harvested while their tops are still fresh and green and the bulbs have not cured in the field to develop their familiar papery skins. Very young "tiny spring onions" are small, the whole plant 6 to 8 inches (15 to 20 cm) long. They have a milder, grassier flavor than "green onions," which aren't necessarily babies but can be used anywhere I suggest tiny spring onions. Further down the road to maturity, a spring onion's bulb is more fully formed and larger, and retains a juicy, mild, fresh tenderness.

KIGELACH WITH LONG-COOKED LEEKS

MAKES 12 MUFFINS

MEAT, DAIRY, OR PAREVE

At Passover, everyone in the family looked forward to my mother-in-law Florence's *kigelach*, Yorkshire pudding–like muffins made from *matzah farfel* (matzah crumbles). She and my father-in-law, Lou, doubled and quadrupled the recipe to make enough for their growing clan. After Fuff passed away, I found her shorthand recipe notes: "heat the CF in the MT" (heat the chicken fat in the muffin tin). Here's her original recipe with my addition of long-cooked leeks, a traditional Sephardic vegetable for Passover. Leeks are at their best this time of year and make these little muffins even more tender and luscious. Serve with roast chicken and gravy, or as a savory snack or brunch accompaniment any time of the year. Use the fat of your choice according to the rest of your meal.

2 large leeks

6 tablespoons (90 g) schmaltz (page 24), butter, or mild oil, such as avocado, grapeseed, or safflower

1½ cups (110 g) matzah farfel

2 eggs

2 tablespoons finely chopped fresh Italian parsley

Kosher or sea salt

Cut off the tough green tops from the leeks and reserve for making stock. Chop the white portions; you should have about 2 cups (180 g). In a medium skillet, heat 2 tablespoons of the schmaltz or oil over medium heat. Add leeks and a little salt, stir well, and cook until their color brightens, 3 to 5 minutes. Reduce heat to medium-low, cover, and cook leeks slowly, stirring occasionally, until very tender, about 25 minutes. Reduce heat as needed to prevent leeks from browning. If the leeks begin to stick, add a bit of water. You should have about 1 cup (100 g) cooked leeks. Set aside to cool. (Leeks can be prepared up to 2 days ahead, covered, and refrigerated.)

Preheat oven to 375°F (190°C). Place farfel in a bowl, cover with water to soften, about 2 minutes, and drain well. While the farfel is soaking, in a large bowl, use a fork to whisk eggs with 1 teaspoon salt. Stir farfel, cooled leeks, and parsley into the eggs.

Place 1 teaspoon schmaltz in each cup of a 12-cup muffin pan. Place the pan in the oven to melt and heat the fat, about 3 minutes. Fill each muffin cup three-fourths full with the batter (about 2 heaping tablespoons).

Bake muffins until puffed and golden brown and a toothpick inserted into the center comes out clean, about 30 minutes. Remove pan from the oven and turn muffins out onto a wire rack. They should release easily. Serve warm or let cool on the rack before mounding in a bowl or basket. (The muffins can be refrigerated overnight and reheated, uncovered, in a 350°F (180°C) oven.)

SPRING GREENS SAUTÉ

MAKES 8 SERVINGS

PAREVE/VEGAN

This bright green medley captures a variety of flavors and textures. Use leafy greens (lettuce, chard, spinach, escarole, pea shoots), alliums (spring onions, leeks, green garlic), something with crunch (asparagus or broccoli), and a few peas or beans for accent. If you observe Ashkenazic kashrut, omit the legumes during Passover and add sprouting broccoli, also known as broccolini or baby broccoli, to the mix. I've given quantities here, but the choices are up to you.

1 pound (450 g) fava beans in the pod, about
    ½ cup (75 g) shelled

1 large onion, 2 leeks, or 1 bunch good-size spring
    onions, about ¾ pound (340 g) total

4 or 5 green garlic plants (see page 136)

1 bunch white-stemmed Swiss chard, ½ pound (225 g)
    spinach or pea shoots, or 1 head escarole or lettuce

1 bunch thick asparagus

1 pound (450 g) English peas in the pod (1 cup (145 g)
    shelled), ½ pound (225 g) sugar snap peas, or
    ½ pound (225 g) sprouting broccoli

2 tablespoons avocado, grapeseed, or extra-virgin
    olive oil

1 to 2 tablespoons chopped fresh mint or dill

1 Meyer or Eureka lemon

Kosher or sea salt and freshly ground white pepper

Prepare the vegetables for cooking, keeping each separate (this can be done a day ahead and refrigerated). Shell the fava beans and cook them in boiling salted water until the skins are loose and the beans are tender but still bright green, about 3 minutes. Drain and let cool until they can be handled, then slip the skins off of the beans and discard. You should have about ½ cup (75 g).

Cut the onion into bite-size pieces. If using the leeks or long spring onions, thinly slice crosswise. Thinly slice the green garlic, including about 5 inches (13 cm) of the tender green tops. If using chard, strip the leaves from the stems as directed on page 17. Chop the stems as you would celery and set aside. Cut the greens crosswise into ribbons 1 inch (2.5 cm) wide. If using spinach, tear any large leaves. If using pea shoots, cut into 2-inch (5-cm) lengths, trimming away tough tendrils or stems. If using escarole or lettuce, cut into ribbons 1 inch (2.5 cm) wide.

Snap off and discard the woody ends from the asparagus spears, then cut the spears into 1-inch (2.5-cm) pieces. If using English peas in the pod, shell them. If using snap peas, cut crosswise into thirds. If using the broccoli, cut into small florets.

In a 12- to 14-inch (30.5- to 35.5-cm) sauté pan, heat the oil over medium heat. Add the onion or leek, green garlic, chard stems (if using), and a little salt and cook, uncovered, until onions are softened, 5 to 7 minutes. Stir in the leafy greens, season with salt and pepper, and cook until tender, 5 to 10 minutes, adding 1 to 2 tablespoons water if the pan seems dry and covering the pan halfway during cooking.

Stir in the asparagus, peas or broccoli, and fava beans, cover, and cook just until tender but still bright, 3 to 5 minutes. Remove from the heat and stir in the mint. Using a five-hole zester, and working over the pan, remove the zest from the lemon in long strands, capturing both the zest and the spray of citrus oils in the pan. Season with salt and pepper, then mound on a platter and serve warm or at room temperature.

SHOPPING TIP: Before there were the large hybrid broccoli we are most familiar with today, open-pollinated varieties produced side shoots that were cut from a central stalk, in the manner of Brussels sprouts. Today, the mature but tender shoots of these mostly heirloom types are known as baby, or sprouting, broccoli and broccolini.

CRISPED ARTICHOKES WITH GREMOLATA

MAKES 8 SERVINGS

PAREVE/VEGAN

Pan-fried chokeless tiny artichokes are a modern nod to the Roman Jewish classic, deep-fried *carciofi alla giudia*. Finished with *gremolata*, the indispensable Italian seasoning of finely chopped parsley, garlic, and lemon zest, they are delicious on their own or over braised lamb shanks (page 192). Try baby purple Fiesole or Campania varieties, which retain a lavender blush after cooking. So-called baby artichokes are actually the small offshoots away from the main thistle of the artichoke plant. No matter how tiny your artichokes may be, you must be ruthless about peeling away the tough outer layers to render them fully edible. Although available year-round, small and large artichokes are at their peak in spring.

3 lemons
1 cup (235 ml) water
3 pounds (1.4 kg) small artichokes, about 3 inches
    (7.5 cm) long (not including stalk)
2 cloves garlic
Leaves of ½ bunch Italian parsley
Olive oil
Finishing salt, such as Maldon sea salt or fleur de sel
Freshly ground black pepper

TO MAKE THE GREMOLATA: Using a five-hole zester, remove the zest in long strands from 2 of the lemons. Chop 1 clove of the garlic, then mince it together with the parsley and zest. Set aside.

TO PREPARE THE ARTICHOKES: Juice the 2 lemons into a bowl and add the water. Trim the artichokes (directions follow), then cut each artichoke half into quarters or thirds lengthwise. As you work, drop the pieces into the water.

Remove the artichokes from the lemon water and dry well. Line a sheet pan with paper towels and place near the stove. Heat a large skillet over medium-high heat and swirl in olive oil to a depth of about ⅛ inch (3 mm). When the oil starts to shimmer and a piece of artichoke dropped into it sizzles on contact, add the remaining garlic clove and one third to one half of the artichokes, being careful not to crowd the pan. Cook, turning the pieces as needed, until well browned on both sides and cooked through, 5 to 7 minutes, removing and discarding the garlic from the pan as soon as it is golden brown. Using a slotted spoon, transfer artichokes to the sheet pan and season liberally with salt and pepper. Repeat with remaining artichokes.

To serve, line a platter with parchment or brown paper, if you like, and arrange the artichokes on it. Scatter the gremolata over the top. Cut the remaining lemon into wedges and add them to the platter. The artichokes can be served warm or at room temperature.

SHOPPING TIP: Some artichoke varieties are tulip shaped with slightly flared outer leaves; others are globe shaped with leaves that curl inward. Either way, choose firm, closed artichokes that are heavy for their size. A few dusty frost marks are okay, but avoid artichokes with blackened leaves. Store artichokes loose in the coldest part of the refrigerator and, ideally, use them within a few days.

HOW TO TRIM ARTICHOKES: Bend back the darker green or purple leaves to the point at which they snap off the base. Continue until you reach very pale leaves. Using a paring knife, shave away any dark remnants at the base. Cut off the top of the artichoke to remove the prickly tips, then cut in half lengthwise. Tiny artichokes, 2 to 3 inches (5 to 7.5 cm), should be choke-free (the inedible fuzzy core). Slightly larger artichokes may have a bit of fuzz at their core that you can scoop out with a paring knife or grapefruit spoon. Large artichokes have large chokes that must be cut away.

GREEN GARLIC AND LEEK MATZAH BREI
WITH SMOKED SALMON AND HORSERADISH CREAM

MAKES 6 SERVINGS

FISH

There are two schools of thought when it comes to matzah brei: the softer scrambled eggs style and the firmer frittata style. My family prefers the latter, and we usually think of matzah brei as a Passover version of French toast, eating it with maple syrup and a sprinkle of salt for breakfast or a light supper. But sometimes I turn this humble dish into an elegant savory main course that incorporates the delicate young green garlic and leeks sold at farmers' markets this time of year. Topped with silky smoked salmon and horseradish-spiked crème fraîche, this matzah brei is too beautiful to serve only during the eight days of Passover.

Green or spring garlic is the mild, immature garlic plant harvested before the familiar bulb forms and whose tops are tender enough to eat, as are those of young leeks no thicker than a green onion. You can use both or just one here, or use more common, mature leeks and garlic.

FOR THE HORSERADISH CREAM

½ cup (115 g) crème fraîche or plain Greek yogurt
1 to 3 tablespoons prepared horseradish (brands vary in strength)
Kosher or sea salt and freshly ground white pepper

FOR THE MATZAH BREI

½ bunch each young leeks and green garlic, about 10 plants total, or 2 large leeks, white part only, and 1 or 2 cloves garlic
2 tablespoons butter
2 tablespoons olive oil
4 sheets matzah
4 eggs
¼ pound (115 g) sliced smoked salmon
A few dill sprigs, snipped
1 lemon

TO MAKE THE HORSERADISH CREAM: In a small bowl, stir together the crème fraîche, horseradish to taste, and a pinch of salt. Cover and refrigerate.

TO MAKE THE MATZAH BREI: Cut off the root ends of the young leeks and green garlic. Trim away the tough green leek tops and discard or save for making stock. Cut the leeks and garlic in half lengthwise, then chop crosswise into ¼- to ½-inch (6- to 12-mm) pieces. You should have about 2 cups (180 g). If using large leeks and mature garlic, cut the white part of each leek into the same-size pieces and mince the garlic.

In a 12-inch (30.5-cm) skillet, heat 1 tablespoon each of the butter and olive oil over medium heat. Add the leeks and garlic, season with salt and pepper, and reduce the heat to medium-low. Cook uncovered, stirring occasionally, until the colors brighten, about 3 minutes. Cover and continue to cook, stirring occasionally and reducing the heat as needed to prevent browning, until very tender, 7 to 8 minutes. Transfer the mixture to a bowl and set aside. Reserve the skillet.

Break the matzah sheets into small pieces into a medium bowl and pour in water to cover. In another medium bowl, whisk together the eggs, ½ teaspoon salt, and a few grinds of pepper until the eggs are well blended. Drain the matzahs (don't be too fussy; just tilt the bowl to pour off the excess water, using your hand to prevent them from tumbling out). Stir the egg and leek mixtures into the matzahs.

Reheat the skillet with the remaining 1 tablespoon each butter and oil over medium heat. The pan is hot enough when a bit of matzah mixture dropped into it sizzles on contact. Pour in the matzah brei batter and smooth the top and edges. Cook, reducing the heat to medium-low as needed to prevent scorching, until the underside is set and golden, about 5 minutes.

continued »

Use the edge of a pancake turner or spatula to cut the matzah brei into 6 wedges. Flip each wedge, rotating the pan as you go so that the pieces fit back into the pan nicely. Continue to cook until the matzah brei is cooked through but not dry, about 3 minutes more. (If you must add more fat to the pan during cooking, tilt the pan, add the fat to the side of the pan still resting on the burner, and hold the pan at this angle for a moment to heat the fat. Then, use your spatula to lift the edge of the matzah brei and tilt the pan in the opposite direction to let the warmed fat run under the matzah brei before you set the pan back squarely on the burner to finish cooking.)

TO SERVE: Place a wedge of matzah brei on each plate. Drape each wedge with salmon, top with a spoonful or two of horseradish cream, and shower with dill. Use a five-hole zester to zest long strands of lemon peel over each serving and add a squeeze of lemon.

SIMCHA'S RICE WITH ALMONDS AND RAISINS

MAKES 6 SERVINGS

PAREVE/VEGAN

Make this Yemenite rice whenever you want to add contrasting sweetness and crunch to your main course. This recipe comes from cook and housekeeper Simcha Pinhas, who works for my cousin Milka Laks, a retired pianist who played for the Israel Philharmonic Orchestra.

2½ cups (600 ml) water

2 cups (370 g) long-grain white rice

Kosher salt

3 tablespoons mild oil, such as grapeseed, safflower, or avocado

⅔ cup (55 g) slivered blanched almonds

1 large onion, chopped

⅓ cup (45 g) raisins

In a medium pot fitted with a lid, bring the water to a boil over high heat. Stir in the rice, 1 teaspoon salt, and 1 tablespoon of the oil. Cover, lower the heat slightly, and return to a boil. Turn the heat to low and steam the rice, stirring once about halfway through the cooking, until all the liquid is absorbed and rice is tender, 15 to 20 minutes.

While the rice is cooking, heat a medium skillet over medium heat. Add the almonds and toast, shaking the pan occasionally, until golden, about 5 minutes. Pour the nuts onto a plate to cool.

Add the remaining 2 tablespoons oil to the skillet over medium heat. Add the onion and a little salt and cook until the onion is tender and golden, about 10 minutes, adding the raisins to the pan during the last 2 minutes or so of cooking.

Stir the onion mixture into the rice. Cook over low heat to blend the flavors, about 10 minutes. Stir in the almonds just before serving.

OVEN-BRAISED ROMANIAN CHICKEN

MAKES 6 TO 8 SERVINGS

MEAT

Use the best chicken you can buy (well, you should anyway), because this miraculous braise is all about the bird. There's not much for the chicken to hide behind. My grandmother Mina added only onions and salt to the pot, although you would never believe it from the gravy that formed during the slow cooking. Everyone in my mother's family still makes some version of this dish. Generations in Israel and the United States have variously added cumin, paprika, black pepper, garlic, bay leaves, and/or potatoes to the original. My cousins, my mother, my daughter Rebecca, and my son Adam cook this on top of the stove. My daughter Jessica and I prefer the leave-it-and-go oven method. Either way, serve it with something to sop up the juices: Basic White Rice (page 21), Sarah's Steamed Potatoes (page 221), Schmaltz-Roasted Potatoes (page 136), latkes (page 94), egg noodles, or a nice challah.

1 chicken, 4 pounds (1.8 kg), cut into serving pieces, or 6 whole chicken legs (thigh and drumstick)

Kosher or sea salt (sel gris is nice here as a cooking salt) and freshly ground black pepper

2 to 3 tablespoons extra-virgin olive oil

3 large onions, thinly sliced

4 bay leaves

Preheat the oven to 300°F (150°C). Pat the chicken very dry and season with salt and pepper. In a large, wide ovenproof pot fitted with a lid, heat 2 tablespoons of the oil over medium to medium-high heat and brown the chicken. Work in batches to avoid crowding the pot. Start the pieces skin side down and turn each piece once the skin is deep golden, about 7 minutes. Transfer the chicken pieces to a platter.

Pour off all but 2 tablespoons of the fat in the pan. Add the onions and a little salt and cook over medium heat, stirring from time to time and scraping up any brown bits, until the onions are pale golden, about 10 minutes.

Scatter the bay leaves in the pan. Return the chicken, skin side up, to the pot, nestling the pieces to fit. Cover and braise in the oven until the chicken is exceptionally tender and juices at least 1 inch (2.5 cm) deep have formed in the bottom of the pot, 2 to 3 hours. Check the pot from time to time. If it seems dry, add a little water to prevent sticking. You don't want to boil the chicken; you want it to stew in its own juices.

Serve the chicken hot with the pot juices. (The dish can be made a day or two ahead, covered, and refrigerated, then reheated on the stove or in a 350°F/180°C oven.)

ONE-PAN STRIPED BASS
WITH FENNEL, POTATOES, AND CREAM

MAKE 6 TO 8 SERVINGS

FISH

My mother's 1963 copy of the Burbank Temple Emanuel Sisterhood's cookbook featured many fish-and-cream casseroles. Was it because cream makes even the simplest dish "fancy" or because it was an opportunity to combine dairy and "animal" protein in one pan? Whatever the reason, all apply to this elegant one-pan bake. Other firm, non-oily fish such as scrod, halibut, or barramundi also work well. To use skinless fillets, see the note below. Blanching the fennel and potatoes ensures they will get tender in the oven without the fish overcooking.

2 pounds (900 g) fennel bulbs with tops
    (about 4 good-size bulbs)
2 pounds (900 g) medium-to-large waxy or
    all-purpose potatoes, such as French fingerling,
    Yukon Gold, Red Rose, or White Rose
1 large onion
Kosher or sea salt and freshly ground white pepper
1¾ pounds (800 g) skin-on striped bass fillets
    (2 fillets), each ¾ to 1 inch (2 to 2.5 cm) thick
2 tablespoons butter
¾ cup (180 ml) heavy cream
2 tablespoons snipped dill sprigs
2 bay leaves

Preheat the oven to 375°F (190°C). Cut off the stalks from the fennel bulbs and reserve for another use. Discard the tough outer layers from each bulb, then quarter each bulb from the stem to the core end and cut crosswise into slices ¼ inch (6 mm) thick. Peel the potatoes, halve lengthwise, and then cut crosswise into slices ¼ inch (6 mm) thick. Cut the onion in half through the stem end, then cut each half crosswise into slices ¼ inch (6 mm) thick.

Cook the fennel and potatoes together in generously salted boiling water until crisp-tender, about 2 minutes

after the water has returned to a boil. Drain and return them to the pot over medium heat briefly to remove any moisture. Season with salt and pepper.

Pat the fish dry. Now you have a choice: Leave fillets whole, which makes a more dramatic presentation, plus the fillets are less likely to overcook. But, they are slightly more difficult to serve. Or, cut the fillets into 6 to 8 serving-size pieces. Season them with salt and pepper. Have a plate or tray handy. Heat a 12-inch (30.5-cm) ovenproof heavy skillet over medium-high heat. Add 1 to 2 teaspoons butter to the pan. When the butter is sizzling, place the fillets, skin side down, in the pan and cook without moving them, until the skin is crisped and brown and releases easily from the pan, 3 to 4 minutes. Transfer fish, skin side up, to the plate.

Reduce heat to medium and add the remaining butter, if any, to the skillet. When the butter is hot, add the onion and a little salt and sauté until softened and translucent, 5 to 7 minutes, lowering heat as needed to prevent browning. Turn off the heat. Add potatoes, fennel, and dill to the pan and mix together with the onion. Season with salt and pepper. Pour cream evenly over the vegetables and tuck in the bay leaves.

Nestle the fish, skin side up, on the vegetables. Bake until the cream is bubbling and the vegetables and fish are tender and browned in places, about 30 minutes. Remove from the oven and let stand for 5 minutes before serving directly from the pan. If you left the fillets whole, remove them to a cutting board and cut into serving-size pieces.

TO MAKE THIS DISH WITH SKINLESS FILLETS: Brown the pretty side of the seasoned fillets, about 2 minutes. Before sautéing the onion, toast 1 cup (45 g) fresh bread crumbs in the skillet. Remove from the pan. Proceed as above, nestling the fillets on the vegetables, browned side up. Top with the bread crumbs and bake as directed.

BRAISED LAMB SHANKS WITH CRISPED ARTICHOKES AND GREMOLATA

MAKES 6 SERVINGS

MEAT

When the Israelites were about to make their escape from Egypt, they were commanded to eat a last meal, standing, dressed, and ready to run. The shank bone on the Seder plate is a vestige of that meal of fire-roasted lamb, unleavened bread, and bitter herb. The commemorative Passover meal, as set forth in the Bible, on the other hand, is to be the exact opposite, leisurely with plenty of time for storytelling. A main course of slow-braised (do-ahead) lamb shanks reinforces the difference between this and all other nights. Lamb and artichokes are a natural pairing throughout the spring season. Serve with Basic White Rice (page 21) or Sarah's Steamed Potatoes (page 221).

3 tablespoons olive oil

6 meaty lamb shanks, about 1¼ pounds (570 g) each

Kosher or sea salt and freshly ground black pepper

1 onion, finely chopped

1 carrot, peeled and finely chopped

2 ribs celery, finely chopped

¼ cup (15 g) chopped fresh Italian parsley

Several thyme sprigs

2 bay leaves, preferably fresh

2 large cloves garlic, minced

1 cup (240 ml) dry white wine

Grated zest and juice of 1 lemon

2 cups (480 ml) beef stock (page 66), or 1 cup (240 ml) canned beef broth diluted with 1 cup (240 ml) water

Crisped Artichokes with Gremolata (page 184)

Heat a large, wide pot over medium-high heat and add 1 tablespoon of the oil. Season the lamb shanks with salt and add them to the pot, working in batches to avoid crowding. Brown well on all sides, 10 to 12 minutes. Transfer the shanks to a plate and drain the fat from the pan.

Reduce heat to medium-low and add the remaining 2 tablespoons oil along with the onion, carrot, celery, parsley, thyme, and bay leaves. Season vegetables with salt and pepper, stir to scrape up any brown bits, and cook, stirring occasionally, until the vegetables are tender, about 10 minutes. Add garlic and cook for 1 minute more. Pour in the wine, raise the heat to high, and bring to a boil. Cook until the wine has reduced by half, about 5 minutes. Stir in the lemon zest and juice.

Return the lamb to the pot, nestling the shanks together to fit; overlap the bony ends if necessary. At this point, the liquid in the pan should reach no more than halfway up the sides of the shanks. Add a little of the stock if needed. Cover and braise the meat, turning the shanks once after the first hour, until very tender, about 1½ hours. Check the meat every 30 minutes during cooking to be sure there is sufficient liquid, adding stock as necessary to keep the shanks covered about halfway, and that the liquid is simmering rather than boiling vigorously.

Transfer the shanks to a plate. Remove and discard bay leaves and thyme sprigs and pour the sauce and vegetables into a liquid measure or a bowl. You should have about 2 cups (480 ml). Using a large spoon, skim off the fat from the surface of the sauce. Return the meat and sauce to the pot and heat, adding a little stock or water if you feel there isn't enough sauce, and reheat to serving temperature. Or, refrigerate the sauce and shanks until closer to serving time; the fat will harden and be easy to lift off. Reheat on the stove or in a 350°F (180°C) oven.

Serve the lamb shanks family style or plated, topped with the artichokes and gremolata.

CHOCOLATE PAVLOVAS WITH TANGELO SORBET AND SEVILLE ORANGE SAUCE

MAKES 10 SERVINGS

PAREVE

Chocolate and orange are a beloved combination in Israel, where citrus is king. Here, tangelos, a flavorful, colorful cross between a mandarin and a grapefruit, produce a vivid sorbet to crown sweet meringues shot through with dark chocolate. Seville oranges, the sort used for marmalade, add contrast. The components of this gluten- and dairy-free showstopper are easy to make and can be done ahead. Use high-quality natural cocoa, and if you are making this dessert for Passover, use potato starch in place of cornstarch. By all means, enjoy the elements in other ways: chocolate Pavlovas with fresh berries, tangelo sorbet with vanilla ice cream and orange sauce for a grown-up 50/50 sundae, or the orange sauce over Semolina and Walnut Oil Cake with Coffee Hawaij (page 243).

FOR THE PAVLOVA SHELLS

2 ounces (55 g) bittersweet chocolate (70 percent cacao mass), coarsely chopped

4 tablespoons (22 g) unsweetened natural cocoa powder

1½ cups (300 g) superfine sugar

2 egg whites, at room temperature

1 teaspoon potato starch or cornstarch

1 teaspoon distilled white vinegar or strained fresh lemon juice

½ teaspoon vanilla extract

¼ cup (60 ml) boiling water

FOR THE SAUCE

5 tangelos

⅔ cup (215 g) Seville orange marmalade

2 tablespoons Cointreau

Tangelo Sorbet (recipe follows)

1 cup (125 g) coarsely chopped salted roasted pistachios or almonds

TO MAKE THE PAVLOVA SHELLS: Preheat oven to 350°F (180°C). Draw 5 well-spaced 3-inch/7.5-cm circles on each of 2 pieces of parchment cut to fit 2 large sheet pans. Line pans with parchment, drawing side down. In a food processor fitted with a metal S blade, pulse the chocolate, 2 tablespoons of the cocoa, and 1 tablespoon of the sugar until the chocolate is pulverized to a fine crumb.

Put the egg whites, remaining sugar, potato starch, vinegar, and vanilla in an impeccably clean bowl of an electric mixer fitted with the whisk attachment. Turn mixer to medium speed to blend the ingredients, about 15 seconds. With the mixer running, add the boiling water. Increase speed to high and beat until the meringue is very stiff and glossy, 7 to 15 minutes, depending on the power of your mixer.

Remove the bowl from the mixer. Sprinkle the chocolate-sugar mixture over the meringue and use a large rubber spatula to gently and quickly swirl it into the meringue. You should have a pale cocoa–colored mixture with streaks of dry chocolate mix ribboned through.

Using a large serving spoon, scoop 10 dollops, each about ½ cup of the meringue mixture, in the center of each circle. Use the back of the spoon to create rounds about 3 inches (7.5 cm) in diameter, swirling the edges of the meringues into free-form peaks and creating a small "valley" in the center of each. Sift a little of the remaining cocoa over each of the Pavlovas.

Bake for 10 minutes. Reduce the oven temperature to 250°F (120°C) and bake for 30 minutes longer in an electric oven or for 45 minutes longer in a gas oven. Turn off the oven, set the oven door ajar, and let the meringues cool completely for at least 3 hours or up to overnight. The shells will have honeycombed ribbons and chocolate crevasses. (The shells can be stored in an airtight container at room temperature for up to 2 weeks.)

continued »

TO MAKE THE SAUCE: Using a five-hole zester, remove the zest from the tangelos in long strands and set aside to use for garnish. Set a sieve over a medium bowl. Peel and segment the tangelos as directed on page 17, allowing the segments to drop into the sieve as you work. Reserve the segments (suprêmes) in a separate bowl. You should have ¾ to 1 cup (180 to 240 ml) juice in the bowl. In a small pot, stir together the marmalade and ½ cup (120 ml) of the juice, taste, and add more juice to balance the sweet and bitter flavors to your liking. Bring to a simmer over medium heat and cook for 1 minute. Stir in the Cointreau and set aside to cool. (The sauce can be kept at room temperature for several hours.)

TO ASSEMBLE THE DESSERT: Place the shells on individual dessert plates. Scatter 4 or 5 tangelo segments around each shell. Top each shell with a scoop of the sorbet, then drizzle about 2 tablespoons of the sauce over each dessert. Scatter about 1 ½ tablespoons nuts over each serving and garnish with the tangelo zest.

KITCHEN NOTE: To make serving these Pavlovas or other individual sorbet or ice cream desserts to a crowd easier, scoop balls of sorbet or ice cream onto a parchment paper–lined sheet pan ahead of time and place in the freezer. When ready to assemble the dessert, use a pancake turner or offset spatula to transfer each scoop to the dessert.

TANGELO SORBET

MAKES 1 QUART (1 L)

PAREVE

Tangelos are deep orange, very juicy, and intensely sweet-tart, especially late in the season. Two of the most popular cultivars are Minneola and Honeybell. If you cannot find tangelos, substitute clementines or another flavorful mandarin variety. In summer, make this sorbet with Valencia oranges and substitute Eureka lemons for the Meyers.

6 to 10 tangelos, 3 to 4 pounds (1.4 to 1.8 kg)
1 to 2 Meyer lemons
1 cup (200 g) sugar
2 tablespoons Cointreau

Using a Microplane grater, remove the zest from 3 of the tangelos and place it in a 1-quart (1-L) pot. Juice enough tangelos to yield 3 cups (720 ml) juice. Juice enough Meyer lemons to yield ¼ cup (60 ml) juice.

Add the sugar to the pot. Using the back of a spoon, a muddler, or a pestle, mash the sugar and zest together until the sugar is tinted orange and moistened by the citrus oils. Stir in 1 ½ cups (360 ml) of the tangelo juice. Bring to a simmer over medium heat and cook, stirring frequently, until the sugar is completely dissolved and the mixture is translucent and glossy, 1 to 2 minutes longer. Remove from the heat.

In a medium bowl, stir together the remaining 1 ½ cups (360 ml) tangelo juice, the lemon juice, and the Cointreau. Add the hot tangelo-sugar syrup and stir to mix well. Cover and chill thoroughly for several hours or up to overnight.

Before processing the mixture in your ice cream maker, place it in the coldest part of your freezer for 20 minutes to super-chill it. Then pour into an ice cream maker and freeze according to the manufacturer's instructions. Transfer to a chilled container, cover tightly, and freeze, preferably at least several hours. Remove from the freezer 10 to 15 minutes before serving to make scooping easier.

SALTED ALMOND AND CHOCOLATE MERINGUES WITH MATZAH SHARDS

DAIRY OR PAREVE

Salty-sweet matzah shards add the sort of addictive crunch that crisped rice cereal gives to a chocolate bar. If you are gluten-free, skip the matzah, or replace it with an equal amount of unsweetened flaked coconut. Serve these on your grandmother's prettiest cut-glass tray alongside a bowl of the season's first strawberries or a bowl of fragrant mandarins. Use fully, rather than "lightly," salted nuts to achieve the right balance of salty and sweet. Avocado and almond oils are good nondairy choices here.

2 sheets matzah

3 tablespoons butter, melted, or avocado or
    almond oil

¾ cup (150 g) sugar

½ teaspoon fleur de sel

1 cup (135 g) salted roasted almonds, hazelnuts,
    or pecans, coarsely chopped

4 ounces (115 g) bittersweet chocolate (70
    percent cacao mass), coarsely chopped

3 egg whites, at room temperature

Pinch of kosher or sea salt

Position racks in middle and upper third of oven. Preheat the oven to 350°F (180°C). Place the matzah sheets on a baking sheet. Brush both sides of each sheet with the butter and sprinkle the tops with 1 tablespoon of the sugar and the fleur de sel.

Toast the matzahs in the oven until crisped and lightly browned, about 10 minutes. Remove the pan from the oven and reduce the oven temperature to 200°F (95°C). When the matzahs are cool, break them into 1- to 2-inch (2.5- to 5-cm) pieces no wider than 1 inch (2.5 cm). In a small bowl, toss together the almonds, chocolate, and 3 tablespoons of the sugar.

Line 2 sheet pans with parchment paper or with foil, shiny side down. Place the egg whites in an impeccably clean bowl of an electric mixer fitted with the whisk attachment. Beat on medium-high speed until thickened and opaque. Increase the speed to high and continue to beat, adding the salt and the remaining ½ cup (100 g) sugar over a couple of minutes until the whites are very stiff and have developed a sheen.

Using a large rubber spatula, gently fold the chocolate-almond mixture into the egg whites just until no white streaks are visible. Fold in the matzah shards and any crumbs. For each meringue, drop about 2 tablespoons of the batter onto the prepared pans, spacing them 1 to 2 inches (2.5 to 5 cm) apart. Verticality is good here.

Bake the meringues for 1 ½ hours, switching the pans top to bottom and front to back halfway through the baking to ensure the meringues bake evenly. Remove a meringue from the oven and allow it to cool. If it is dry and crisp throughout, turn off the oven. If it is still chewy, bake for another 15 to 30 minutes, and test again. Once the meringues are done, turn off the oven and leave the meringues in the oven until completely cool and crisp, 2 to 3 hours or up to overnight.

Carefully peel off the meringues from the parchment. They will keep in an airtight container at room temperature for up to 1 week.

THE OVERNIGHT WAY: There's a favorite version of meringue cookies that has been floating around for decades, that I learned from my friend, Jane Bard. Prepare meringues as above but leave the oven at 350°F (180°C). Turn off the oven as soon as you put in the meringues. Leave them untouched for at least 4 hours, or overnight. Test for crispness; if necessary, return meringues to a 200°F (95°C)-oven until done as above.

MEYER LEMON POPPY SEED TART
WITH **ROASTED RHUBARB** AND **STRAWBERRIES**

MAKES ONE 9-INCH (23-CM) TART, 8 SERVINGS

DAIRY

This is not your 1970s lemon–poppy seed Bundt cake from a mix. Three favorite flavors from the Jewish Diaspora come together in this modern spring tart: rhubarb (Syria and Iran), poppy seeds (eastern Europe), and lemon (California). I've used the Meyer lemon here, the sophisticated and hauntingly floral cross between a sweet orange and a tart lemon discovered in China in 1905 by fruit explorer Frank N. Meyer. Sweets expert Alice Medrich has brilliantly streamlined the classic curd-making technique: no more standing over the stove beating in bits of butter. If you've assembled all the filling ingredients before you start the crust, you'll have enough time to prepare the filling while the crust bakes.

FOR THE CRUST

1 Meyer lemon

1 cup (125 g) unbleached all-purpose flour

¼ cup (20 g) ground almonds (see page 18)

¼ cup (50 g) sugar

2 tablespoons poppy seeds

¼ teaspoon salt

½ cup (115 g) butter, cut into small pieces

FOR THE FILLING

2 to 3 Meyer lemons, plus the lemon from the crust
   (enough to yield ¾ cup/180 ml strained juice)

4 egg yolks

2 eggs

¾ cup (150 g) sugar

½ cup plus 1 tablespoon (130 g) butter, cut
   into pieces

Roasted Rhubarb and Strawberries
   (recipe follows)

TO MAKE THE CRUST: Preheat the oven to 375°F (190°C). Using a Microplane grater, grate the zest from the lemon. In a medium bowl, stir together the flour, almonds, sugar, poppy seeds, lemon zest, and salt. Scatter the butter pieces over the flour mixture and, using your fingertips or a pastry blender, cut in the butter until the mixture is uniformly crumbly and resembles coarse cornmeal. The mixture will look dry but will stick together when pressed between your fingers.

Pour the mixture into a 9-inch (23-cm) tart pan with 1 inch (2.5 cm) sides and a removable bottom. Use gentle fingertip pressure to press the dough up the sides of the pan, no more than ¼-inch/6 mm-thick, allowing some of the dough to extend above the rim. Gently press the dough evenly over bottom of the pan, making sure to press well where the bottom meets the sides to keep thickness even. For a clean edge, use a sharp knife to shave off the excess dough, holding the blade horizontal to the rim of the pan. Chill the crust for 20 minutes or, if you have the time, up to overnight.

Bake the crust until pale golden, 15 to 20 minutes. Remove from the oven and use the back of a soup spoon to smooth out any cracks that may have formed or to push the crust back up the sides of the pan if it has slumped. This should take only a few seconds. Lower the oven temperature to 350°F (180°C) and return the tart pan to the oven until the crust is golden, 10 to 15 minutes longer. Let cool completely on a wire rack.

TO MAKE THE FILLING: Set a sieve over a medium bowl and place near the stove. Using the Microplane grater, remove the zest from 1 lemon. Halve and juice enough lemons to yield ¾ cup (180 ml) strained juice. In a medium pot, whisk together the egg yolks, eggs, and sugar until blended. Whisk in the lemon juice, lemon zest, and sugar, and stir in butter pieces.

Bring to a simmer over medium heat, stirring constantly, until thickened and just beginning to bubble around the edges, about 3 minutes. Immediately scrape into the waiting sieve. To avoid pushing any bits of cooked egg through, give the sieve a few good side-to-side shakes to help the lemon mixture pass through the mesh without pressing on it. Scrape the underside of sieve to capture any filling that has not dropped into the bowl. You should have about 1½ cups (360 g) curd. (The filling can be made 1 to 2 days ahead; cover with plastic wrap, pressing it directly onto the surface of the curd, and refrigerate, then let it stand at room temperature for a few minutes before spreading it into the tart shell.)

Pour the filling into the crust and cool completely. The filling will continue to set as it cools. Adorn each serving with a spoonful of the rhubarb-strawberry condiment.

ROASTED RHUBARB AND STRAWBERRIES

MAKES 1½ CUPS (480 G)

PAREVE

Preheat the oven to 400°F (200°C). Trim off and discard the dry ends and any greens (which are toxic) from the rhubarb stalks. Cut the rhubarb into ½-inch (12-mm) pieces. Don't worry about peeling the strings away; they will soften up during cooking. Hull the strawberries; leave small berries whole and halve or quarter larger ones.

Place the rhubarb and strawberries in a nonreactive 9-x-13-inch (23-x 33-cm) baking pan or dish. Sprinkle with the sugar and with the black pepper, if using, then toss to coat evenly and spread more or less in a single layer.

Roast until the strawberries and rhubarb are tender and browned in places and the sugar and strawberry juices have caramelized, 25 to 30 minutes. If strawberries have released too much liquid to allow browning, pour off the liquid and reserve, then continue roasting until browned and caramelized. Scrape the mixture, including any brown bits, into a bowl. It will be a dusty rose, thick, chunky, and perfumed. Stir in the reserved juices for a more sauce-like condiment. Serve warm or at room temperature.

Technically a vegetable, rhubarb grows most abundantly in cold climates and is often paired with strawberries in spring desserts. Although I usually prefer rhubarb on its own, in this recipe, the strawberries are the necessary bridge to marry the tangy topping with the lemon tart. Roasting rhubarb with a bit of brown sugar preserves its ruby color and creamy texture. Add a little black pepper to this conserve and it becomes a great accompaniment to cheeses or smoked meats, a sort of spring equivalent to quince paste. This condiment is prettiest the day it is made.

¾ pound (340 g) rhubarb stalks (about 4 large)
1½ cups (215 g) ripe strawberries
⅓ cup (75 g) firmly packed light brown sugar
Several grinds of black pepper (optional)

SHOPPING TIPS: Look for shiny, juicy rhubarb stalks. Some rhubarb varieties produce mostly green stalks, which cook down to a not-so-pretty shade of olive. When the color in a finished dish is important, choose stalks that are as red as possible.

Strawberries should be completely red inside and out (a few rare varieties are pinkish rather than red) with no dulling or soft spots. Small or medium-size berries are usually the most flavorful. Avoid extra-firm, overly large fruits that have white shoulders and, often, a hollow core, indicators that they have been overwatered and grown for shipping and storage capability rather than for flavor. Strawberries are best used within a couple of days of purchase and should be refrigerated unwashed on paper towels in an airtight container. Use water sparingly to clean them just before using.

GRANNY'S CITRUS SPONGE CAKE

MAKES ONE 10-INCH (25-CM) CAKE, 12 TO 16 SERVINGS

PAREVE

Baking expert and culinary historian Greg Patent spent his World War II childhood in Shanghai's International Settlement, where he and his family lived with his grandmother in a one-room apartment. There, Greg's granny turned out the most amazing baked goods, including this delicate sponge cake for which she whipped the egg whites with a fork on a platter! Greg shares a modern version of her recipe here, scented with orange and made using an electric mixer. And, after countless experiments, Greg has converted his grandmother's cake into an amazingly light version suitable for Passover (see the variation at the end of this recipe). The exacting Greg says the secret is to reduce the amount of matzah cake meal, which loves to absorb moisture and can render baked goods heavy, and compensate with potato and tapioca starches. For two more tips for success, follow food scientist Shirley Corriher's advice to rinse the tube pan with hot water before adding the batter and Greg's to start the cake in a cold oven. A perfect sponge cake—moist, tender, light—is the little black dress of desserts, especially at Passover. Serve this one with seasonal berries or any of the suggested accompaniments below.

1 to 2 large oranges
1 large lemon
1⅓ cups (265 g) sugar
¼ teaspoon salt
8 large eggs, separated
1½ cups (150 g) sifted cake flour
1 teaspoon cream of tartar

Have ready a two-piece 10-x-4-inch (25-x-10-cm) tube pan (either aluminum or nonstick will work), preferably with "feet." Position an oven rack in the lower third of the oven but do not turn the oven on.

Using a Microplane grater, grate the zest from 1 of the oranges and the lemon. You should have about 2 tablespoons zest total. Juice the orange(s) to yield 6 tablespoons (90 ml) juice and set aside. Set aside ⅓ cup (65 g) of the sugar to whip with the egg whites. Using the back of a spoon, a muddler, or a mortar and pestle, mash 3 tablespoons of the remaining 1 cup (200 g) sugar and the zest together until fragrant and the sugar is moist and tinted from the citrus oils.

In a bowl, using an electric mixer fitted with the whisk attachment or a handheld mixer, beat the egg yolks on medium speed until they thicken slightly, about 2 minutes. Beat in the citrus sugar and the salt. Continuing to beat on medium speed, gradually add the remainder of the 1 cup (200 g) sugar, sprinkling it into the yolks in a steady stream. Then, increase the speed to medium-high and beat the yolk mixture until it is very thick and pale and falls in a slowly dissolving ribbon when the beater is raised, 3 to 4 minutes longer. On low speed, beat in the orange juice and then the cake flour, beating only until incorporated. Scrape the yolk-and-flour mixture into a large wide bowl and reserve.

Thoroughly wash and dry the whisk attachment or beaters. In an impeccably clean bowl, whip the egg whites on medium speed until frothy, about 1 minute. Add the cream of tartar and beat on medium speed until the beater leaves traces in the whites and the whites hold soft peaks when the beater is raised. On medium speed, beat in the reserved ⅓ cup (65 g) sugar in 1-tablespoon additions, beating about 10 seconds after each addition. Increase the speed to medium-high and continue beating

continued »

until the whites are thick and shiny—with a creamy texture like marshmallow crème—and hold firm peaks.

Fold one-fourth of the whites into the yolk mixture to lighten; then fold in the remaining whites in two batches just until no white streaks show. Rinse the tube pan under running hot water and shake out the excess water. Scrape the batter into the tube pan and spread the surface level. Place the pan into the cold oven.

Turn on the oven to 325°F (165°C) and bake the cake until it has risen almost to the top of the pan, is golden brown, and springs back when gently pressed, 45 to 50 minutes. Remove from the oven and, if using a footed cake pan, immediately invert the pan onto your countertop. If your tube pan lacks feet, support the pan upside down on the neck of a wine bottle. Don't worry, the cake won't fall out of the pan while your back is turned. Let cool completely upside down, about 3 hours.

To remove the cake from the pan, run a thin-bladed knife or spatula around the inside edge of the pan to loosen the cake sides. Lift the cake out of the pan by the tube, then run the knife around the central tube and between the cake and the bottom of the pan and invert the cake onto a cake plate. The cake will now be upside down. Lift away the bottom of the pan and the cake is ready to serve. Cut into portions with a serrated knife. Well wrapped, the cake will stay nice and moist for 2 to 3 days at room temperature.

PASSOVER VARIATION: Accuracy in measuring dry ingredients is key to success. See the directions for measuring flour, by both volume and weight, on page 20 and apply one or the other to the dry ingredients here. For the cake flour, substitute ½ cup matzah cake meal (2.3 ounces/63 g), ¼ cup potato starch (1.6 ounces/45 g), and ¼ cup tapioca starch (1.2 ounces/32 g). Whisk the cake meal, starches, and salt together thoroughly. You will have a total of 5 ounces (140 g). Reduce the orange juice to ¼ cup (60 ml). Substitute 1 teaspoon fresh lemon juice for the cream of tartar.

DELICIOUS ACCOMPANIMENTS DEPENDING ON THE SEASON

Strawberries and Roses and/or Rose Geranium Cream (page 242)

Fresh Berries and Fresh Raspberry Sauce (page 289) or Quick Dark Chocolate Sauce (page 289)

Summer Fruit Compote with Lemon Verbena (page 283)

Roasted Autumn Fruit (page 68)

Peppered Red Wine Fruit Compote (page 112)

May & June

FIRST FRUITS

We have come to the first big harvest of the year. The days between the barley harvest at Passover and the spring wheat ingathering seven weeks later are counted off in anticipation of Shavuot, the holiday that commemorates this harvest and the giving of the Torah.

The change of season waits in the wings, as well. The big bold crops of summer are yet to come, and no matter how warm the weather may turn or when the holiday may occur during these two solar months, for Jewish Israelis, summer begins only after Shavuot.

This prelude to summer is an opportunity to notice subtler forms of seasonality and flavor. Milk is especially plentiful in May and June after spring calving. Strawberries, sugar snap peas, spinach, asparagus, and wild ferns and ramps are at their peak. In some regions, early cherries and green tomatoes make their first appearance. All are perfect partners with the barley, wheat, milk, and cheeses of Shavuot, and all are showcased here.

May & June

FRESH GRAPE LEAVES STUFFED WITH THREE CHEESES

MAKES 8 SERVINGS

DAIRY

In late spring and early summer, grape growers trim back new shoots whose tangy leaves are tender enough to use fresh instead of brined. Wrapped around a Balkan cheese filling and grilled, these are an entirely fresh take on dolmas. If you live where grapes are grown, ask local farmers to bring cuttings to the farmers' market. You especially want leaves that aren't deeply lobed (indented or fingered), so you have more leaf space to wrap your filling securely, and so it won't leak during grilling. These tender, savory packets are a rustic-elegant start to an early-summer meal, delicious with a glass of Viognier, a wine that northern Israeli boutique wineries produce extremely well. If fresh grape leaves aren't available, you may substitute Swiss chard, beet tops, or radicchio. Semifirm kashkaval (see page 11) is a Balkan grating cheese. Greek kasseri or a young pecorino cheese is a good alternative.

16 large, young grape leaves, preferably
    6 to 7 inches (15 to 17 cm) across
1½ cups (185 g) grated kashkaval cheese
    (about 6½ ounces)
¾ cup (140 g) crumbled feta cheese
    (about 5 ounces)
½ to ¾ cup (115 to 170 g) fromage blanc or quark
¼ teaspoon Aleppo pepper
½ cup (120 ml) extra-virgin olive oil
Ground sumac for finishing (optional)

Soak grape leaves in ice water to cover for 30 minutes. Meanwhile, use a fork to mash together the kashkaval and feta cheeses. Stir in enough fromage blanc to bind the cheeses together to a thick paste. Stir in the Aleppo pepper. You should have about 2½ cups (450 g) filling.

Drain the leaves, pat dry, and snip off the stem at the base of each leaf. Lay a leaf, dull underside up and with the base of the leaf closest to you, on a work surface and brush with olive oil. Depending on the size of the leaf, place 1 to 2 tablespoons of the cheese mixture in a horizontal log about 1 inch (2.5 cm) from the base of the leaf. Fold the stem end of the leaf over the cheese, fold in the sides, and roll up the package from stem end to top. Place seam side down on a plate. Repeat with the remaining leaves. Because leaf size can be so variable, you may have leftover filling. Cover and chill for at least 30 minutes or up to 1 day ahead.

Heat a grill to medium-high. Place the grape-leaf packets, seam side down, on the grill rack. Grill, turning once, until leaves are scored on both sides and no longer bright green, about 2 minutes per side. Use a spatula and tongs to handle the packets carefully. Transfer them to a platter and let rest for a few minutes for the cheese to settle.

Serve warm or at room temperature, sprinkled with sumac for added tartness, if desired.

TO USE SWISS CHARD, BEET TOPS, OR RADICCHIO: Cut away any stem that would prevent easy rolling. Dip the leaves in hot water to soften, then pat dry. Place each leaf cupped side up and fill, roll, and grill as directed. Radicchio will lose its red color when cooked.

A SMART WAY TO USE EXTRA FILLING: Spread any leftover filling on toasted or grilled slices of country bread and run under a broiler until the cheeses are bubbly and browned.

Shavuot

A SPRING HARVEST CELEBRATION

Shavuot, literally "weeks," marks the culmination of counting the seven week period that begins on the second night of Passover, a holiday that commemorates the Exodus from Egypt, to the time when Moses received the Ten Commandments on Mount Sinai, a sort of Torah birthday. The only holiday with no fixed date given in the Bible, its timing coincides with the spring barley harvest at Passover and the wheat and first fruit harvests of Shavuot.

Unless you are a very religiously observant Jew, Shavuot, which is celebrated in May or June, is barely a blip on the American Jewish calendar. What a shame, because this is one of the great, happy, eating holidays that showcases the foods of late spring, especially milk, which is more plentiful after spring calving and tastes of young grass.

For secular Israelis, the agrarian and food aspects of the holiday are joyously celebrated. Girls dress in white and adorn their hair with flower garlands. Families take field trips to local dairies, farming kibbutzim have tractor parades through the fields, and everyone indulges in luscious foods based on cheese and cream: blintzes, cheesecakes, quiches, and cheesy pasta bakes. Desserts are often sweetened with honey, a nod to the sweetness of the gift of the Torah.

If at all possible this time of year, try to find fresh spring cheeses from local dairies that pay homage to a "land flowing with milk and honey" (Exodus 3:8), and which remind us that to every food there is a season, even milk.

Lag b'Omer

A NIGHT OF BONFIRES

The seven weeks of waiting are a period of anxious anticipation for very observant Jews. They do not dance, wed, or cut their hair during this time. The national Israeli calendar echoes the mood; few concerts or festivals are held, and the Holocaust Memorial Day, Yom HaShoah, and Veteran's Day, Yom HaZikaron, fall during this period, as does Israel's Independence Day.

But partway through the seven weeks of counting the *omer* (the sheaves of barley), there is a night of utter respite—Lag b'Omer—when Orthodox Jews hold weddings, make music, and get haircuts; and those who follow kabbalistic teachings, make pilgrimages to Meron, near Safed, to honor the beginnings of the mystical movement. For secular Jewish Israelis, Lag b'Omer is a national holiday, an excuse for a bonfire, an all-night party, and *kartoshkes*—potatoes roasted in the embers.

"MANTA RAY" CEVICHE

MAKES 6 SERVINGS

FISH

This ceviche is named for the casual-chic Tel Aviv beachfront restaurant owned by Ofra Ganor, an Alice Waters–like food pioneer, where I first tasted a Mediterranean interpretation of the Latin American classic. Its secret ingredient is sumac, the ground dark red to bright purple berries of the sumac shrub, which makes the dish deliciously tart without being overly sour. Manta Ray uses grey mullet, an oil-rich regional favorite, but other fairly firm fish, such as halibut, mahimahi, and white seabass, are good here. The key is to use supremely fresh, preferably local, fish that you buy, prepare, and eat all on the same day. Serve the ceviche with a chilled rosé to begin an outdoor dinner or include it on a mezze table.

1 pound (450 g) firm-fleshed, skinned very fresh
    fish fillets, such as halibut, mahimahi, or white
    seabass

1½ cups (360 ml) fresh lime juice (from about
    6 large limes)

½ cup (120 ml) fresh lemon juice (from about
    2 large lemons)

½ small red onion

¼ cup (12 g) snipped fresh chives, in ⅛-inch
    (3-mm) pieces

1 to 2 tablespoons extra-virgin olive oil

1 teaspoon ground sumac, or more to taste

½ teaspoon Aleppo pepper, or ¼ teaspoon red
    pepper flakes

½ teaspoon sel gris, or more to taste

Pita Triangles with Za'atar (see page 161) or
    crackers for serving

Pat the fish dry. Check for any hidden bones and remove them. Cut away the blood line and any other dark patches and discard. Cut the fish across the grain into slices ⅛ to ¼ inch (3 to 6 mm) thick. Cut the slices into ¼- to ¾-inch (6-mm to 2-cm) pieces. Place in a glass bowl, add the citrus juices, and stir to mix. Cover and refrigerate, stirring occasionally, until the fish is completely opaque, 2 to 3 hours.

Cut the onion half in half again vertically and then cut each piece crosswise into paper-thin slices. In a small bowl, soak the slices in cold water to cover for 30 minutes. Drain well and pat dry.

Drain the fish thoroughly and place in a clean bowl. Add the onion, chives, olive oil, sumac, Aleppo pepper, and sel gris and toss well. Taste and adjust the seasoning. Serve with the pita triangles.

BOUIKOS: BULGARIAN CHEESE PUFFS

MAKES ABOUT FIFTY 2-INCH (5-CM) PASTRIES

DAIRY

Bouikos, a classic Bulgarian Jewish snack, are popular throughout the Balkans and Israel with good reason: they bake up crisp and golden on the outside and moist and tender on the inside. They are so fragrant that everyone in the house will demand to know what's in the oven. This version comes from Vicky Zipory, my cousin Tami Schneider's mother-in-law, and it conveniently works with whatever chunks of cheese you have in the refrigerator. Black, peppery nigella seeds add an aromatic finish.

3 cups (375 g) unbleached all-purpose flour

1 tablespoon baking powder

¾ teaspoon salt

½ cup plus 3 tablespoons (155 g) butter, at room temperature

¾ cup (185 g) plain whole-milk yogurt

1 cup (250 g) quark, fromage blanc, or ricotta or cottage cheese that has been drained in a sieve of its excess liquid

1⅔ cups crumbled (255 g) feta cheese (about 9 ounces)

1 cup (135 g) grated kashkaval, Emmentaler, or young pecorino cheese (about 4¾ ounces)

2 eggs

Nigella seeds or black sesame seeds for sprinkling

Preheat the oven to 350°F (180°C). Line 2 or 3 baking sheets with parchment paper.

In a medium bowl, stir together the flour, baking powder, and salt. In an electric mixer fitted with the paddle attachment, beat the butter on medium-high speed until light and creamy. Add the yogurt, quark, feta, and kashkaval cheeses and beat until combined, then beat in 1 of the eggs until incorporated. On low speed, add the flour mixture in three batches, beating after each addition just until blended. The dough will be sticky.

Roll the dough into 2-inch (5-cm) balls and place 2 inches (5 cm) apart on the prepared baking sheets. In a small bowl, whisk the remaining egg until blended. Brush the tops of the balls with the egg and sprinkle with nigella seeds.

Bake pastries until the undersides are golden brown and the tops are shiny and golden, about 25 minutes. The pastries will be crisp on the outside and moist and tender at the center. Serve warm. Leftover pastries can be stored in an airtight container at room temperature up to 2 days and refreshed in a 350°F (180°C) oven.

SPINACH AND AVOCADO SALAD WITH A LOT OF LEMON

MAKES 8 TO 10 SERVINGS

PAREVE/VEGAN

When Israelis say spinach, they mean a hot-weather-friendly, drought-resistant New Zealand type, with thick, curling raw leaves that are meltingly delicious in a salad. In cooler climates a meaty Savoy spinach is the way to go. All shades of green are at play in this salad, offering a refreshing contrast to spicy Middle Eastern dishes.

2 bunches New Zealand or Savoy spinach,
    about 1½ pounds (680 g) total
3 or 4 cucumbers, preferably Persian, about
    ¾ pound (340 g) total
1 bunch green onions
⅓ cup (3 g) fresh dill sprigs (about 1 small bunch)
Extra-virgin olive oil
1 lemon
Kosher or sea salt or finishing salt, such as
    Maldon sea salt
Freshly ground black or white pepper (optional)
1 large ripe avocado

Pluck the spinach leaves from their stems and discard the stems or save for Testine di Spinaci, page 230. Rinse the leaves in several changes of water and pat dry. You should have 8 to 9 cups (240 to 270 g) of lightly packed leaves. Coarsely chop the large leaves and place them all in a salad bowl. Peel the cucumbers or leave them unpeeled if you prefer. Cut them in half lengthwise and use a small spoon to scrape out the seeds. Cut the halves crosswise into pieces ¼ inch (6 mm) thick and add to the bowl. Cut the green onions crosswise into very thin slices, including the tender green tops. Chop the dill and add it and the onions to the bowl. (The salad can be made 6 hours ahead up to this point, covered, and refrigerated.)

Drizzle the salad with a healthy glug of olive oil. Halve the lemon and squeeze most of the juice over the salad. You want this salad to be refreshingly tart. Season the salad with salt and with pepper, if using, then toss until the leaves are evenly coated with a fine sheen of oil and the salad has reduced slightly in volume. Mound the salad on a pretty platter or in a shallow bowl.

Halve, pit, and peel the avocado, then cut into thin wedges or chunks. Place the pieces on the salad with their deeper green edges facing up and serve.

BEETS AND BERRIES

MAKES 8 SERVINGS

PAREVE/VEGAN

I first encountered the genius pairing of late-spring beets, which are at their sweetest, with early-summer berries, which are on the tart side, from chef Jeremy Fox at Santa Monica's Rustic Canyon restaurant. Here's my take on this inspired combination: roast beets two different ways for textural, visual, and taste contrast and finish them with pomegranate molasses, the Middle Eastern equivalent of a balsamic reduction. Chioggia and golden beets are especially pretty in this salad. If you cannot find beets with the greens attached, use wild arugula or Swiss chard in place of the greens.

3 pounds (1.4 kg) medium-size beets with leafy tops
    attached (about 2 pounds/450 g without the tops)
Olive oil
Kosher or sea salt and freshly ground black pepper
1 cup (20 g) wild arugula or baby Swiss chard,
    (optional)
1 pint (290 g) mixed berries, such as blueberries,
    blackberries, and raspberries (2 cups)
Finishing salt, such as Maldon sea salt or fleur de sel
3 tablespoons pomegranate molasses

POMEGRANATE MOLASSES

Widely available at Middle Eastern markets, a sweet-tart pomegranate reduction can also be made at home. Boil pomegranate juice with a little fresh orange juice until it has reduced to a syrup, watching carefully toward the end so the mixture does not burn. The syrup will continue to thicken as it cools. The sugars in the orange juice help caramelize the more-tart pomegranate juice.

Position oven racks in middle and upper third of oven. Preheat the oven to 375°F (190°C). Cut off the greens from the beets, leaving about 1 inch (2.5 cm) of the stem attached, and reserve the greens. Scrub the beets and set aside 2 of the larger beets. Cut the remaining beets into halves or quarters so that all the pieces are about same size.

Place the beets on a sheet pan, drizzle with 2 to 3 teaspoons olive oil, sprinkle with salt and pepper, and toss to coat evenly. Spread the beets in a single layer, cover the pan tightly with foil, and roast on the center oven rack until tender when pierced with a knife, 30 to 40 minutes. Set aside to cool.

Meanwhile, using a Japanese mandoline or a sharp knife, shave the 2 reserved beets into rounds about $\frac{1}{16}$ inch (2 mm)—and no thicker than $\frac{1}{8}$ inch/3 mm—thick. You should have about 36 rounds. Transfer the rounds to a sheet pan, drizzle with 1 to 2 teaspoons olive oil, sprinkle with salt, and toss to coat evenly. Move the first pan of beets to a higher rack to finish roasting and roast beet rounds on center rack until the edges are crisped, curled, and browned in places, about 15 minutes. Remove from the oven and let cool.

Select the most tender beet greens and cut the leaves crosswise into ribbons $\frac{1}{4}$ inch (6 mm) wide. Alternatively, use the arugula.

When the beet pieces are cool enough to handle, peel them and cut into cubes or wedges (I like to leave the stem ends attached). Place them in a bowl along with the berries and greens and toss gently with a small amount of olive oil, the finishing salt, and several grinds of pepper.

Divide the dressed beets among 8 salad plates or mound them on a platter. Scatter the beet "chips" over the salad(s). Drizzle the pomegranate molasses artistically around and over the salad(s).

GOLDEN BORSCHT WITH BUTTERMILK AND GINGER

MAKES 8 SERVINGS

DAIRY

Traditional dairy borscht is often little more than boiled beets and their greens with a dollop of sour cream. This chilled soup is true to the spirit of the original but uses a ginger-infused steaming liquid and tangy buttermilk to create a refreshing bowl of sunshine. Look for fresh, juicy-looking beets, and try to find small-batch cultured buttermilk, or if you have access to a butter producer, the kind with flecks of butter in it.

1¾ pounds (800 g) medium-to-large golden beets with leafy tops attached (about 1¼ pounds/570 g without tops)
3 cups (720 ml) water
Juice of 2 lemons
1½-ounce (40-g) piece fresh ginger, peeled and sliced
2 tablespoons honey
Kosher salt
1½ to 2 cups (360 to 480 ml) buttermilk

Cut off the greens from the beets, reserve the tenderest, prettiest leaves, and set aside. Scrub beets and cut into halves or quarters so all the pieces are about the same size.

Put the water, juice of 1 lemon, and ginger in the bottom of a pot fitted with a steamer basket. Place beets in the steamer basket, cover pot, and bring to a boil. Reduce heat to keep water simmering and steam until beets are tender when pierced with the tip of a knife, 20 to 25 minutes.

While the beets are cooking, cut enough of the reserved stems and leaves crosswise into pieces ¼ inch (6 mm) wide to equal about 1 cup (40 g). When beets are tender, transfer them to a tray to cool. Add the greens to the steamer basket, cover, and steam until tender but still bright, 3 to 5 minutes. Transfer greens to a small bowl and reserve. Strain the steaming liquid and reserve ginger and liquid. You should have about 2 cups (480 ml) golden cooking liquid.

Trim off and discard any stem and root ends from the beets, then peel the beets. Using a food processor fitted with a grating disk, grate the beets. Transfer them to a bowl large enough to hold all the ingredients. Fit processor with metal S blade, and with the motor running, drop in ginger slices to mince. Return roughly half the shredded beets to the work bowl, along with 1 cup (240 ml) cooking liquid, the honey, and 1 teaspoon salt, and puree until the mixture is smooth. Scrape mixture into the bowl of grated beets.

Stir in the remaining 1 cup (240 ml) cooking liquid, the juice of the second lemon, and 1½ cups (360 ml) of the buttermilk. The soup should taste refreshingly tart, with a hint of sweetness and a warm glow from the ginger. Cover and refrigerate the soup and greens until well chilled.

Taste the soup and add salt and remaining buttermilk as desired. Stir greens into soup just before serving.

KITCHEN NOTE: Common purslane pops up in gardens everywhere this time of year. Its succulent young leaves add another tart note to the soup. Quickly sauté 8 to 10 small sprigs in a little butter and use to garnish the borscht.

GOLDEN BORSCHT WITH BUTTERMILK
AND GINGER, TOP;
VELVET CELERY ROOT AND POTATO SOUP
(PAGE 180), BOTTOM

BARLEY PILAF WITH GARLIC SCAPES, FIDDLEHEADS, AND SHIITAKE MUSHROOMS

MAKES 8 SERVINGS

MEAT OR PAREVE/VEGAN

Barley is the first important crop to be harvested around Passover. As the harbinger of the wheat crop that will be ready seven weeks later, barley (*omer*) sheaves are counted each day of the *omer* as a tally, an anxious countdown to the coming harvest, and a symbolic enumeration of the days in the desert, following the Exodus from Egypt. Barley loves garlic. Pair it with shiitake mushrooms, which have a hint of garlic, and garlic scapes (shown above), the tender flower stems that must be trimmed away from the base of the developing garlic plant to allow the bulb to form. Resourceful farmers show up at May farmers' markets with these cuttings, which have a grassy, mild garlic flavor and aroma. You may use green garlic (the whole immature garlic plant), garlic chives, or leeks and garlic in place of scapes. Coiled, young wild fiddlehead fern fronds are gathered in cool climates this time of year. Since fiddleheads have an asparagus-like quality,

feel free to use easier-to-find asparagus in their place. To keep the vegetables bright, add them just before the pilaf is ready. Barley is delicious cooked with either meat or vegetable stock, and any leftovers can be thinned with additional stock for a delicious soup.

1 cup (200 g) pearled or whole-grain barley

½ pound (225 g) fresh medium-size shiitake mushrooms, or 2 ounces (55 g) dried, soaked in hot water to cover to reconstitute

1 large leek, white part only, chopped (about 1 cup/90 g)

Kosher or sea salt and freshly ground black pepper

Extra-virgin olive oil

4 cups (960 ml) chicken, beef, or vegetable stock or water

Large handful of thin garlic scapes (8 to 10), 1 bunch green garlic or garlic chives, or 2 leeks and 2 cloves garlic

½ pound (225 g) fiddlehead ferns, or 1 pound (450 g) asparagus

If using pearled barley, pick over to remove any debris, then rinse. If using whole-grain barley, soak as directed on page 18. Separate the stems from the mushroom caps. Cut the caps into slices ¼ inch (6 mm) wide. If using fresh mushrooms, cut off and discard the dry ends of the stems, then chop the stems. If using dried shiitakes, the stems may be too tough to chop; save them for making stock.

In a wide pot large enough to hold all the ingredients, cook the leek with a little salt in 2 tablespoons olive oil, stirring occasionally, until bright green and softened, 5 to 7 minutes. Add the mushroom caps and stems and a little salt and pepper and turn up the heat to medium-high. Cook until the mixture is fragrant and glistening and the vegetables have reduced by about half, 2 to 3 minutes. Transfer the contents of the pot to a bowl.

Add the barley and 3 cups (720 ml) of the stock to the pot and bring to a boil over high heat. Reduce the heat to low, cover, and simmer, adding more stock if the pot runs dry, until tender, about 40 minutes for pearled barley. Return the cooked leeks and mushrooms to the pot after the first 20 minutes of cooking. If using whole-grain barley, return the leeks and mushrooms to the pot when barley is almost tender, after 1 to 1½ hours, and cook until the barley is tender, about 30 minutes longer.

While the barley is cooking, prepare the scapes and ferns or asparagus. Trim off and discard the ends of the scapes and cut the scapes crosswise into 1-inch (2.5-cm) pieces. Drop the fiddleheads into boiling salted water and boil for 2 minutes. A lot of "fern debris" will come loose.

Drain the fiddleheads and rinse well in ice water. Trim off the ends and rub away any remaining brown film clinging to the ferns. If using asparagus, snap off the woody stems and discard or save for stock. Cut the asparagus crosswise into ½-inch (12-mm) pieces, leaving the tips whole.

Shortly before you are ready to serve, heat a medium skillet over medium heat. Swirl in a little olive oil and add the garlic scapes and the fiddleheads or asparagus. Season with salt and pepper, cover the pan, and cook until bright green and just tender, 3 to 5 minutes. Stir scapes and ferns or asparagus into the barley, heat briefly, and serve.

RAMPS VARIATION: In place of the garlic scapes, use ramps, small wild leeks with broad, tender tops and a slight garlic flavor. They are gathered in late spring in cool climates and sold at selected markets.

SARAH'S STEAMED POTATOES

8 SERVINGS

DAIRY, PAREVE, OR MEAT

Depending on which fat you use, this versatile side dish changes its nature, becoming the perfect companion to a vegan, meat, or dairy meal. My aunt Sarah taught me a clever trick with potatoes: the onion and fat start the potatoes browning, and the steam in the covered pot makes the potatoes tender and flavorful. Try some of the wonderful potato varieties available at farmers' markets, especially any of the season's new potatoes. If you'd like, add a woody herb, such as rosemary, thyme, or bay leaves, to the pot. If using schmaltz, add a good scattering of *gribenes* (page 24).

3 pounds (1.4 kg) all-purpose potatoes

4 tablespoons (55 g) butter or schmaltz or (60 ml) olive oil

½ onion, chopped

1 or 2 rosemary sprigs (optional)

Kosher or sea salt

Scrub or peel the potatoes and cut into quarters or 2-inch (5-cm) chunks, depending on their size. In a deep pot fitted with a lid, melt the butter (or other fat) over medium heat. Scatter the onions over the fat, add the potatoes and the rosemary, if using, and season with salt. Cover, raise the heat to medium-high, and cook, shaking the pot a few times, until the onions are light golden, 3 to 5 minutes.

Turn the heat to low and steam the potatoes, stirring occasionally and adding a little water if needed to prevent sticking, until they are very tender, 25 to 30 minutes. Place a folded wet dish towel on a heatproof surface, set the pot on the towel, and let stand for 5 minutes. The steam that is created will loosen any crusted brown bits. Stir the brown bits into the potatoes and serve. (The dish can be made a few hours ahead and kept at room temperature. To reheat, add a little water to the pot, cover, and steam over medium heat.)

THE JEWISH FARM MOVEMENT IN THE UNITED STATES

There are farmers who happen to be Jewish, and there are farmers who farm "Jewish." Nati Passow—midthirties, full beard, loosely tied rope of brown dreadlocks, well-worn patrol cap—is one of a new breed of Jewish farmers in the United States who seek to connect the agricultural and social justice lessons in the Torah to today's concerns about sustainability, the environment, food safety, and feeding the hungry.

Nati, cofounder and executive director of the Jewish Farm School (JFS), teaches practical sustainability skills within a Jewish context from his home in west Philadephia: permaculture, beekeeping, food preservation (including "shtetl" skills such as fermentation), and how to create and run urban community gardens.

JFS is one of a loosely affiliated national network of organizations, many of which are supported by Hazon, the country's largest nonprofit devoted to creating eco-conscious Jewish communities (see page 299 for some listings). These projects are often urban based and interfaith, working from a shared ancient history toward a "practical application of the [Bible's] agricultural laws that were designed to protect social and food justice," as Nati puts it. The projects may differ in focus, but their work stems from the same three biblical tenets, which are intertwined with lessons of empathy and empowerment and sound remarkably current:

A SABBATH FOR THE LAND (*shmita***).** Today, we talk about cover crops and field rotation as naturally sustainable practices that restore and enrich soil to increase productivity. The books of Exodus, Leviticus, and Deuteronomy mandate *shmita*, a year of rest for the land every seventh year that, if followed, protects land from overuse and promises future abundance. To survive a year without actively farming, farmers would set aside a portion of the sixth year's harvest and were allowed to gather anything that grew perennially. In other words, they practiced permaculture, one of today's key sustainability efforts. *Shmita* is having a renaissance. As I

write these words in fall 2014, a sabbatical year has just begun, and visionaries like Yigal Deutscher, founder of the 7Seeds Project, weave together Jewish tradition with permaculture teaching.

LEAVINGS (*shikcha***) AND GLEANINGS (***peah***).** Google "gleaning projects" and you'll get over 200,000 results. Faith-based, governmental, and nonprofit agencies across the United States practice what was commanded in Leviticus and Deuteronomy: to leave the fallen fruit and forgotten sheaves of a harvest for the poor. Gathering leftovers from field crops, urban fruit trees, farmers' markets, and community-supported agriculture organizations (CSAs) has become one of the most popular and direct solutions to provide fresh food to communities in need. Leviticus and Deuteronomy also command that we leave the unreaped edges of our fields for those in need to harvest for themselves, the purpose of many community gardens. Today's activists design farms with "corners," or *peyot*, whose harvests are designated for food pantries.

STEWARDSHIP. When we talk about being good stewards of the land, we are talking about caring for the earth's topsoil and protecting it for future generations so that it will continue to yield abundant food. The role of steward reminds us we aren't the end users of natural resources, a concept laid out in Leviticus: the land doesn't belong to us but to God (or, for many today, a more general universe). We cannot own the land in perpetuity; we are its guardians. And furthermore, we cannot sell but must preserve "the unenclosed land about [the] cities." That would be a call for greenbelts and parklands today.

FIRST CAME THE CHICKEN FARMERS. . .

Before the current new age of spiritual farming, there was a different sort of American Jewish farm movement prompted by another kind of social justice. Beginning in the early 1880s, idealistic agricultural colonies were

and Petaluma, California, that Jewish farmers were selling hundreds of millions of eggs per year, especially during the movement's peak from the 1930s through the 1950s.

Petaluma's sandy soil and its fame as site of the invention of the egg incubator in the late nineteenth century had already established the Sonoma County town as the Egg Basket of the World by the time Russian Jewish farmers started trickling in from abroad and the East Coast. Indeed, early-twentieth-century California cookbooks and menus listed "Petaluma chickens" much as many menus today note the provenance of ingredients. The heirs of Levi Strauss contributed heavily to the establishment of a Jewish community in Petaluma, as Baron de Hirsch had done a generation before in the East, funding the building of synagogues and community centers. Petaluma was considered an important enough Jewish center that Golda Meir paid it a visit in the 1930s, perhaps to scout asylum for refugees, engage in fund-raising for the establishment of the State of Israel, or to pick up some farming tips to take to the fledgling country.

Although many of these farming communities had rabbis and kept kosher, they were primarily secular endeavors that evolved from the socialist and communist ideologies many of the founding Russian Jews brought with them. Labor exploitation and profit motives were the social justice issues of their day, setting the stage for today's conscientious farming with Jewish intent.

Jewish family egg farms thrived until the 1960s, when large-scale industrial egg production and commodity crop subsidies were introduced. Small operations could not compete, and many farmers sold their land to developers. The Jewish Agricultural Society and its publication, *The Jewish Farmer*, closed its doors in the early 1970s. Although Petaluma is no longer an important egg production center and few in its Jewish community still farm, older locals keep the history alive, and the area remains an agricultural center, primarily dairy. With today's small-farm renaissance and with a growing interest in closed-loop and permaculture practices in which chickens and chicken manure play a big role, Petaluma and other historic Jewish farming communities could be poised to reclaim the title Egg Basket of the World.

established across the country to offer a new life to Russian Jews fleeing pogroms, and later, escaping crowded tenements and factory jobs in their new homeland. Many of these utopian settlements were funded by German Jewish philanthropist Baron Maurice de Hirsch through the Jewish Agricultural Society. And most of these early ventures failed due to their collective structure.

By the early twentieth century, the Jewish Agriculture Society was funding individual family farms with far greater success. With $2,000 seed money, a person could buy a five-acre (two-hectare) farm, chicks, and a coop and be in business within a few months. With a second influx of Jews after World War I, and another during and after the Holocaust, there were so many small-scale chicken farms, particularly in New Jersey, Connecticut,

LATE SPRING CHICKEN-IN-A-POT

MAKES 6 SERVINGS

MEAT

This is a lighter version of the traditional deli favorite that also solves the age-old problem of how to cook white and dark meat together and have both done to perfection. Splaying the chicken legs allows them to braise in the cooking liquid while the delicate breast meat steams above, resulting in plump white meat infused with the aromatics in the pot. There are many vegetable options to try; the choice is up to you. Here, red carrots, purple potatoes, and green pea shoots beautifully capture the season. If you include spinach, use one with meaty leaves, such as a sweet Savoy type like Bloomsdale. You can include potatoes in the vegetable mix, or serve the chicken over egg pasta, such as *pappardelle* or *garganelli*, to soak up the delicious juices. And don't forget the challah.

1 chicken, 3½ to 4 pounds (1.6 to 1.8 kg)

Kosher or sea salt and freshly ground white pepper

1 large onion, preferably a spring onion with tops
   still attached

8 carrots, preferably red (about ¾ pound/340 g)

¼ pound (115 g) morel mushrooms

½ pound (225 g) sugar snap peas, stringed, or
   1½ cups (220 g) shelled English peas or fava beans

About 2 cups (55 g) pea shoots or Savoy spinach,
   such as Bloomsdale (about 2 ounces)

1 pound (450 g) waxy or all-purpose potatoes,
   such as Russian Banana, La Ratte, French, or
   Rose Finn Apple Fingerlings or Yukon Gold

1 tablespoon olive, grapeseed, or avocado oil

1 cup (240 ml) dry white wine

1 to 2 cups (240 to 480 ml) water

2 tablespoons snipped fresh dill, chervil, or parsley

Pat the chicken dry. Use a sharp knife to make an incision in the skin at the point at which each leg joins the body of the bird, then bend the legs outward until they lie open. Season the chicken inside and out with salt and pepper.

Chop the onion into 1-inch (2.5-cm) pieces. If using a spring onion, include some of the tender neck. Scrub or peel the carrots, then halve them lengthwise, leaving a little of the stem attached because it's pretty and tastes delicious. Halve or quarter the mushrooms lengthwise, and brush well to loosen any grit. Check the snap peas for strings and strip away any you find. Remove and discard the tough stems from the pea shoots or spinach; if using pea shoots, discard any long, tough tendrils. Scrub or peel potatoes. Cut small fingerlings in half lengthwise, or cut larger potatoes into 1- to 2-inch (2.5- to 5-cm) cubes.

In a large, wide pot, heat the oil over medium-high heat. Add the chicken, breast side up. Brown the underside of the chicken, pressing down on the legs so that they come in full contact with the hot pot. Cook until the chicken is fragrant and is light golden when you lift a drumstick to check, about 10 minutes.

Arrange the onion, carrots, and mushrooms around the chicken, adding them in that order so that the mushrooms are on top. Lower the heat to medium, season with salt and pepper, and cook, stirring occasionally, until the onion is softened and translucent, the carrots have deepened in color, and the mushrooms have released any moisture, about 7 minutes.

Add the wine, raise the heat to medium-high, and cook until the wine has reduced by about one third and the juices are starting to thicken, 3 to 5 minutes. Add water until the liquid in the pot is at a depth of 1 inch (2.5 cm), then add the potatoes. Cover the pot, turn down the heat to low, and cook at a very gentle simmer, basting the chicken occasionally with the pot juices, until the chicken is very tender, 30 to 45 minutes. As the chicken cooks, the pan

continued »

juices will increase. Add water as needed to keep the juices at a depth of at least 2 inches (5 cm). The legs should be mostly submerged, but the breast should be exposed. (The dish can be made ahead up to this point, cooled, covered, and refrigerated and then reheated later in the day.)

Five minutes before serving, add the pea shoots and peas to the pot. Turn up the heat to medium-low and cook until the peas and greens are tender but still bright. Taste and adjust the seasoning, then add the herb of your choice to the pot.

Cut or pull the chicken into serving-size portions and serve in shallow bowls along with some of the broth and vegetables (the chicken skin is not crisped in this dish; you may remove it first, if you prefer).

KTZITZOT: CHICKEN PATTIES

MAKES 6 SERVINGS

MEAT

Pan-fried ground-meat patties—especially from poultry—are one of the most beloved Jewish Israeli comfort foods (the other is chicken schnitzel). The term comes from the verb "to grind"; choose whole parts and ask your butcher to grind them freshly for you. Cookbook author and radio host Lynne Rosetto Kasper advises a mix of turkey and chicken for a richer, capon-like flavor. If you must use white meat, add a little olive oil to the meat mixture to prevent it from drying out. *Ktzitzot* are delicious with other comfort foods, such as Sarah's Steamed Potatoes (page 221) and Gvetch: Roasted Romanian Ratatouille (page 48), or in a sandwich (see the "falafel" sandwiches, opposite).

1 egg

¼ cup (15 g) finely chopped fresh cilantro

3 tablespoons minced onion

1 clove garlic, minced

1 teaspoon salt

1 teaspoon sweet paprika

1 teaspoon ground cumin

¼ teaspoon ground turmeric

Freshly ground black pepper

3 tablespoons dry bread crumbs or cooked rice

1 pound (450 g) freshly ground chicken or turkey, or a mix

¼ cup (60 ml) olive or mild oil, such as safflower, sunflower, or grapeseed

In a medium bowl, lightly whisk the egg with a fork. Stir in the cilantro, onion, garlic, salt, paprika, cumin, turmeric, a few grinds of pepper, and the bread crumbs. Add the meat and mix gently but thoroughly. If you have time, chill the mixture for 1 hour or more.

Form the mixture into 10 to 12 patties, each about 3 inches (7.5 cm) in diameter. The patties may be made several hours ahead and refrigerated.

In a large skillet, heat the oil over medium heat. Working in batches to avoid crowding, add the patties and fry, turning once, until golden brown on both sides and cooked through, about 7 minutes total. Using a slotted spatula, transfer to paper towels to drain briefly. Repeat with the remaining patties. Serve hot.

CHICKEN "FALAFEL" SANDWICHES: Make patties 2 inches (5 cm) in diameter (or cut up leftover large ones). Stuff into pita with raw or cooked seasonal vegetables and the pickle of your choice or Vinegared Cabbage (page 22). Top with Tahini Sauce (page 23) and Smoky Harissa (page 33) or Matboucha (page 32).

FREEKEH, ENGLISH PEAS, AND SMOKED FISH

MAKES 8 SERVINGS

FISH

Freekeh is the product of an ancient processing method for wheat used throughout the Levant. Traditionally, the wheat is harvested while still green, dried briefly in the field, and then fire roasted, yielding a nutrient-rich grain with grassy and smoked flavors. The method for "new ears parched with fire" is described in Leviticus, in a "recipe" for religious offerings of first fruits, making freekeh a perfect dish for Shavuot, the holiday that celebrates the spring harvest, notably of wheat. Here, I've paired the chewy grain with lots of English peas and smoked fish (whitefish, sturgeon, and trout are all good choices). Freekeh is harvested green, and studies show that it contains far more protein, minerals, and fiber than its mature dried counterpart. In large-scale production, freekeh is often oven roasted instead, which yields a less smoky result. It is available as a whole or cracked grain (which must be soaked before cooking) or in finely cracked form.

Kosher or sea salt and freshly ground black or
  white pepper

1 cup (150 g) freekeh, preferably finely cracked

1 bunch thin spring onions with tops or green onions

2 tablespoons butter or mild oil, such as grapeseed
  or avocado

2½ cups (600 ml) hot water

2 cups (300 g) shelled English peas (2 pounds/450 g
  in the pod)

¼ cup (15 g) chopped fresh Italian parsley

2 tablespoons snipped dill

Juice of ½ lemon

1 pound (450 g) smoked whitefish, sturgeon, or trout

Horseradish Cream, optional

½ cup (115 g) crème fraîche or plain Greek yogurt

1 to 3 tablespoons prepared horseradish (brands
  vary in strength)

If using whole grain or cracked freekeh, soak as directed on page 18. If using finely cracked freekeh, skip this step.

Stir together the crème fraîche, horseradish to taste, and a pinch of salt. Cover and refrigerate.

Thinly slice the onions, including most of the green tops, crosswise. In a wide pot large enough to hold all the ingredients, cook onions with a little salt and pepper in 1 tablespoon of the butter over medium heat until they

continued »

are soft and their color has brightened, about 5 minutes. Watch carefully and lower heat to prevent browning.

Add the remaining 1 tablespoon butter to the pot, and once it has melted, stir in the freekeh, raise the heat to medium-high, and cook for 1 minute, stirring to coat. Stir in the water, about ½ teaspoon salt, and several grinds of pepper. Cover, reduce the heat to medium-low, and cook until almost all the water has been absorbed and the freekeh is tender, about 20 minutes. Add the peas, and continue to cook, uncovered, until all the water is absorbed and peas are crisp-tender but still bright green, about 5 minutes longer.

Stir in the parsley, dill, and lemon juice. You now have a choice: Cut the smoked fish into 8 equal pieces and serve alongside the freekeh. Or, flake the smoked fish and gently mix it into the freekeh. Serve warm or at room temperature with the horseradish cream, if desired.

ROMANESCO VARIATION: In place of peas, use lime green Romanesco, an Italian cross between cauliflower and broccoli with fractal-shaped florets. Blanch the florets before adding them to the dish.

PAREVE VARIATION: Omit fish and horseradish cream and use a mild oil instead of butter. Delicious with braised lamb shanks (page 192 sans artichokes and gremolata), a nod to the traditional Syrian dish of lamb, spring peas, and pine nuts.

SALMON, GREEN TOMATOES, AND SORREL WITH TAGLIERINI

MAKES 6 SERVINGS

FISH

When I came upon a recipe for an unripe tomato pasta sauce in Joyce Goldstein's *Cucina Ebraica*, I was inspired to pair the tart tomatoes with mouth-puckering sorrel to serve with fish. The luscious sauce is also delicious as a late-spring or early-summer topping for crostini with fresh goat cheese. *Sel gris* adds the perfect briny finishing note.

2 pounds (900 g) green (unripe) tomatoes (5 to 6 tomatoes)

3 tablespoon extra-virgin olive oil

4 tablespoons (55 g) butter, at room temperature

1 onion (about ½ pound/225 g), chopped

Kosher or sea salt and freshly ground white pepper

1 clove garlic, minced

¼ pound (115 g) lightly packed stemmed sorrel leaves (about 4 cups; about ¾ pound/340 g with stems), finely chopped

Sel gris

1 pound (450 g) salmon fillet, preferably with skin, cut into 6 equal pieces

½ pound (225 g) taglierini or other fresh or dry Italian egg pasta

Core the tomatoes and use a swivel-blade vegetable peeler to peel them. Chop the tomatoes into small pieces no larger than ½ inch (12 mm). Don't worry about seeding them.

In a wide pot, heat 2 tablespoons each of the olive oil and butter over medium heat. Add the onion and a little kosher salt and cook until the onion is translucent, soft, and light golden, 7 to 10 minutes, reducing the heat as needed to prevent browning. Add the garlic and cook for 1 minute. Add the tomatoes, season with salt and pepper, reduce the heat to medium-low, and cook until the tomatoes are meltingly tender, thick, and glossy, 10 to 15 minutes. If the mixture seems too dry during cooking, add a little water and cover the pan.

Remove the pot from the heat and stir in the sorrel until it is wilted. Stir in the remaining 2 tablespoons butter and season to taste with sel gris and pepper. You should have about 3½ cups (840 ml) sauce. (The sauce can be made up to 1 day ahead, cooled, covered, and refrigerated, then reheated.)

Bring a large pot of water, covered, to a boil over high heat. While the water is heating, prepare the fish. Pat it very dry and season with sel gris and pepper. Heat a large, heavy skillet over medium-high heat and swirl in a little of the remaining 1 tablespoon oil. When the oil shimmers, place a piece of the fish, skin side down, in the pan. If you get a strong sizzle, go ahead and put the pieces of fish in without crowding the pan. Cook the pieces, without moving them, until the skin is crisped and brown and the fish releases easily from the pan, 3 to 4 minutes. Turn the fish and cook to desired doneness, 2 to 3 minutes for medium-rare, 4 to 5 minutes for medium-well. (A good rule of thumb is 10 minutes per inch/2.5 cm of thickness to cook through.) Place the fish, skin side up, on a plate.

When the water comes to a vigorous boil, generously salt it, and add the pasta (cooking time will vary depending on whether you are using fresh or dry noodles). Just before the pasta is ready, scoop out about 1 cup (240 ml) of the cooking water and reserve. Drain the pasta and add to the tomato sauce in the pot. Turn the heat to medium and toss the pasta and sauce together, adding about ¼ cup

(60 ml) of the pasta cooking water. Cook until the pasta is well coated and the sauce is thick, about 3 minutes, adding pasta water as needed to create a luscious sauce.

Divide the pasta among shallow bowls and place a piece of salmon, skin side up, on each serving. Season with sel gris and white pepper. Diners should break up the salmon and stir it into their pasta.

RISOTTO VARIATION: When the sauce is ready, stir in 1½ cups (295 g) raw Arborio, Carnaroli, or Vialone Nano rice and cook over medium heat, stirring frequently, until the rice grains are opaque, 2 to 3 minutes. Make risotto in the usual way, adding hot water or vegetable stock, a ladleful at a time, until the rice is creamy and chewy. Place the fish on top of the risotto to serve.

A PASHTIDA: BAKED PASTA WITH SPINACH, RICOTTA, AND BROWN BUTTER

MAKES 8 TO 10 SERVINGS

DAIRY

ashtida is the Israeli word for a noodle or egg casserole. Mac 'n' cheese, quiche, lasagna, and kugel are all *pashtidot*. The word derives from the Italian *pasticcio* and the Ladino *pastida*, originally crusted savory meat pies that graced Sephardic Shabbat tables since medieval times. Today's Israeli *pashtidot* are typically crustless, and every cook has a few handy recipes up his or her sleeve. The most popular are dairy based and served during Shavuot. Use the best-tasting spinach possible, such as the Savoy varieties, which have thick, meaty leaves and little tannin. Available in late spring and early summer at farmers' markets, they often come with their stems still attached at the root. Don't throw those away! Edda Servi Machlin includes an "ancient Venetian-Jewish recipe" for them in *The Classic Cuisine of the Italian Jews* (see opposite). By all means use the best small-batch sheep's or cow's milk ricotta you can find.

½ cup (115 g) plus 2 tablespoons butter

1 pound (450 g) spinach

Kosher or sea salt and freshly ground white or
    black pepper

1 pound (450 g) penne, farfalle, or other short pasta

3 eggs

1 pound (450 g) ricotta cheese

1½ cups (150 g) grated Parmigiano-Reggiano
    cheese

½ teaspoon freshly grated nutmeg

Preheat the oven to 350°F (180°C). Butter a shallow 3-quart (3-L) baking dish with 1 tablespoon of the butter.

Wash spinach well and drain, but do not dry. Stem the spinach and reserve the stems if you like. Heat a wide pot over medium heat and swirl in 1 tablespoon of the butter. Working in batches if necessary, add the spinach, season with salt and pepper, and cook until the spinach has wilted

and released its liquid, 2 to 3 minutes. Transfer to a sieve and drain, pressing out as much liquid as possible. Finely chop the spinach. You should have about 1½ cups (285 g).

Cook the pasta in generously salted boiling water. While the pasta is cooking, in a large bowl, lightly whisk the eggs. Stir in ricotta cheese, half the Parmigiano-Reggiano, the nutmeg, 1 teaspoon salt, and several grinds of pepper. Stir in the spinach.

Heat the remaining ½ cup (115 g) butter in a medium skillet over medium heat and cook, swirling the pan occasionally, until the foam has subsided and the butter is fragrant and nut brown, 7 to 10 minutes. Lower the heat as necessary to keep the milk solids from burning. Stir half the browned butter into the spinach mixture.

Just before the pasta is ready, scoop out about ½ cup (120 ml) of the cooking water and reserve. Loosely drain the pasta and return it to the pot. Add the spinach mixture and pasta water and mix well. Scrape into the prepared baking dish, top with the remaining Parmigiano-Reggiano cheese, and pour the remaining browned butter evenly over the top. (The dish can be prepared up to this point and refrigerated for several hours.)

Bake the casserole until the top is golden brown, about 30 minutes. (If baking a cold casserole, allow an extra 10 minutes or so in the oven.) Serve hot.

SAUTÉED SPINACH STEMS (inspired by Machlin's *testine di spinaci,* "little spinach heads."): Four pounds (1.8 kg) spinach yields 1 pound (450 g) of stems. You can save the hardy stems over a couple of weeks to have enough (they keep well in an air-filled plastic bag in the refrigerator). Clean them and trim off the dangling roots, but leave the stems attached in their clusters. Cook, covered, with a little olive oil, water, salt, and pepper until tender. Add a little red wine vinegar and cook until the vinegar smell disappears. Serve chilled as a little side salad.

CHEESE BLINTZ SOUFFLÉ

MAKES 6 TO 8 SERVINGS

DAIRY

The cheese blintz soufflé recipe in my mother-in-law's sisterhood cookbook was so popular that three versions were included. The casserole called for frozen blintzes, but the best part was the "soufflé"—eggs, sour cream, and sugar—that turned into a puffed, golden custard in the oven. My version begins with delicate, easy-to-make crepes that are layered with the familiar cheese-blintz filling and topped with the magic soufflé. The dish may be assembled the night before and baked just before brunch, supper, or dessert. The recipe can be doubled, and the crepes can be made ahead and frozen. Serve with any of the fruit condiments that follow, according to the season, or with imported Italian or Hungarian preserved cherries. Unlike traditional crepes for blintzes, which are browned only on one side, these crepes are browned lightly on the second side.

FOR THE CREPES

2 eggs, at room temperature

¾ cup (180 ml) whole milk

¼ cup (60 ml) warm water

¾ cup (95 g) unbleached all-purpose flour

1 tablespoon sugar

¼ teaspoon salt

4 tablespoons (55 g) butter, melted

FOR THE CHEESE FILLING

¾ pound (340 g) farmer cheese

½ cup (115 g) fromage blanc or crème fraîche

1 egg, lightly beaten

2 tablespoons sugar

½ teaspoon salt

½ teaspoon ground cinnamon (optional)

2 tablespoons butter, melted, for the baking dish

FOR THE CUSTARD

2 eggs

3 tablespoons sugar

¾ cup (150 g) sour cream

TO MAKE THE CREPE BATTER: In a blender, combine eggs, milk, water, flour, sugar, salt, and 2 tablespoons of the butter and blend until smooth, about 10 seconds. Scrape down the sides of the jar and blend again briefly. You should have 2 cups (480 ml) of batter the consistency of thin cream. Cover and refrigerate for 1 hour or up to overnight.

TO MAKE THE CREPES: Line a sheet pan with parchment paper. Stir the crepe batter to reblend. Heat a 6- or 7-inch (15- or 17-cm) crepe pan or skillet over medium-high heat. When a tiny drop of water flicked into the pan skitters immediately, you are ready to cook. Brush the pan lightly with a bit of the remaining butter. Pour in about 2 tablespoons of the batter and immediately tilt the pan to distribute the batter evenly. Cook until the edges of the crepe are lightly crisped, the top surface no longer looks wet, and the underside is light golden brown, 1 to 2 minutes. Flip the crepe and lightly brown the second side, about 1 minute. Flip the crepe, browner side down, onto the sheet pan.

Repeat with the remaining batter, brushing the pan with melted butter only as needed to keep the crepes from sticking, placing them in a single layer on the sheet pan. Begin stacking the second layer on the coolest crepes. You should have about 12 crepes (you will only need 9 crepes for the dish; consider the extras as insurance or a bonus). When completely cool, the crepes can be arranged in a single stack, covered, and refrigerated for up to 1 day. To freeze the crepes, layer them with parchment paper.

continued »

TO MAKE THE FILLING: Use a wooden spoon or rubber spatula to beat together the cheeses, egg, sugar, salt, and the cinnamon, if using.

TO ASSEMBLE THE DISH: Preheat the oven to 350°F (180°C). Brush the 2 tablespoons melted butter over the bottom and sides of an 8-inch square flameproof baking dish. Lay 3 crepes, browner side down, in a single layer on the bottom and one third the way up the sides of the pan, generously overlapping 2 of the crepes to fit and cutting the third crepe in half to fit, so that the bottom of the baking dish and the lower third of its sides are lined. Spoon half the cheese filling over the crepes and use an offset spatula to smooth the surface. Cover with a second layer of 3 crepes, browner side down. Spoon the remaining filling over the crepes. Top with the remaining 3 crepes, browner side up. (The dish can be made to this point 1 day ahead, covered, and refrigerated. Remove from the refrigerator 1 hour before baking.)

TO MAKE THE CUSTARD: In a small bowl, whisk together the eggs and sugar until thickened, then whisk in the sour cream until well blended. Pour evenly over the casserole.

Bake until the custard is puffed and set, about 45 minutes. Heat the broiler and place the casserole under the broiler until the custard bubbles and is browned in places, about 2 minutes. Cut into squares to serve.

DELICIOUS TOPPINGS FOR CHEESE BLINTZ SOUFFLÉ

Strawberries and Roses (page 242)

Braised Cherries (below)

Summer Fruit Compote with Lemon Verbena (page 283)

Peppered Red Wine Fruit Compote (page 112)

BRAISED CHERRIES

MAKES ABOUT 2 CUPS (500 G)

PAREVE

Inspired by Hungarian and Italian preserved whole cherries, this quick sauce-compote is delicious alongside Cheese Blintz Soufflé (previous page) or Quark Cheesecake (page 240) or over vanilla ice cream. For an unusual pairing, serve it over Carob Molasses Ice Cream (page 151).

1½ pounds (680 g) sweet or tart cherries
⅓ to ⅔ cup (100 to 135 g) sugar (use the larger amount for tart cherries)
1 cup (240 ml) light red wine, such as Beaujolais
1 lemon (optional)

Pit and halve the cherries (leave small tart cherries unpitted and whole if you prefer). Place a large, nonreactive skillet over medium-high heat and sprinkle the sugar evenly over the bottom. When the sugar starts to melt, after 2 to 3 minutes, add the cherries and cook, without stirring, until the sugar is melted and bubbly and the cherries have released their juices, about 2 minutes. Add the wine and cook until the juices are thickened, 3 to 5 minutes longer. Halve the lemon and add a squeeze or two of juice, if desired.

MAMALIGA

MAKES 8 SERVINGS

DAIRY

Mamaliga, a.k.a. polenta, is Romanian *and* Italian comfort food for both Jews and non-Jews. Possibly introduced in the Balkans during the time of the Ottomans (rather than via the Venetians), cornmeal porridge is typically prepared with at least two cheeses, a semihard one and a fresh one, at least one of them of sheep's milk. In Italy, young pecorino and ricotta were and still are used; in Romania, kashkaval and urda (similar to ricotta). Stirring the stiff porridge was considered man's work, so it was my grandfather, in a houseful of women, who made this dish, pouring out the steaming cornmeal onto a wooden board and portioning it with a taut string to serve.

½ pound (225 g) medium-sharp kashkaval,
    kasseri, or young pecorino cheese
1 pound (450 g) sheep's or cow's milk ricotta cheese
    or fromage blanc
7 cups (1.7 L) water
Kosher or sea salt
1 cup (160 g) polenta
4 tablespoons (55 g) butter, at room temperature,
    cut into small pieces
1½ cups (345 g) sour cream or crème fraîche
Kosher or sea salt
Finishing salt, such as fleur de sel
Freshly ground white pepper (optional)

Grate kashkaval cheese on the large holes of a box grater. Stir ricotta cheese to it break up. Have a wooden board or a platter and kitchen twine or a serving spoon handy.

In a wide pot, bring the water to a boil over high heat, season with 1 teaspoon kosher salt, and reduce heat to medium-low. Add the polenta in a slow, steady stream while stirring constantly. Keep polenta at an occasional bubble and cook, stirring frequently, until it comes cleanly away from the sides of the pot and no longer tastes gritty, about 40 minutes. If the polenta seems too stiff, stir in hot water as needed. Beat in the butter.

Working quickly, pour half the polenta in an oblong shape onto the board. Cover with the kashkaval cheese, allowing some of the cheese to scatter onto the board. Pour remaining polenta over the kashkaval, and then spoon large dollops of ricotta cheese onto the polenta. Serve immediately, using a large wooden spoon to scoop servings into shallow bowls (or use the twine method below). Offer sour cream, finishing salt, and pepper at the table.

KITCHEN NOTE: To portion the mamaliga with thin kitchen twine, hold an end in each hand as though you were about to floss. Drag the taut twine under the mound of mamaliga and then "saw" upward to cut a serving. Slide a (traditionally nonmetal) spatula under the portion, then lift and transfer it to a shallow bowl.

SHOPPING TIP: Use stoneground cornmeal or polenta made from flint corn that retains the hull and germ. These are oil-rich, flavorful, and toothsome. If you use a rustic polenta from the excellent Anson Mills, it will absorb more liquid than called for here and it will take longer to cook, but it is well worth the effort.

MAMALIGA VARIATIONS:
• Stir cheeses into the pot of mamaliga and serve in bowls with sour cream.
• Make a do-ahead casserole: Layer hot polenta and kashkaval cheese into a buttered 3-quart (3-L) baking dish. Cool, cover, and refrigerate. Dot with butter, cover with foil, and heat in a 325°F (165°C) oven, 25 to 30 minutes. Serve with ricotta and sour cream.
• Try other cheeses: Gorgonzola, Parmigiano-Reggiano, and mascarpone; or feta, manouri, and Greek yogurt.

CHEESE AND HONEY FILO PIE

MAKES 8 SERVINGS

DAIRY

My grandmother Rachel used to make cheese-filled Iraqi pastries called *kahi* from a puff pastry–like dough that required multiple folds and turns. She added salty cheese to each portion of dough, which she then rolled into large squares and pan-fried to bubbled, golden perfection. My *safta* was way ahead of the salty-sweet curve: She served these many-layered delicacies with a simple sugar syrup.

The memory of this dish so haunted my father—a noncook—that he attempted to re-create it when I was a child. Relying on guesswork, he worked flour and milk together with his hands until it looked and felt "right." My father forgot that cheese was involved and couldn't remember the dish's Arabic name. We dubbed this new version Waky Flaky, because you had to get up pretty early on a weekend morning to create all those layers. Years later, when my grandmother came to visit, we learned the truth about *kahi*: my dad had improved on the original, folding and turning the dough so many more times than she did, there must have been at least a dozen leaves that got more transparent and tender as we cut toward the center of the "package" on our plates.

In any form, *kahi* is extravagantly delicious, but, whew, what a lot of work! I've captured the traditional flavors and textures in a much simpler pie using ready-made filo dough. The focus is on the cheese, with just enough filo to add crisp contrast. Served with salted pistachios and a pour of warm honey, the pie is lovely with an afternoon cup of mint or lemon verbena tea and makes a beautiful dessert or brunch dish on Shavuot. (For more on this holiday, see page 211.)

Use a special honey for this dessert: avocado, chestnut, and orange blossom honeys are all delicious, as is the unusual almond blossom honey, reminiscent of *amaretti*.

2 eggs

¾ pound (340 g) farmer cheese

½ cup (75 g) coarsely grated ricotta salata or aged mizithra cheese (use the large holes of a box grater)

⅓ cup (75 g) labneh, homemade (page 22) or store-bought

¼ cup (85 g) honey, warmed, plus more for serving

½ cup (115 g) butter, melted

8 sheets filo dough, each at least 9 x 13 inches (23 x 33 cm), thawed (see tip below) and at room temperature

Salted pistachios, toasted (see page 17) and chopped, for serving

TO MAKE THE FILLING: In a large bowl, whisk the eggs until well blended. Using a wooden spoon or sturdy rubber spatula, stir in the farmer cheese, ricotta salata, labneh, and honey and mix until thoroughly blended.

TO MAKE THE PIE: Preheat the oven to 375 F (180 C). Have a 9-inch (23-cm) glass pie plate, the filling, the melted butter, and a pastry brush nearby. (Use a soft bristle brush for good coverage and to avoid tearing the dough; avoid silicone brushes, as the "bristles" are too thick and widely spaced.) Gently unfold the 8 filo sheets onto a clean, dry work surface (I like to put the dough on a piece of parchment paper). Cover with a clean dish towel if you like, but as long as you work at a steady pace and the filo dough is properly thawed, it should remain pliable. Using kitchen scissors, trim the stack of sheets into a 9-by-12-inch (23-by30.5-cm) rectangle.

Brush the pie plate with melted butter. Working at a steady pace, brush a filo sheet with butter, using enough to

continued »

cover the sheet completely and evenly, but not so much that you have pools of butter. Ease the sheet of dough into the pie plate so that the dough generally conforms to the shape of the plate and extends evenly on the two longer sides of the sheet. Repeat with 3 more filo sheets, placing them directly on top of the one before. Give the plate a quarter turn. Brush the remaining 4 filo sheets with butter as before, this time setting them into the pan at a diagonal to the first set, so that the overhanging dough more or less creates a star pattern.

Pour the filling into the filo-lined pie plate. Fold each set of points up and over the edges of the filling. Don't worry if some of the layers of dough extend upward. Brush the filo border with melted butter.

Place the pie in the oven and reduce the temperature to 350°F (180°C). Bake the pie until the filo is golden in places and the filling is golden and set but not too firm, about 40 minutes. If you notice that the filo is browning too quickly, lower the oven temperature by 25°F (5°C) to prevent the dough from developing an acrid, burnt flavor.

Let the pie rest in the pie pan on a wire rack for 5 minutes before sliding it, with the help of an offset spatula, onto a serving plate. Or, serve the pie right from the pan. Cut the pie into wedges to serve, drizzle each slice with the warmed honey, and top with the pistachios. The pie can be served warm or at room temperature. Cover and refrigerate any leftovers, then recrisp the filo in a 350°F (180°C) oven before serving.

KITCHEN NOTE: Save your beautiful ceramic or vintage metal pie pans for another use. A simple Pyrex pie dish works best for this recipe. Glass conducts heat more rapidly, which allows the filo to brown properly and the cheese filling to puff and set without overbaking and separating.

WORKING WITH FILO DOUGH

- **Most stores carry only frozen filo dough. Lucky you if you live near a Middle Eastern or Greek bakery that sells it fresh. Standard filo leaves, which this recipe uses, are almost translucent, yet surprisingly sturdy, and typically measure 9 x 13 inches (23 x 33 cm) or 13 x 18 inches (33 x 46 cm). There is also a "rustic" style with thicker leaves; use fewer of this type than called for in this recipe.**

- **To prevent the dough from cracking, thaw the unopened package overnight in the refrigerator. Two to three hours before you are ready to bake, remove a roll of dough from the box (but leave it in its protective wrapper) and place it on the counter to warm to room temperature. Have all your supplies close at hand. Remove the dough from its wrapper and unfold it. If the dough resists or feels cold, stop, cover the dough, and wait until it warms up enough to unfold easily. Count out the number of sheets you need and place the stack on a clean, dry work surface (I like to use a sheet of parchment paper). Cover the remaining dough with a towel.**

- **I prefer to use butter for its flavor, but you can also use a mild oil, such as avocado or grapeseed. Melt more butter than you'll need, so that you don't run out midassembly.**

- **Rewrap any unused filo, using plastic wrap to keep it from sticking, and store in the refrigerator for up to 1 week.**

CHERRY AND GOAT CHEESE TART

MAKES ONE 10-INCH (25-CM) TART, 8 TO 10 SERVINGS

DAIRY

The grassy tang of goat cheese makes a sophisticated partner to sweet cherries, whose deep pepper notes are accented with a hint of white pepper in the custard. The press-in cookie crust is as easy as, well, pie. This is a lovely way to celebrate both Shavuot and the arrival of the first stone fruits of the year.

FOR THE CRUST

1 cup (125 g) unbleached all-purpose flour

¼ cup (25 g) ground almonds (see page 18)

¼ cup (50 g) sugar

¼ teaspoon salt

½ cup (115 g) butter, cut into small pieces

FOR THE FILLING

2 eggs

¼ cup (50 g) sugar

¼ to ½ teaspoon freshly ground white pepper

¾ cup (200 g) fresh goat cheese, at room temperature

½ cup (120 ml) heavy cream

1 pound (450 g) sweet cherries, such as Bing, Garnet, Lambert, or Black Tartarian, pitted and halved

TO MAKE THE CRUST: Preheat the oven to 375°F (190°C). In a medium bowl, using a fork, stir together the flour, almonds, sugar, and salt. Scatter the butter pieces over the flour mixture and, using your fingertips or a pastry blender, cut in the butter until the mixture is uniformly crumbly and resembles very coarse cornmeal. The mixture will look dry but will stick together when pressed between your fingers.

Pour the mixture into a 10-inch (25-cm) tart pan with 1 inch (2.5 cm) sides and a removable bottom. Use gentle fingertip pressure to press the dough up the sides of the pan, then gently press the remaining dough evenly over the bottom of the pan.

Bake the crust until pale golden, 15 to 20 minutes. Remove from oven and use the back of a soup spoon or the bottom of a small glass to smooth out any cracks that may have formed or to push crust back up the sides of the pan if it has slumped. This should take a few seconds.

TO MAKE THE FILLING: While the crust is baking, in a medium bowl, whisk together the eggs, sugar, and pepper until completely blended. In a separate bowl, beat the goat cheese with a wooden spoon or spatula to soften it, then gradually stir the cream into the cheese, mixing well. Stir the egg mixture into the cheese mixture to blend.

Reduce the oven temperature to 350°F (180°C). Scatter the cherries over the crust. Pour the cheese filling evenly over the cherries. Bake until the edges of the crust are deep golden and the filling is slightly puffed and just set, about 30 minutes. Cool in the pan on a wire rack for at least 30 minutes. The tart can be kept at room temperature for up to 8 hours. Refrigerate any leftovers.

QUARK CHEESECAKE

MAKES ONE 10-INCH (25-CM) CAKE, 12 TO 16 SERVINGS

DAIRY

Korcarz bakery and Finkelsztajn deli in the Marais, Paris' historic Jewish district, bake great pans of not-too-sweet, dense cheesecake that they sell by the slab. After long, slow baking, the cake's milk sugars burnish to a rich golden crust that I find irresistible. The cake bears little resemblance to American-style cream cheesecakes. This is classically Ashkenazic, and it shows up wherever European Jews have settled. The French make the cake with fromage blanc; the Italians, ricotta. Israelis use *gvinah levanah*, literally "white cheese," that derives from German quark, introduced by the Templers in the late nineteenth century, and that no home in Israel today would be without. All are fresh cheeses that work well in this recipe. Bake this cake the day before you want to serve it to allow the texture to "cure." For Shavuot, you can gild the lily with Strawberries and Roses (page 242), but I love it unadorned with an afternoon cup of strong tea.

FOR THE FILLING

3½ cups (750 g) quark

1 cup (230 grams) sour cream

6 eggs

¼ cup (30 g) cornstarch, sifted

¼ cup (30 g) unbleached all-purpose flour

¼ teaspoon baking powder

¼ teaspoon salt

1 cup (200 g) sugar

1 teaspoon vanilla extract

FOR THE CRUST

7 ounces (200 grams) Petit Beurre or Biscoff cookies, or vanilla wafers

7 tablespoons butter (100 grams), melted

Finely grated zest of 1 lemon

The night or morning before you want to make this cake, line a sieve with cheesecloth and set it over a bowl. Spoon the quark and sour cream for the filling into the prepared sieve, then transfer to the refrigerator to drain overnight.

The next day, preheat the oven to 400°F (200°C). Adjust the oven racks to the lowest and middle levels. Separate the eggs, placing the whites in the impeccably clean bowl of an electric mixer fitted with the whisk attachment and the yolks in a large bowl.

TO MAKE THE CRUST: Put the cookies in a large resealable plastic bag and crush to crumbs with a rolling pin. Put the crumbs in a medium bowl and stir in the butter and lemon zest. Pour into a 10-inch (25-cm) springform pan. Pat the mixture onto the bottom and halfway up the sides of the pan, pressing it into the corners so you get a sharper angle. The bottom of a small glass is perfect for this task.

TO MAKE THE FILLING: In a small bowl, sift together the cornstarch, flour, baking powder, and salt. Whip the egg whites on medium speed until foamy. Increase the speed to high and gradually add ½ cup (100 g) of the sugar until the egg whites mound in soft peaks. Lightly whisk the egg yolks. In the following order, whisk in the remaining ½ cup (100 g) sugar, the vanilla, and the quark and sour cream.

Fold one-fourth of the whipped egg whites into the cheese mixture to lighten, then gently fold in the flour mixture in 3 batches alternately with the remaining egg whites in 2 batches, beginning and ending with the flour and folding after each addition just until blended. Pour the filling into the prepared pan. Tap the pan on the counter once or twice to settle the filling.

Place a shallow pan of water on the lowest rack of the oven. Place the cake in the center of middle rack and bake for 5 minutes. Reduce the heat to 325°F (165°C) and

continue to bake until the top edges of the cake are golden brown and firm and the center is pale gold and jiggles slightly when the pan is shaken, 45 to 50 minutes. Turn off the oven and let the cake cool completely in the oven before removing it.

When the cake is cool, run a thin-bladed knife or spatula around the inside edge of the pan to loosen the cake sides, then unlatch and remove the pan ring. Cover the cake and refrigerate overnight. Remove from the refrigerator at least 30 minutes before serving. (The cake will keep refrigerated for up to 5 days.)

NICE ACCOMPANIMENTS FOR QUARK CHEESECAKE

Strawberries and Roses
(page 242)

Summer Fruit Compote with Lemon Verbena
(page 283)

Fresh Raspberry Sauce
(page 289)

Peppered Red Wine Fruit Compote
(page 112)

STRAWBERRIES AND ROSES

MAKES 6 SERVINGS

PAREVE

FOR THE ROSE GERANIUM SYRUP

1 cup (200 g) sugar

1 cup (240 ml) water

2 large rose geranium sprigs (with 4 or 5 leaves each)

4 cups (575 g) ripe strawberries

Handful of unsprayed fragrant rose petals

TO MAKE THE ROSE GERANIUM SYRUP: In a medium pot, whisk together the sugar and water and bring to a boil over medium-high heat. Simmer until the sugar is completely dissolved and the syrup is clear, 1 to 2 minutes. Remove from the heat. Tear the leaves from the rose geranium sprigs and crush or rub them with your fingers to release the oils. Drop them into the syrup along with the stems, cover the pot, and let stand until cooled, about 20 minutes. Strain through a mesh sieve and discard the solids. You should have about 1 cup (240 ml) syrup. (The syrup will keep refrigerated for up to 1 week.)

TO ASSEMBLE THE DISH: Hull the berries, quarter lengthwise, and place in a serving bowl. Add ½ cup (120 ml) of the cooled syrup. Let stand for 15 to 30 minutes. Use a fork to mash some of the berries. Add the rose petals and serve.

Think of this as a fresh, yet romantic nod to the eastern Mediterranean's traditional affection for rose-infused sweets. Strawberries and roses paired together intensify the berry's floral notes (makes sense; they are distant cousins). But instead of rose water, which can be too perfume-like, or even roses, which offer more visual than culinary power, this simple recipe uses fragrant rose geranium leaves to create a rose-forward syrup to enhance the ripe strawberries. Fresh rose petals are strewn over at the end for a gorgeous presentation. (Be sure to use unsprayed organic fragrant rose varieties suitable for culinary use.) Rose geranium has long been a garden favorite. Thomas Jefferson planted it at Monticello, and the native South African plant lined Victorian garden pathways, so that its leaves' fragrance was released when brushed by women's skirts. Rose geranium is available in late spring and summer at farmers' markets. Use leftover rose geranium syrup to sweeten iced tea or lemonade.

DAIRY VARIATION: Top individual servings of Strawberries and Roses with a cloud of rose geranium cream. Stir together 1 cup (240 ml) heavy cream and 3 tablespoons sugar. Bruise the leaves from 2 rose geranium sprigs and add to the cream. Cover tightly and infuse for 1 hour. Strain the cream through a mesh sieve and discard the solids. Whip the cream to soft peaks.

SEMOLINA AND WALNUT OIL CAKE WITH COFFEE HAWAIJ

MAKES ONE 5-BY-9-INCH (13-BY-23-CM) LOAF CAKE, 12 SERVINGS

PAREVE

Coffee *hawaij* is a Yemenite spice blend of ginger, cardamom, and cinnamon used to flavor coffee (not to be confused with savory *hawaij* for soups). Ground, it's great for baking (you can create your own blend, below). Together with coarse semolina and walnut oil, it makes this blond loaf unique. Walnut oil is a key ingredient here, so use a well-crafted, untoasted one with no off flavors. Coarse semolina is available at Greek markets; regular Cream of Wheat can be substituted. To make a nut-free version of this cake, use another oil, such as avocado, and omit the walnuts.

Mild oil, such as grapeseed or safflower, for the pan
1 cup (125 g) unbleached all-purpose flour
⅔ cup (146 g) coarse semolina
1 teaspoon baking powder
4 teaspoons coffee hawaij, or 1½ teaspoons each
    ground ginger and brown cardamom and
    1 teaspoon ground cinnamon
1 teaspoon salt
⅔ cup (165 ml) untoasted walnut oil
1 cup sugar
3 eggs
⅓ cup (40 g) chopped walnuts, lightly toasted

Preheat the oven to 350°F (180°C). Oil a 5-by-9-inch (13-by-23-cm) loaf pan.

Sift together flour, semolina, baking powder, hawaij, and salt. In an electric mixer fitted with the paddle attachment, beat together walnut oil and sugar on medium speed until thoroughly blended and creamy, 1 to 2 minutes. Add the eggs, one at a time, beating well after each addition until mixture is thick and creamy, 2 to 3 minutes total. On low speed, add the flour mixture in three batches, mixing after each addition just until blended. Pour the batter into the prepared pan and sprinkle the nuts evenly over the top.

Bake the cake until the top is golden, springs to the touch, and a toothpick inserted into the center comes out almost clean, about 45 minutes. Let cool in the pan on a wire rack for 5 minutes. Run a thin-bladed knife or spatula around the inside edge of the pan to loosen the cake sides. Invert the pan onto the rack, lift off the pan, and turn the cake top side up. Let cool completely before serving.

AFTERNOON COFFEE IN BEIT JANN

Inviting guests to afternoon coffee is an act of great hospitality in the Middle East. On a trip to northern Israel, I enjoyed the Druze version of the custom—twice in one afternoon. My husband Ralph and I accompanied my cousins to visit a friend in Beit Jann, an ancient Druze village clinging to a steep mountainside. (The Druze are an Arabic-speaking tightly knit sect whose religion includes elements of Islam, Christianity, and Judaism.) After a lavish late lunch, we retired to the living room for dessert and coffee scented with cardamom. Like Turkish, Greek, and Arab versions, the thick coffee was prepared in a long-handled *finjan* and served in tiny cups. Later, on a walk, we met another acquaintance who was renovating his home. Still spattered with cement, he insisted we come for coffee, leading us through the construction to the balcony, where his wife quickly assembled the traditional tray. As the sun set, we sat on the porch, sipping coffee and chatting in a mix of languages.

July & August

THE LONG, HOT DAYS OF SUMMER

Summer ingredients, hot days, balmy nights, and the bold flavors of Israel and the eastern Mediterranean are a match made in heaven. Brined pickles and salted snacks whet the appetite for meats, fish, and vegetables straight from the grill. Cold summer soups, crisp salads, and refreshing dessert sorbets and sundaes are exactly what we want now.

But this is also the season when farmers worry most about dwindling water. Grasses turn straw yellow, hillsides are parched, and the risk of fire is great. In the midst of this comes Tisha b'Av, the remembrance of the destruction by fire of the first and second Temples in Jerusalem during Babylonian and Roman rule, respectively. For observant Jews, it is a time of mourning and fasting that concludes with a forward look to the coming new year, when the year's cycle of seasons will begin again.

July & August

PICKLED OKRA

MAKES 1 QUART OR 2 PINT JARS

PAREVE/VEGAN

Okra, with its asparagus-like flavor, is a favorite Sephardic vegetable from the late summer through fall, and is often braised and served over rice. Think Middle Eastern gumbo without the pork or shellfish. A member of the mallow family (the original source for marshmallows), okra acts as a thickener in stews. But not everyone likes its mucilaginous texture. One way to minimize this quality is to turn okra into crisp pickles, accented with lemon zest and juice and red jalapeño chiles. Use the firmest, smallest okra pods you can find, preferably no bigger than your pinkie. A mix of purple or red and green okra is pretty; just know that the brine will bleach the purple ones a pale lavender.

1 pound (450 g) small okra, 2 to 3 inches
    (5 to 7.5 cm) long
1 to 2 large lemons
2 to 3 red (ripe) jalapeño chiles
4 large cloves garlic, sliced
¾ cup (180 ml) white wine vinegar
1½ cups (360 ml) water
3 tablespoons kosher salt
1 tablespoon sugar

Rinse the okra and rub dry with paper towels to remove the sticky fuzz. Trim the stem ends, but do not cut away the caps. Pack the okra into a 1-quart (1-L) jar or two 1-pint (500-ml) jars, with the pointed tip of some of the pods upward and others downward to fit. Use a vegetable peeler to remove the zest of the lemons in long, wide strips. Push the strips vertically into the jar(s), using a bamboo skewer if needed to guide them. Squeeze enough juice from the lemon(s) to equal ¼ cup (60 ml).

Cut the chiles lengthwise into quarters, leaving the stems attached for effect. Slide the peppers, including their seeds if you like your pickles spicy, into the jar(s), using a bamboo skewer to guide them. Scatter in the garlic slices and give the jar(s) a shake to help the slices settle in.

In a medium pot, combine vinegar, water, lemon juice, salt, and sugar and bring to a boil over high heat. Cook for 2 minutes, then pour the hot brine over the okra, leaving ½-inch (12-mm) headspace. Rotate the jar a few times and push down on the okra to release air bubbles.

Cap jar(s) tightly and let stand in a sunny spot for the day. Refrigerate okra 1 to 2 days before serving. It will keep in the refrigerator for up to 1 month. (For more on quick pickles, see Kitchen Note, page 125.)

PICKLED GREEN TOMATOES

MAKES 1 QUART (1 L)

PAREVE

These quick pickles offer the taste and crunch of the deli favorite, yet retain a summer freshness. Although ready after a day of brining, the pickle continues to develop flavors over time. Unripe tomatoes range from rock-hard green to those with a blush of color and juice. If you have the former, allow an extra day of brining to get a satisfying pickle. For an interesting variation, pickle red but not-quite-ripe tomatoes in brine for about an hour as a colorful and sweeter contrast to tangier green pickled tomatoes.

1½ pounds (680 g) green (unripe) tomatoes (4 or 5)

4 large cloves garlic, sliced

8 whole dill sprigs (including stems)

1 cup (240 ml) cider vinegar

1½ cups (360 ml) water

3 tablespoons kosher salt

1 tablespoon sugar

1 teaspoon celery seeds

½ teaspoon mustard seeds

Core the tomatoes, then cut each tomato through the stem end into 6 or 8 wedges. Pack the wedges into a 1-quart (1-L) jar or two 1-pint (500-ml) jars along with the garlic and dill. In a saucepan, combine the vinegar, water, salt, sugar, celery seeds, and mustard seeds and bring to a boil over high heat. Boil for 2 minutes, then pour the hot brine over the tomatoes, leaving ½ inch (12-mm) headspace. You may have leftover brine, but make sure that all the celery and mustard seeds get into the jar(s).

Cap the jar(s) tightly and place in a sunny spot for the day. Refrigerate the tomatoes for at least 24 hours before serving. They will keep in the refrigerator for up to 1 month. (For more about quick pickles, see Kitchen Note, page 125.)

THE MEZZE TABLE

Mezze (also spelled meze) are small savory dishes typically offered as an assortment. According to Middle Eastern and Levantine cooking expert Claudia Roden, mezze are meant to whet the appetite and accompany aperitifs. Another Middle Eastern culinary expert, Clifford Wright, asserts that mezze are not hors d'oeuvres but a table of savories from which diners convivially help themselves according to taste. Either way, the concept is perfect for today's small-plate style, whether as one or two appetizers before dinner or as an abundant buffet meal. Put together a mix of sours (pickles, olives), spreads, salads, cheeses, cured or salted fish or meats, and flatbreads. The obvious choices are the seasonal starters and salads throughout this book, but many side and main dishes can also be adapted for this purpose as you can see in the following photo. Mezze-friendly foods are well suited to gin or vodka cocktails—cucumber martini (Eastern Standard and Eastside), Negroni, or Tom Collins—as well as the more traditional pairing of anise-flavored arak, ouzo, or pastis.

FROM LEFT:
TOP ROW: LABNEH (PAGE 22), ISRAELI SALAD (PAGE 264), ISRAELI EGGPLANT CAVIAR (PAGE 253),
OLIVES WITH ZA'ATAR AND CITRUS (PAGE 82)

MIDDLE ROW: MARINATED CHICKPEA SALAD (PAGE 261), AUTUMN SLAW (PAGE 41),
PICKLED OKRA (PAGE 248), "MANTA RAY" CEVICHE (PAGE 212)

BOTTOM ROW: MATBOUCHA (PAGE 32), QUICK-PICKLED BABY TURNIPS AND BEETS (PAGE 125),
PICKLED GREEN TOMATOES (PAGE 249), PITA TRIANGLES WITH ZA'ATAR (PAGE 161)

ISRAELI EGGPLANT CAVIAR WRAPS

MAKES 2 CUPS (540 G) CAVIAR, ENOUGH FOR 24 BITE-SIZE WRAPS, 8 SERVINGS

PAREVE/VEGAN OR DAIRY

This isn't baba ghanoush, the Middle Eastern smooth eggplant-tahini dip. This is a chopped eggplant "caviar," loaded with lemon, garlic, cilantro, parsley, and mint. You can scoop this dip with pita, but for an exciting and more flavorful presentation (not to mention, lower calorie and gluten-free), serve with a mound of fragrant summer basil or tart sorrel leaves to make bite-size wraps. Feta cheese is a nice addition.

2 medium globe eggplants, about 1 pound
    (450 g) each
3 or 4 large cloves garlic, slivered
1 teaspoon ground cumin
Kosher or sea salt and freshly ground black pepper
¼ cup (60 ml) extra-virgin olive oil
1 to 2 lemons
¼ cup (15 g) chopped fresh cilantro and mint, or
    oregano, or Italian parsley
24 to 30 medium or large fresh basil leaves or
    other small wrapping green, such as lettuce,
    sorrel, or radicchio
Feta cheese, in chunks, for serving (optional)

Preheat the oven to 400°F (200°C). Cut the eggplants crosswise into slices ½ inch (12 mm) thick. Make 2 parallel slits each about 1 inch (2.5 cm) long in the center of each slice. Insert 1 garlic sliver into each slit, then season the eggplant slices with the cumin and salt. Slather the olive oil in the bottom of a baking pan large enough to accommodate the slices (or use 2 baking pans). Arrange the slices snugly in the pan(s)—a little overlapping is okay—turning each slice to coat it with the oil.

Roast the eggplant slices until they are soft and the bottom sides are browned, about 30 minutes. Using a spatula, turn the slices and continue to roast until quite tender, about 10 minutes more.

Pile the roasted eggplant in a bowl to steam and soften. Squeeze the juice of half a lemon into the pan(s), scrape up any brown bits, and add to the bowl. When the eggplant is cool enough to handle, chop it finely and place in a serving bowl. Stir in cilantro and mint. Season with salt, pepper, and with additional lemon juice if needed.

If time permits, let the caviar stand for 1 hour to allow the flavors to blend. Taste and adjust the seasoning with lemon juice, pepper, and/or salt if needed. (The caviar can be made up to 1 day ahead, covered, and refrigerated. Bring to room temperature before serving.)

Serve with a mound of basil leaves and feta cheese. To eat, place about 2 teaspoons caviar and a bit of cheese on each leaf, wrap, and pop the packet into your mouth.

SHOPPING TIP: Just-picked eggplants that aren't overly mature will have no trace of bitterness. Eggplants come in many colors, shapes, and sizes at farmers' markets from midsummer through early fall. My favorite is the purple-and-white-skinned Rosa Bianca, which has creamy white flesh and few seeds. Look for firm, shiny eggplants that are heavy for their size, are free of any soft spots, and have a fresh-looking calyx.

SALT-GRILLED FRESH CHICKPEAS IN THEIR PODS

MAKES 6 TO 8 SERVINGS

PAREVE/VEGAN

Before they turn the familiar tan as they mature and dry, young chickpeas are bright green, tender, and delicious raw or cooked. They show up at farmers' markets and Middle Eastern and Indian groceries in early summer, in their pods and still on the branch. Partially bury the little pods in coarse salt in a skillet and put it on the grill for a great cocktail-hour nibble (think peanuts in the shell). Salty snacks, *pitzuchim* in Hebrew, are popular in Israel, where vendors at traditional markets, like Shuk Levinsky or HaCarmel in Tel Aviv, offer an astonishing array. The grill adds the element of smoke, but you can also prepare fresh chickpeas on the stove or in the oven. The salt-grilling technique is also terrific with shishito or Padrón peppers.

3 to 4 cups fresh chickpeas in their pods
    (about 1 pound/450 g on the branch)
½ cup (115 g) sel gris, or ⅓ cup (100 g) kosher salt

Heat a grill to medium-high (or preheat the oven to 425°F/220°C). Toss the chickpeas and salt together in a cast-iron skillet or other heatproof, ovenproof shallow pan (a paella pan works great). Place the pan on the grill rack and cook the pods, tossing them occasionally, until they are blackened in spots and slightly dusty from the salt, about 10 minutes or 15 minutes in the oven.

Serve directly from the skillet. The pods should be easy to split open to reveal the 1 or 2 chickpeas nestled inside.

GRILLED FIGS WITH POMEGRANATE MOLASSES AND AGED SHEEP'S MILK CHEESE

MAKES 6 FIRST-COURSE OR 12 COCKTAIL SERVINGS

DAIRY

Full of contrasting flavors and textures, this is a lovely appetizer or cheese course on a hot night, served with a lightly fruity Sauvignon Blanc or rosé. Years ago, Karen Bates, daughter of the founding family of the French Laundry in Yountville, California, taught me the trick of toasting black peppercorns to release their fruity notes. The recipe calls for 1 tablespoon peppercorns, far more than you'll need here. Save the rest to use wherever you'd like a little toasted warmth.

1 tablespoon black peppercorns

1-pint (500-ml) basket ripe figs (about 9 figs)

About 2 tablespoons extra-virgin olive oil

Kosher or sea salt

6 ounces (170 g) aged sheep's milk cheese, such as Manchego, kashkaval, kasseri, or Abbaye de Belloc

Finishing salt, such as Maldon sea salt or fleur de sel

2 to 3 tablespoons pomegranate molasses

In a small skillet, toast the peppercorns over medium heat until they are fragrant and begin to pop, 5 to 7 minutes. Let cool briefly, then crush with the back of a spoon or broad knife handle.

Heat the grill to medium-high, or place a stove-top grill pan over medium heat. Cut the figs in half lengthwise, brush both sides of each half with oil, and season the cut sides with kosher salt and a little of the pepper.

Place the fig halves, cut side down, on the grill rack and grill until they are caramelized on the underside, about 2 minutes. Turn and grill on the second side until lightly browned, 1 to 2 minutes. Place cut side up to cool.

To serve as a first course, cut the cheese into 6 equal slabs or break into chunks, then divide evenly among 6 plates. Divide the figs, cut side up, among the plates. Season the figs and the cheese with the finishing salt and pepper. Add an artistic drizzle of pomegranate molasses over the figs. Or, assemble all the components on a platter and serve family style.

SHOPPING TIP: Figs do not ripen or sweeten off the tree, so look for ones that are appetizingly soft and use them within a day or two of purchase. A few sugar cracks are a good sign, but avoid figs with signs of mold. Black Mission and green Kadota and Adriatic are flavorful fig varieties. The grilling and glazing methods in this recipe will improve less-than-fabulous figs, but if all you can find are very firm (and expensive) figs, use another fruit. Juicy white peaches or nectarines are also delicious prepared this way.

BLANCHED AMARANTH WITH OLIVE OIL AND LEMON

MAKES 8 SERVINGS

PAREVE/VEGAN

Ancient amaranth is an often-overlooked green that deserves attention. Like its relative quinoa, amaranth produces high-protein seeds that are used in cooking and ground into flour. The nutritious leaves have a nut- or grain-like flavor and are a favorite ingredient in many cuisines, from the Caribbean to Southeast Asia. In the Mediterranean region, amaranth is often steamed or blanched and simply dressed with a good olive oil and a squeeze of lemon. This dish comes from Mary Sue Milliken, chef-owner of Border Grill restaurants, and is very nice with a piece of feta cheese on the side for a dairy lunch on a hot day.

4 pounds (1.8 kg) red or green amaranth
Extra-virgin olive oil for drizzling
Kosher or sea salt and freshly ground black pepper
1 lemon
¼ pound (115 g) feta cheese, cut into 8 slices
    (optional)

Pluck the amaranth leaves from their stems (you can leave the ones at the tender top part of the stems attached). Cook the amaranth in a pot of boiling salted water for 2 minutes. Taste a stem, if you have included any. If the stem is not yet tender, cook the amaranth for 1 to 2 minutes longer. Drain well and spread the leaves and a handful of ice cubes on a towel so the leaves cool quickly. Discard the ice and transfer the leaves to a clean towel to dry.

Arrange the amaranth on a platter or individual salad plates, drizzle with 1 to 2 tablespoons olive oil, and season with salt and pepper. Just before serving, halve the lemon and add a generous squeeze of lemon juice. Serve cool with the feta cheese, if desired.

SHOPPING TIP: Red and variegated amaranth leaves will "bleed" when cooked; stick with the green variety if this bothers you. Look for lush bunches with stalks that haven't yet produced a lot of seed-laden flowers, an indication that the leaves are already overly mature. Amaranth is available at Asian and Latin groceries and farmers' markets.

VINEGARED POTATOES WITH BAY LAUREL, GARLIC, AND ALEPPO PEPPER

MAKES 8 SERVINGS

PAREVE/VEGAN

Cooking potatoes in vinegar allows the tang to permeate the potato fully and prevents overcooking (the pectin in the potato breaks down more slowly in an acidic environment), so that potatoes hold up well in salads. It's a technique I learned from Italian cooking expert Giuliano Bugialli at his home overlooking the Great Synagogue of Florence (Tempio Maggiore). Call this a salad or a side; either way, it is delicious, intriguing, and mayo-free.

5 cups (1.2 L) water

1 cup (240 ml) plus 2 tablespoons red wine vinegar

Kosher or sea salt

3 pounds (1.4 kg) waxy or all-purpose potatoes, such as Yukon Gold, Red Rose, or French Fingerlings

6 cloves garlic, peeled but left whole

⅓ cup (75 ml) extra-virgin olive oil

½ to 1 teaspoon Aleppo pepper or sweet, hot, or smoked paprika

6 bay leaves

½ cup (30 g) chopped fresh Italian parsley

In a wide pot, combine the water and 1 cup (240 ml) of the vinegar, bring to a boil over high heat, and add 2 tablespoons salt. Peel the potatoes, halve them, and cut into slices ¼ inch (6 mm) thick. Add the potatoes and garlic to the boiling water, cover, and cook until the potatoes are tender, 15 to 20 minutes. Drain well. Mince the garlic.

In the same pot or in a large skillet, heat the olive oil over medium-low heat. Stir in the remaining 2 tablespoons vinegar along with the garlic, Aleppo pepper, bay leaves, parsley, and 1 teaspoon salt. Add the potatoes and cook, tossing gently to coat the potatoes evenly, until the dish is warmed through, 1 to 2 minutes.

Serve warm or at room temperature. Taste and season with salt, pepper, and olive oil as desired. (This dish may be made several hours ahead and kept at room temperature.)

MARINATED CHICKPEA SALAD (FACING PAGE) WITH (FROM LEFT) TAHINI (PAGE 23), LEMON SAUCE (PAGE 23), AND MATBOUCHA (PAGE 32)

MARINATED CHICKPEA SALAD WITH TAHINI AND LEMON SAUCE

MAKES 8 TO 10 SERVINGS

PAREVE/VEGAN

Think of this as a deconstructed falafel sandwich with all the robust flavors—fresh, pickled, spicy—and textures of the eastern Mediterranean's favorite street food, but without the deep-frying. Lemon sauce is a popular condiment for Arab-style hummus and adds a nice jolt to this salad (and other dishes!). This summer salad is robust enough for a main dish and zesty enough for a mezze table. It is divine with home-cooked chickpeas (see page 18), but good-quality canned chickpeas, such as Al Wadi brand, will do. In winter, skip the tomatoes and cucumbers and serve the salad on Tu b'Shvat or Purim—legend has it that Esther subsisted on chickpeas to avoid breaking kashrut.

3 cups (490 g) drained cooked chickpeas, or 2 cans (1 pound/450 g each) chickpeas, drained and rinsed

⅓ cup (75 ml) olive oil

1 teaspoon ground cumin

½ teaspoon ground brown cardamom

½ teaspoon Aleppo pepper, or more to taste

1 teaspoon salt

2 cloves garlic

2 tablespoons fresh lemon juice

1 pita bread, split into 2 rounds and dried in the oven, or a handful of Pita Triangles with Za'atar (page 161)

2 medium tomatoes (about ½ pound/225 g), diced

1 to 2 cucumbers, preferably Persian, about ¼ pound (115 g) total, diced

1 cup (150 g) Vinegared Cabbage (page 22)

½ cup (70 g) diced dill pickles, in ¼-inch (6-mm) pieces

¼ cup (45 g) Quick-Pickled Baby Turnips and Beets (page 125) or other spicy pickled vegetable, in thin slices or batons

⅓ cup (20 g) chopped fresh Italian parsley

¼ cup (15 g) chopped fresh cilantro

Tahini Sauce (page 23)

Lemon Sauce (page 23)

½ cup (120 ml) Matboucha (page 32), optional

Place the chickpeas in a nonreactive bowl large enough to hold all the ingredients. In a small pot, combine the olive oil, cumin, cardamom, Aleppo pepper, and salt. Crush the garlic with a garlic press and add to the pot. Warm the oil mixture over medium-low heat. When hot, remove from the heat, let stand for 5 minutes, and then pour over the chickpeas along with the lemon juice. Let stand for at least 30 minutes (use this time to prepare the remaining ingredients) or up to 4 hours.

At least 10 minutes before serving, break the pita into large bite-size pieces and add to the bowl. Add the tomatoes, cucumbers, cabbage, pickles, turnips and beets, parsley, and cilantro and toss well. Top with a generous pour of Tahini Sauce or serve on the side along with the Lemon Sauce and with Matboucha, if desired.

TOMATOES WITH SARDINES AND RICE

MAKES 6 TO 8 SERVINGS

FISH

ere's a fresh take on traditional stuffed and baked tomatoes. Made with ripe raw tomatoes and canned sardines (or tuna), this is a substantial first course or, accompanied by hard-boiled eggs and an arugula side salad, a delightful summer supper. Canned sardines are a favorite pantry item in Jewish kitchens everywhere. Use good-quality ones from Spain, Portugal, or California. I like a starchy medium-grain rice here, such as the varieties used for risotto. Although you can prepare the components a few hours ahead, the dish is best assembled just before serving. You can easily halve this recipe or omit the fish for a pareve/vegan meal.

6 to 8 ripe tomatoes, preferably with stems attached, 3 pounds (1.4 kg) total

Kosher or sea salt

1 cup (200 g) rice for risotto, such as Arborio, Carnaroli, or Vialone Nano

1 medium-size red or yellow onion, chopped

4 tablespoons (60 ml) extra-virgin olive oil

2 tablespoons red wine vinegar

Sel gris and freshly ground black pepper

½ cup (15 g) fresh Italian parsley leaves, chopped

3 cans (4 ounces/115 g each) good-quality sardines, drained

Slice off the stem end of each tomato at the point where the tomato widens; reserve the caps. Using a paring knife and a grapefruit spoon or a vegetable drill (see page 20), scoop out the pulp and juices, leaving a shell ¼ inch (6 mm) thick. Reserve the pulp and juices. Season the tomato cavities with kosher salt and let stand, cut side up, to draw out the juices, about 15 minutes. Turn cut side down on a rimmed plate to drain for 15 minutes. Add any juices that accumulated to the reserved pulp.

Meanwhile, cook the rice in boiling salted water until cooked through but still chewy, about 12 minutes. Pour into a sieve to drain. You should have about 3 cups (560 g) rice.

In a large skillet, cook the onion in 2 tablespoons of the oil with a little salt and pepper over medium heat until soft and pale golden, 7 to 10 minutes, lowering the heat as needed to keep the onion from browning. Add the tomato pulp and juices, breaking up any large pieces of tomato. Add the vinegar and ½ teaspoon sel gris. Turn the heat to medium-high and cook until the juices thicken, 2 to 3 minutes. Stir in the rice and cook until it is well coated and tinted pink, about 2 minutes. Stir in the parsley, 1 to 2 tablespoons olive oil to moisten, and sel gris and pepper to taste. Set aside to cool. (The rice mixture may be made 1 to 2 hours ahead and kept at room temperature.)

Break the sardines into chunks. When the rice is cool to the touch, gently fold in the sardines. Stuff the mixture into the tomatoes, using ⅓ to ½ cup (65 to 95 g) for each tomato. Place the caps at a jaunty angle. The dish may be fully assembled up to 1 hour before serving.

KITCHEN NOTE: Canned sardines are also delicious smashed on black or whole grain bread. Season with a squeeze of lemon and a pinch of finishing salt, and top with slivered radishes.

CAULIFLOWER "STEAKS" WITH HAWAIJ AND TAHINI

MAKES 6 TO 8 SERVINGS

PAREVE/VEGAN

Cauliflower and tahini are a popular pairing in Israel, and rightly so, for they share a nutlike flavor. Hawaij, a Yemenite spice blend of cumin, black pepper, turmeric, and cardamom (and sometimes coriander or cinnamon), accents the meaty nature of cauliflower, making this a terrific pareve or vegan center of the plate for a summer barbecue. (And use a grill pan on the stove to make this dish all winter long.) *Sel gris*, the briny French sea salt, is an especially delicious finishing accent here.

2 large cauliflowers (about 4 pounds/1.8 kg) total
⅔ cup (165 ml) olive oil
1 tablespoon hawaij spice blend
1½ teaspoons kosher or sea salt
Finishing salt, such as sel gris
Tahini Sauce (page 23)
Chopped fresh Italian parsley
1 lemon, cut into wedges

Cut the cauliflowers through the stem end into slabs ½ to ¾ inch (12 mm to 2 cm) thick, leaving the greens attached. Cut off and discard the tough stem end from each slab, but leave enough of the stem attached to keep each slab intact. You'll get 3 or 4 large "steaks," 5 or 6 smaller "medallions" 2 to 4 inches (5 to 10 cm) in diameter, and some extra small bits from each cauliflower.

Line a sheet pan with paper towels and set near the stove. Bring a large skillet or sauté pan of water to a boil and salt generously. Working in batches, add the cauliflower and cook until just crisp-tender, about 3 minutes. Using tongs or a large spatula, carefully lift out the steaks and medallions and place on the prepared pan. Use a slotted spoon or spider to remove any small cauliflower bits and set aside. (This step can be done up to 1 day ahead and the cauliflower stored covered in the refrigerator.)

Heat the grill to medium-high. In a small pot, warm together the olive oil, hawaij, and kosher salt. Remove the pot from the heat and let stand for a few minutes. Place the steaks and medallions in a single layer in a shallow pan. Pour the oil mixture evenly over the cauliflower and use a brush to distribute the seasonings. Turn the cauliflower and brush the other side with the mixture that has collected in the pan.

If you like, pan-fry the extra bits of cauliflower in a little oil and salt until nicely browned.

Grill the cauliflower, using a large spatula to turn the pieces once halfway through the cooking, until tender and browned, about 4 minutes on each side. Season with sel gris and top with Tahini Sauce, parsley, and the browned cauliflower bits. Serve with lemon wedges on the side.

ITALIAN VARIATION: Liberally brush parboiled cauliflower with olive oil seasoned with kosher or sea salt and freshly ground black pepper. Grill as above and serve with salsa verde (see Blistered Chicories with Tuna and Salsa Verde, page 144).

ISRAELI SALAD

MAKES 6 TO 8 SERVINGS

PAREVE/VEGAN

This is the go-to salad for any Israeli meal, especially breakfast, where it accompanies fresh cheeses, omelets, or pickled fish. The salad always includes tomatoes, cucumbers, and parsley, but may also contain kohlrabi, a bit of onion, and red or green sweet peppers. The choice is yours. My Iraqi family often adds minced hot pickled peppers to the mix. One thing you won't find here is lettuce; that's a different salad altogether. Some people dress the salad, others simply season with salt. Israeli salads are judged by the quality of their ingredients and the fineness of the dice. Here's a recipe to give you an idea of quantities.

1 pound (450 g) ripe tomatoes or large, oblong cherry tomatoes, such as Juliet

½ pound (225 g) cucumbers, preferably Persian (about 4 small)

6 ounces (170 g) kohlrabi (3 to 4 ounces/85 to 115 g peeled)

1 medium red bell pepper

Small piece of red onion (about 1 ounce/30 g)

¼ cup (15 g) chopped fresh Italian parsley, or more to taste

2 small pickled peppers, minced (optional)

Extra-virgin olive oil

1 lemon

Kosher or sea salt

Freshly ground black pepper (optional)

Cut the tomatoes into ½-inch (12-mm) dice and place in a salad bowl. Leave the cucumber unpeeled or peel, as you like, cut into ½-inch (12-mm) or smaller dice, and add to the bowl. Do the same for the kohlrabi and the bell pepper. Cut the onion into very small dice and add to the bowl along with the parsley and pickled peppers, if using. Drizzle the salad with olive oil and add a healthy squeeze of lemon juice. Season with salt and pepper and toss.

SHOPPING TIP: There are many more kinds of cucumbers available than the shrink-wrapped English hothouse type. I like Persian cucumbers, which are typically small-to-medium size, sweet (for a cucumber), and crisp-tender. Look for firm cucumbers with no soft spots or shriveling. Plant stress and cold weather trigger bitterness, so if you are buying very fresh, not overly large cucumbers in summer, you should be fine. Their high water content makes cucumbers perishable; use within a few days of purchase, and don't store them in plastic. Instead, to absorb excess moisture, wrap cucumbers in paper towels before refrigerating.

HAND-GRATED CHILLED TOMATO SOUP WITH "ISRAELI SALAD" TOPPING

MAKES 6 SERVINGS

PAREVE/VEGAN

The same ingredients you find in a classic Israeli salad—tomatoes, cucumbers, onions, parsley, and salt—deliver a completely different result here. This chilled soup is all about fully ripe tomatoes, plus a little something for crunch. Use juicy tomato varieties with a good sweet-acid balance, such as Early Girl or Celebrity hybrid types or Brandywine heirlooms. (Avoid meaty Roma-type tomatoes for this dish, which taste better cooked and will produce a puree that is too thick.) You can adjust the flavors of the soup by adding a few sweet or acidic tomatoes to your mix. Using a box grater and sieve is a simple way to seed and puree tomatoes. You can also use a food mill, or peel and seed tomatoes and hand chop finely. But don't use a blender for this recipe, which will make the soup too frothy.

FOR THE SOUP

4 to 5 pounds (1.8 to 2.3 kg) ripe tomatoes
1 to 2 teaspoons kosher salt
1 teaspoon red wine vinegar (optional)

FOR THE TOPPING

1 or 2 medium-size cucumbers, preferably
    Persian, about ¼ pound/115 g total
Small piece of red onion, minced
¼ cup (15 g) finely chopped Italian parsley
1 small jalapeño chile or pickled pepper, minced
A squeeze of lemon
Extra-virgin olive oil for finishing
Finishing salt, such as Maldon sea salt or fleur de sel

TO MAKE THE SOUP: Set a sieve over a large bowl. Cut the tomatoes in half crosswise. Holding each tomato half over the sieve, use your finger to scoop out the seeds so that any juices fall into the bowl. Using the back of a spoon, push through any pulp remaining in the sieve. Remove the sieve from the bowl and discard the seeds.

Set a box grater in the bowl and grate each tomato half on the cut side, rubbing it over the large holes until you reach the skin. You should have about 5 cups (900 g) of grated tomato. Discard the skins. Stir in 1 teaspoon of the salt. Cover and let stand at least for 1 hour, refrigerating for part of the time to chill the soup lightly.

TO MAKE THE TOPPING: Halve the cucumbers lengthwise, then seed, peel, and chop very finely. Transfer to a bowl, add the onion, parsley, chile, and lemon juice, season with salt, and mix well.

When ready to serve, taste the soup. It should have a good sweet-acid balance. Add the vinegar if needed, or a touch more salt. If the soup seems too thick or intense, stir in a few ice cubes. Ladle the soup into individual bowls and top each serving with a small mound of the topping, a drizzle of olive oil, and a sprinkle of salt.

GREEN MELON AND TOMATO GAZPACHO

MAKES 8 SERVINGS

PAREVE/VEGAN

Sweet-savory melon salads, with or without tomatoes, are an Israeli summer favorite that have become popular in many parts of the world. I've taken the concept and turned it into a summer soup that is as refreshing to look at as it is to eat. Use Israeli green-fleshed melons, such as Ha'Ogen and Galia, or a ripe honeydew, and ripe green tomatoes, such as Evergreen or Green Zebra, or any yellow variety.

4 cups (680 g) ripe green melon pieces, from 1½- to 2-pound (680- to 900-g) melon, such as Ha'Ogen, Galia, or honeydew

1 pound (450 g) ripe Green Zebra or Evergreen tomatoes

1 small white onion, coarsely chopped

1½ cups (115 g) torn crust-free, stale French bread

Leaves from 4 mint sprigs (about 12 leaves)

Juice of 3 to 4 limes

1 tablespoon avocado or other mild oil

½ to 1 small jalapeño chile, cut into small pieces

1 to 1½ teaspoons kosher or sea salt

1 cup (240 ml) water

1 Persian cucumber

Set aside ½ cup (85 g) of the melon pieces and place the remaining melon in a blender. Peel the tomatoes (page 17). Cut the tomatoes in half crosswise and squeeze out the seeds over a sieve set over the blender jar to catch the juices. Cut the tomatoes into chunks.

Add the tomatoes, onion, bread, mint, juice of 3 limes, the oil, half the chopped chile, 1 teaspoon of the salt, and ½ cup (120 ml) of the water to the blender. Blend to a rough puree, adding water as needed to create a soup-like consistency. Cover and chill for at least 1 hour.

Taste the soup and add more salt and lime as needed. Meanwhile, mince the remaining chile pieces, cut the reserved melon into tiny dice, and place them in a medium bowl. Halve the cucumber lengthwise, then seed, peel, cut into tiny dice, and add to the bowl. Stir to mix.

Serve the gazpacho in iced bowls or mugs and top each serving with a little of the chile-melon-cucumber mixture.

CANTALOUPE VARIATION: Make this soup with cantaloupe or other orange-fleshed melons and use ripe red, orange, or yellow tomatoes.

CHILLED SORREL AND CUCUMBER SOUP

MAKES 6 TO 8 SERVINGS

DAIRY

Evocative of the Bulgarian yogurt soup *tarator* and the eastern European *schav* (sour spinach or sorrel soup), this soup combines all things tart—sorrel, lemon, yogurt, and sumac—with the delicate aroma and refreshing qualities of cucumber plus the earthy undertones of nuts and dill. Add kasha, egg, and potatoes to turn this soup into a main course. Use Persian cucumbers if possible; they are flavorful and crunchy.

1½ pounds (680 g) French (common) sorrel (about 3 large bunches)

1½ pounds (680 g) cucumbers, preferably Persian (about 6 cucumbers)

2 small cloves garlic, peeled but left whole

2 tablespoons finely chopped fresh dill

Kosher or sea salt

3 cups (735 g) whole-milk or low-fat plain yogurt

⅓ to ½ cup (75 to 120 ml) cold water

1 lemon

2 teaspoons ground sumac

¼ teaspoon finishing salt, such as fleur de sel

Walnut oil for finishing

½ cup (25 g) snipped fresh chives or garlic chives, or a mix

½ cup (65 g) toasted (see page 18) and chopped walnuts

Stem the sorrel by holding the stem in one hand and pulling down the leaf with the other. Peel the cucumbers, halve lengthwise, and scrape out the seeds with a small spoon. Cut the cucumbers crosswise into chunks.

Fit a food processor with a metal S blade. With the motor running, drop in the garlic cloves to mince. Add the sorrel, cucumbers, dill, and 1 teaspoon salt and process to a rough puree. Add the yogurt and process to a smooth, light green puree flecked with herbs.

Scrape the mixture into a large bowl or pitcher. Stir in enough cold water to thin the soup to the consistency of light cream. Add a generous squeeze of lemon juice. Taste, then add kosher salt and/or lemon juice as needed for a tasty, refreshing flavor balance. Cover and chill thoroughly. (The soup can be made to this point up to a day ahead and refrigerated.)

In a small bowl, stir together the sumac and finishing salt. Taste the soup and adjust the seasoning with kosher salt. Pour the soup into individual bowls and top each serving with a drizzle of walnut oil and about 1 tablespoon each of the chives and walnuts. Sprinkle a good pinch of the sumac salt over each serving.

MAIN DISH VARIATION: Stir 2 cups (340 g) cooked buckwheat groats—kasha, (see page 9)—into the soup. Ladle into bowls and top as above, adding ½ hard-boiled egg, chopped, to each serving. Sprinkle the sumac salt over the egg, and serve with a side of cold boiled potatoes.

KITCHEN NOTE: The sumac-and-finishing-salt seasoning mix is a terrific condiment any time you want to add a tart and salty note to savory dishes.

SNAP BEAN AND RED QUINOA TABBOULEH

MAKES 6 TO 8 SERVINGS

PAREVE/VEGAN

Every "tabbouleh culture" has strong opinions about how to prepare this dish: the ratio of bulgur to herbs, how to chop the parsley and mint. This refreshing tomato-less version breaks all the rules. It uses protein-rich, gluten-free quinoa (red is prettiest and most flavorful in this dish) and height-of-the-season summer snap beans. It's more like a green bean salad with quinoa than the other way around. The dish is inspired by one I ate at Dallal, a Tel Aviv restaurant named for the famous dance school founded by Susanna Dallal.

1½ cups (360 ml) water

⅔ cup (125 g) red quinoa, well rinsed

¾ pound (340 g) snap beans, stemmed and cut into ¼-inch (6-mm) pieces

½ pound (225 g) cucumbers, preferably Persian (2 to 4)

1 bunch skinny green onions

Leaves from 1 bunch Italian parsley

1 small bunch mint

1 to 2 lemons

Kosher or flaky sea salt, such as Maldon sea salt, and freshly ground black pepper

¼ cup (60 ml) extra-virgin olive oil

In a covered 2-quart (2-L) pot, bring the water to a boil over high heat. Stir in the quinoa, bring back to a boil, re-cover, reduce heat to medium, and cook until the grains have absorbed all the water and the small tails of the outer germs begin to spiral out, about 12 minutes. Remove from the heat and stir quinoa with a fork to fluff. Cover the pot and let stand for 15 minutes. Uncover and cool completely.

While the quinoa is cooking, cook the snap bean pieces in (or steam over) salted boiling water until the color brightens and beans are crisp-tender, about 2 minutes. Drain and shock in a bath of ice and cold water to stop the cooking and preserve the color. Drain well, pat dry, and place in a large bowl.

Halve the cucumbers lengthwise, then seed, peel, and cut crosswise into slices ¼ inch (6 mm) thick. Add the slices to the bowl with the beans. Cut the onions crosswise into slices ¼ inch (6 mm) thick, including several inches (about 10 cm) of the green (you should have ⅓ to ½ cup/35 to 50 g), and add to the bowl. Finely chop the parsley leaves (you should have about ¾ cup/40 g) and add to the bowl. Chop enough mint to yield ¼ cup (15 g) and add to the bowl along with the quinoa. Using a Microplane grater, and working over the salad, grate the zest from 1 lemon into the salad, catching both the zest and the spray of citrus oils in the bowl.

Squeeze enough lemon juice into a small bowl to yield ⅓ cup (75 ml) juice. Season with 1 teaspoon salt and several grinds of pepper, then whisk in the olive oil. Pour the dressing over the salad, toss to coat evenly, and serve. (The components of the salad can be prepared early in the day and refrigerated. Toss the salad with the dressing up to 1 hour before serving.)

DAIRY VARIATION: This makes a lovely light lunch on a hot day with crumbled feta cheese, labneh (homemade, page 22, or store-bought), or Shanklish (page 101).

PENNE WITH ZUCCHINI SAUCE

MAKES 6 TO 8 SERVINGS

PAREVE/VEGAN OR DAIRY

"Melted" zucchini is a favorite Italian Jewish approach to summer squash. It is also a famously wonderful pasta specialty of the small village of Nerano on the Amalfi Coast. Sautéed in good olive oil with only onion and garlic, the squash melts into a luscious sauce that coats each noodle in creamy goodness and reminds you just how special this ubiquitous summer ingredient is. Because so few ingredients are used in this dish, the quality of the squash, pasta, and olive oil makes all the difference. Use tender, medium-size green zucchini, pale green marrow squash, or white (Lebanese) zucchini. Any non-egg dried pasta shape works well in this recipe.

1 onion, chopped

Kosher or sea salt and freshly ground black or white pepper

4 to 6 tablespoons (60 to 90 ml) extra-virgin olive oil

2 cloves garlic, minced

2 pounds (900 g) medium-size zucchini or marrow squash (4 to 5 squash per pound/450 g), cut into ½-inch (12-mm) pieces

1 pound (450 g) small or regular penne, farfalle, or other short pasta

Grated Parmigiano-Reggiano cheese (optional)

Put a large pot of water on to boil. In another wide pot large enough to accommodate all the ingredients, sauté the onion with a generous pinch of salt in 1 to 2 tablespoons of the oil over medium heat until the onion is softened and translucent, 5 to 7 minutes. Stir in garlic and cook for 1 minute. Add zucchini, a little more oil, ½ teaspoon salt, and a few grinds of pepper. Cook uncovered, stirring occasionally, until the color of the squash deepens and the mixture starts to get shiny, about 3 minutes.

Cover the pot, reduce the heat to low, and cook until the zucchini are extremely tender, even melting in places, and have released their liquid to make a sauce, about 15 minutes. Check the pot from time to time just in case you need to add a little water. The sauce can be made ahead and reheated before you are ready to serve.

Meanwhile, generously salt the boiling water and add the pasta. Just before the pasta is ready, scoop out about ½ cup (120 ml) of the cooking water and reserve. Loosely drain the pasta and stir it into the zucchini sauce. Raise the heat to medium, stir in 1 to 2 more tablespoons olive oil and about ¼ cup (60 ml) of the pasta water, and season with salt and pepper. Cook over medium heat, stirring, until the pasta is nicely coated with sauce, about 2 minutes, adding the remaining pasta water as needed to achieve a nice consistency. Stir in cheese to taste and serve.

SHOPPING TIP: Select shiny, firm, unblemished squash with their stem ends still attached. The color of the squash should be bright rather than faded. Medium-size zucchini (about 4 or 5 to a pound/450 g) are easy to work with and are likely to have fully developed flavors. The flesh should be juicy looking, not dry or woody.

GRILLED FISH THREE WAYS

Nothing says summer dinner like fish on the grill, especially at the beach. Here are three ways to capture the Mediterranean in your own backyard. Feel free to mix and match fish, seasonings, and grilling techniques (as I've done, opposite). A grill basket helps you turn the fish more easily and prevents it from falling apart and into the coals. Serve the fish with grilled or roasted small, whole red sweet peppers, cherry tomatoes, and potatoes, and a refreshing side of Parsley and Celery Salad (page 36).

WHOLE FISH WITH PRESERVED LEMON AND HERBS

MAKES 6 TO 8 SERVINGS

FISH

Sea bream, also known as *denise, daurade,* and *orata,* is one of the most highly regarded fish in Mediterranean cooking. Its flesh is plump, meaty, and tender and tastes wonderful grilled. A 1½-pound (680-g) fish will serve two. European seabass (*lavrak, spigola, branzino, loup de mer, bar*) is also a good choice. And for something altogether different, try this method with fresh sardines. Using preserved lemons, in place of fresh, adds a briny accent to grilled fish, as I discovered at Manta Ray, a casual-chic Tel Aviv beachfront restaurant. Purchase good-quality preserved lemons, make your own, or use Tunisian Lemon Rind Salad (page 31). In winter, stuff the fish with Quick-Preserved Kumquats (page 129 and roast in a hot oven. Fish takes about 10 minutes per inch (2.5 cm) of thickness to cook, especially with whole, bone-in fish.

Mild oil, such as grapeseed or safflower for the grill

4 whole white-fleshed fish, such as sea bream
    or sea bass, about 1¼ pounds (570 g) each,
    or 12 sardines, about ¼ pound (115 g) each,
    cleaned and scaled

½ cup (50 g) finely chopped preserved lemons

6 tablespoons (90 ml) extra-virgin olive oil

¼ cup (15 g) finely chopped fresh herbs, such as
    Italian parsley, rosemary, or thyme, or a mix

8 cloves garlic, peeled but left whole

Sel gris and freshly ground black pepper

Heat the grill to medium-high. Pat the fish dry inside and out. If using the larger fish, make 3 evenly spaced slashes, ¼ inch (6 mm) deep, on the fleshiest part of both sides of each fish. Omit this step if using sardines.

In a small bowl, stir together the preserved lemons, olive oil, and herbs. Smash the garlic cloves to release their oils. Place the fish in a shallow nonreactive pan. Place 1 generous tablespoon of the lemon mixture and 2 cloves garlic in the cavity of each fish (use less for sardines). Rub any remaining lemon mixture liberally over the outsides of the fish, making sure to fill the slashes. Cover and refrigerate for at least 15 minutes or up to 40 minutes.

Season the fish with sel gris and pepper. Oil a grill basket, if using, or the grill rack. Arrange the fish in the basket, leaving ample room between them. Grill the fish, turning them once halfway through the cooking, until the skin is crisped and the fish is cooked through, 5 to 7 minutes on each side for the larger fish and 2 to 3 minutes on each side for the sardines. Present fish on a platter or transfer to individual plates to serve.

BUTTERFLIED WHOLE FISH WITH "FISH SPICE"

MAKES 6 TO 8 SERVINGS

FISH

Hazaken Vehayam (The Old Man and The Sea) is a popular Arab fish restaurant in Jaffa Port that serves an astonishing twenty-five-dish refillable mezze of salads and sours to accompany grilled, roasted, or fried fresh fish. Each week, the restaurant goes through giant tubs of its secret fish seasoning mix—basically a magical combination of salt, cumin, and hot paprika. Make extra; it's great on chicken and roasted potatoes, too. Feel free to adjust the spice ratios to suit your taste. Butterflied whole fish take less time to cook than whole fish, a good choice with larger fish. Ask your fishmonger to butterfly the fish for you.

FOR THE FISH SPICE

3 tablespoons ground cumin

2 tablespoons hot paprika

1 tablespoon sweet paprika

1 tablespoon kosher or sea salt

½ cup (120 ml) extra-virgin olive oil

2 whole white-fleshed fish, such as daurade or European seabass, 1½ to 2 pounds (680 to 900 g) each, cleaned, scaled, and butterflied

1 lemon, cut into 6 or 8 wedges, or Lemon Sauce (page 23)

TO MAKE THE FISH SPICE: In a small bowl, stir together cumin, paprika, and salt.

TO PREPARE THE FISH: Heat the grill to medium-high. Oil 1 or 2 grill baskets.

Measure 5 tablespoons (40 g) of the fish spice into a small bowl. Reserve the remainder for another use. Add the olive oil and stir to mix. Place the fish in a shallow non-reactive pan and liberally brush on both sides with the spice oil. Cover and refrigerate for 10 to 40 minutes.

TO GRILL THE FISH: Lay the fish flat in the grill basket(s) or directly on the grill rack and grill, turning once halfway through the cooking, until cooked through, about 5 minutes on each side. Serve with lemon wedges.

GRILLING TIPS

• For maximum cooking control, create direct (hotter) and indirect (cooler) areas of heat. In the recipes in this book, assume direct heat unless otherwise stated.

• Gas grills usually have multiple controls; turn one section (preferably the middle area) to low or off to create an indirect-heat area.

• For a kettle-type charcoal grill, mound most of the charcoal to one side, or make two equal piles, one on either side, and put the food over the cooler area for indirect-heat grilling.

• For Santa Maria–type grills, raise and lower the pulley-operated grill grates to control the distance of the food from the heat.

• Wait to begin cooking until the coals are glowing and covered with white ash, 30 to 40 minutes after lighting (hardwood charcoal takes longer than briquettes).

• Grill quick-cooking foods such as steaks and burgers over direct heat and delicate fish over indirect or medium direct heat. If using a charcoal grill, you'll soon learn where direct "high" and "medium" heat areas are.

• Grill whole chickens or roasts over indirect heat to allow them to cook all the way through without burning. Move the food to the hotter part of grill at the end of the cooking to crisp.

• Test meat for doneness by pressing it with your fingertip. If it is blood-rare, it will feel squishy; if is medium-rare, it will be springier and have some give; and if it is medium-well, it will be heading toward firm. Pull the meat off of the heat before it reaches the feel you want. It will continue to cook from its own residual heat.

FISH FILLETS WRAPPED IN LEAVES

MAKES 6 TO 8 SERVINGS

FISH

Fresh fig or grape leaves add a tart note while keeping fish fillets moist on the grill, a technique especially helpful with fish that dries out quickly, such as halibut. No leaves? Make camp-style foil packets instead.

6 or 8 fish fillets, each about 1 inch (2.5 cm) thick,
   1½ to 2 pounds (680 to 900 g) total
Sel gris and freshly ground black pepper
8 large fresh fig leaves, or 16 to 20 fresh grape leaves
Extra-virgin olive oil

Pat fish dry and season with sel gris and pepper. Snip off the stem at the base of each leaf. Place a fig leaf, dull side down, on a work surface and smear with olive oil. Lay a fillet across the leaf, about 2 inches (5 cm) from the bottom. Fold the bottom of the leaf up and over the fish. Fold in the sides and then roll up the fillet in the leaf. Place seam side down on a plate or sheet pan. Repeat with remaining fillets and fig leaves. If using grape leaves, overlap 2 or 3 of them, dull side up, to make a rectangle larger than the fillet. Brush with olive oil and lay a fillet across the leaf rectangle. Fold in the sides, then roll up the fillet, bottom to top. Refrigerate for 10 minutes or up to 1 hour.

Heat the grill to medium-high. Place the packets, seam side down, on the grill and cook, turning once halfway through the cooking, until the fish is cooked through, about 5 minutes on each side. Serve the fish in their packets.

GRILLED CORN WITH ZA'ATAR

MAKES 8 SERVINGS

PAREVE/VEGAN

Vendors on Israel's beaches used to sell steaming ears of deep yellow corn from big metal drums. They seasoned the corn with coarse salt and served it up on a piece of husk to protect customers' fingers. I like to boil ears of corn briefly to plump the kernels and then finish them on the grill, mopping them with a blend of za'atar, salt, and olive oil. Supersweet white corn is all the rage, but I prefer a meatier white-and-yellow calico type.

8 ears corn
¾ cup (180 ml) extra-virgin olive oil
2 tablespoons za'atar
1½ teaspoons kosher or coarse sea salt

Bring a large pot of water to a boil over high heat. Shuck the corn and save some of the husks, if you like. Drop the corn into the boiling water and cover the pot. When the water returns to a boil, turn off the heat. Let stand for a few minutes, then remove corn from the water, and pat dry.

Heat the grill to medium-high. In a shallow dish or pan large enough to accommodate the corn ears, stir together the olive oil, za'atar, and salt. Roll the corn in the oil mixture, making sure some of the za'atar adheres.

Grill corn, turning as needed, until nicely browned in places, 10 to 12 minutes. Brush hot corn with additional za'atar oil, then mound on a platter or serve on the reserved husks (use remaining oil as a dip for bread).

LAMB KEBABS WITH PARSLEY, MINT, AND TAHINI SAUCE

MAKES 6 TO 8 SERVINGS

MEAT

Shishlik, shashlik, and kebab all mean the same thing—skewered and grilled meats that have been enjoyed throughout the Balkans and Middle East for centuries. Once made strictly from chunks of lamb, kebabs are now made from a variety of cubed or ground meats, as in these herb-rich lamb skewers with tomatoes and onions. Use lamb shoulder, which has a bit of fat to it, and ask the butcher to grind it not too finely. You may also use ground beef or turkey. *Sans* skewers, these become *mititei,* Romanian for "little ones."

1 large onion

1½ pounds (680 g) freshly ground lamb

¾ cup (35 g) packed fresh Italian parsley leaves

⅓ cup (15 g) packed fresh mint leaves

⅓ cup (45 g) pine nuts, coarsely chopped

1 tablespoon minced garlic (about 3 cloves)

1½ teaspoons kosher or sea salt

Freshly ground black pepper

1 lemon

24 good-size cherry tomatoes, stemmed

Pita bread

Tahini Sauce (page 23)

Israeli Salad (page 264)

Pickled Green Tomatoes (page 249)

Cut the onion into 1- to 2-inch (2.5- to 5-cm) chunks. Mince enough of the onion to equal 3 tablespoons. Cook the remaining onion in boiling salted water for 1 minute. Don't worry if the onion pieces separate into layers. Drain and set aside.

In a bowl, combine the lamb, minced onion, parsley, mint, pine nuts, garlic, salt, and several grinds of pepper. Using a Microplane grater, grate the zest from the lemon into the bowl. Mix together thoroughly but gently. Cover and chill the mixture for at least 30 minutes to make it easier to handle. Form the meat into 14 to 16 torpedo-shaped logs each about 3 inches (7.5 cm) long. Cover and chill until ready to grill.

Heat the grill to medium-high. Have ready 6 to 8 metal or bamboo skewers, each 14 inches (35.5 cm) long. Without crowding, thread the tomatoes, blanched onion pieces, and lamb kebabs onto each skewer, using 2 kebabs, 3 tomatoes, and a generous amounts of onion for each skewer and beginning and ending with onion (spear a few onion layers each time you use onion).

Grill the kebabs, turning once halfway through the cooking, until nicely browned and cooked to desired doneness, about 7 minutes total for medium. Transfer the kebabs to a platter.

Season the kebabs with additional salt and a squeeze of the reserved lemon. Serve with the pita, Israeli Salad, Tahini Sauce, and pickled tomatoes.

GRILLED SPATCHCOCKED ROCK CORNISH GAME HENS

MAKES 6 TO 8 SERVINGS

MEAT

The parsley, rosemary, lemon, and garlic marinade for these hens is one you'll turn to again and again for poultry *and* lamb. Small birds cook quickly on the grill, especially if they are spatchcocked, a new-old term for butterflying. Some sustainable producers raise young birds, or *poussins*, and Cornish game hens, but if you prefer, use a large chicken. If you're a person of a certain age, you grew up thinking that Rock Cornish game hens were fancy food and something more than chicken. What they are is a cross between a Cornish game chicken and a White Plymouth Rock hen, developed in the 1950s by a Mrs. Makowsky and promoted by musician and comedian Victor Borge, né Borge Rosenbaum. Since observant Jews don't eat hunted game, Mrs. Makowsky's birds were likely a "kosher" substitute.

4 game hens, about 1½ pounds (680 g) each

FOR THE MARINADE

2 lemons

4 large cloves garlic, peeled but left whole

½ cup (25 g) packed fresh Italian parsley leaves

¼ cup (7 g) fresh rosemary needles

1 small onion, chopped

2 teaspoons sweet or hot paprika, or 1 teaspoon each sweet and hot paprika

Kosher salt and freshly ground black pepper

½ cup (120 ml) extra-virgin olive oil

TO PREPARE THE HENS: Use kitchen scissors to cut from the tail end up along one side of the backbone of a bird. Open the bird, skin side up, on a work surface. Make a small cut in the neck near the top of the breastbone. Press down hard on breastbone with your palm to flatten the breast. Cut the thigh skin at the joint, so the legs can lie open, and pop the joint. Loosen skin from the breasts, thighs, and legs by running your finger between skin and meat, and place hen in a nonreactive pan. Repeat with remaining hens.

TO MAKE THE MARINADE: Using a Microplane grater, grate the zest from the lemons. Squeeze the juice from one half a lemon. Cut the remaining lemon half and whole lemon into large wedges and reserve. Fit a food processor with the metal S blade. With the motor running, drop the garlic through feed tube to mince. Turn off the processor and add the parsley, rosemary, lemon zest, lemon juice, onion, paprika, 2 teaspoons salt, and several grinds of pepper. Pulse until finely ground. With the motor running, add the oil through the feed tube and process until a thick, opaque, rough puree forms. You should have about 1½ cups (360 ml).

TO MARINATE AND GRILL THE HENS: Set aside half of the seasoning mix for basting. Use the other half to stuff under the loosened skin of the birds, then rub the excess over the outside of the birds. Cover and let stand for 1 hour before grilling or refrigerate up to 6 hours, removing from refrigerator 1 hour before grilling.

Heat the grill to medium, creating direct (hotter) and indirect (cooler) areas. Season the birds with salt and grill, skin side up, over indirect heat until the meat is fairly firm and the underside is nicely browned, about 35 minutes. Spoon reserved seasoning mix over the birds. Turn birds skin side down over direct heat to crisp the skin, 5 to 10 minutes.

Transfer to a platter, season with salt and pepper, and serve with the lemon wedges.

LAMB CHOP VARIATION: Use 3 pounds (1.4 kg) rib, blade, or shoulder chops for 6 to 8 servings. Place in a nonreactive pan, pour over the seasoning mix, and turn to coat evenly. Cover and let stand for 1 to 2 hours at room temperature, or refrigerate for 6 to 8 hours, removing them from the refrigerator 1 hour before grilling. Heat grill to medium-high. Grill chops to desired doneness, turning them once halfway through the cooking. Season with salt and lemon juice to serve.

STEAK "DAK DAK"

MAKES 6 TO 8 SERVINGS

MEAT

The term *dak dak* is onomatopoeic slang for "chopped," and this is a meat-and-herb chopped salad, good in a pita or plated, where every bite is a mix of textures and flavors. The recipe is inspired by the version I ate at Ha Miznon in Tel Aviv, where chef Eyal Shani has elevated the pita sandwich to a fine art (there's also a branch in Paris). Thin slices of steak seared quickly on a grill or a *plancha* (griddle) yield a high ratio of crisped crust to meat. Depending on my mood, I season the meat before grilling simply, with salt, or with *baharat*, the aromatic Arab spice blend of black and red peppers, cloves, cinnamon, and nutmeg. Accompany the salad with an array of self-serve condiments—chile oil, grated tomato, pickled cabbage, sel gris, and tahini sauce—and pita pockets.

2 medium-size Persian cucumbers, about ½ pound (225 g) total, halved and seeded

1 medium-size kosher pickle

1 small kohlrabi, about 3 ounces (85 g), peeled

3 or 4 medium-size red radishes

¼ small red onion

½ cup (15 g) lightly packed fresh Italian parsley leaves

½ cup (15 g) lightly packed fresh cilantro leaves

¼ cup (3 g) dill sprigs

6 to 8 pita breads

1½ pounds (680 g) boneless beef steak, such as sirloin or rib, thinly sliced (¼ to ½ inch/6 to 12 mm thick)

Extra-virgin olive oil

1 to 2 teaspoons baharat

Kosher or sea salt

Sel gris

FOR THE CHILE OIL

¼ cup (40 g) minced hot green chile, such as jalapeño (about 2 large chiles), in ⅛-inch (3-mm) pieces, including the seeds for added heat, if desired

FOR THE GRATED TOMATO

¼ cup (60 ml) extra-virgin olive oil

½ pound (225 g) ripe tomatoes (about 1 large)

Kosher salt

Vinegared Cabbage (page 22)

Tahini Sauce (page 23)

Cut the cucumbers, pickle, kohlrabi, radishes, and onion into fine julienne and place in a bowl. (This step can be done early in the day and the vegetables covered and refrigerated individually.) Coarsely chop the parsley, cilantro, and dill and add to the bowl. Set aside.

Cut one-third off of the edge of each pita. Open pita pockets and line with pita wedges to reinforce the bottom.

To prepare the meat, brush the beef slices on both sides with olive oil, then season on both sides with the baharat and kosher salt. Grill, griddle, or panfry the meat over high heat, turning once, until browned on both sides, about 1 minute on each side.

Transfer the beef slices to a cutting board and cut into narrow strips. Add the beef to the vegetables and herbs, toss well, and return to the cutting board. Preferably using a cleaver, chop the mixture into small pieces. Return it to the bowl, add a little olive oil and sel gris, and toss well. Serve with the pita and condiments.

TO MAKE THE CHILE OIL: Stir together the chile and olive oil. Let stand for a couple of hours to infuse the oil. The oil will keep, tightly covered and refrigerated up to 1 week. Bring to room temperature before using.

TO MAKE THE GRATED TOMATO: Cut the tomato in half crosswise. Use a finger to scoop out and discard the seeds. Grate the cut side of each tomato half on the large holes of a box grater until you reach the skin. Discard the skin. You should have about ½ cup (90 g). Season with salt.

FARMING IN ISRAEL

Israel has "local" down to a science. The tiny country raises 95 percent of its own produce. When Israelis say a crop is "imported," they usually mean it was grown in a different region of the country from their own: cherries, blueberries, and raspberries brought from the mountainous north to Tel Aviv; peppers, tomatoes, and eggplants from the Negev Desert in winter.

In one long afternoon, it is possible to drive the entire growing region of the northern half of the country, the Jezreel and Jordan Valleys and the Galilee, zigzagging east from the central coast to the Jordan River and north to within a few kilometers of the Lebanese and Syrian borders. An intense Eden-like patchwork of groves—mango, citrus, lychee, avocado, almond, pecan, banana, date—give way to undulating fields of sunflowers, cotton, wheat, corn, and row crops, including the newly popular *kale-im*. Soon you're in Israel's notable (and burgeoning boutique) wine country, where rows of Viognier, Chardonnay, Rhône and Italian varietals, Cabernet Franc, and more cling to hillsides. Finally, you reach the far north, where there are enough winter chill hours to grow a dozen different cherry varieties, glowing crimson and yellow among their long leaves. Interspersed throughout the landscape are scraggly olive and fig trees, grazing cattle, and the water-catch and desalinization plants that make Israel a leader in water collection and reuse.

At the opposite, southern, end of the country sprawling the length of the Arava, the southeastern portion of the Negev Desert, family-farm cooperatives make up the core of Israel's agricultural export industry that supplies the European Union, Russia, Ukraine, and the eastern United States with tomatoes, peppers, and exotic fruits.

Innovation is the hallmark of modern Israeli agriculture, from computerized water recycling and milking systems to the plant breeding that has given us Galia and Ha'Ogen melons, seedless mini-watermelons, and bite-size seedless sweet peppers.

Modern Israeli farming has its roots in the Jewish emancipation and enlightenment of the late nineteenth century, the same period when Russian Jews were settling in New York's Lower East Side and California was becoming known for its agricultural industry. (As with California, the orange was Israel's first and defining major crop, and its Jaffa and Shamouti oranges have mythic status for Israelis.) Motivated by a desire to shed the old ways, the mostly Russian first wave of farming pioneers embraced the rugged outdoors; a more secular life; ancient Hebrew, turning it into a living, modern language; and socialist ideals.

Israeli agriculture is built on a foundation of (once) wholly communal kibbutzim and family-oriented moshavim. In the spirit of Leviticus, which reminds us that we are stewards, not owners, most agricultural land is still nationally owned and leased to farming communities for forty-nine-year periods, a nod to the "seven times seven" Jubilee year when all land debts are to be forgiven.

Today, there is a rising interest in organic and biodynamic practices, but in Israel, as elsewhere, these efforts account for only a small portion of the production methods and consumer support. Israelis interested in farmer-direct sustainably raised food purchase their groceries at hipster small urban groceries or at rural farm stands. Or, urbanites engage in hyperlocal projects, such as Tel Aviv's Zvulun Balagan, a network of rooftop gardens orchestrated by a group of Jewish and Bedouin Israelis in an effort to achieve food self-sufficiency through permaculture, annuals, and raising chickens.

The jewel in the crown of the budding locavore movement is the farmers' market at Namal Tel Aviv (Port of Tel Aviv), overlooking the shimmering Mediterranean. Started by Israeli food celebrity Michal Ansky, and most closely resembling San Francisco's famed Ferry Plaza Market, the Namal Market is a twice-weekly farmers' market coupled with a repurposed wharf building housing high-end eateries, permanent produce stalls, and artisanal food producers of halvah, pickled fish, cheeses, and baked goods, notably those from Lechamim, an internationally known bakery with a branch called Breads (a direct translation) in Manhattan.

SUMMER FRUIT COMPOTE WITH LEMON VERBENA

MAKES 8 SERVINGS

PAREVE

Known as *louisa* in the Middle East, lemon verbena has haunting floral and citrus notes that are one of the region's defining summer scents. In this compote, seasonal fruit is cooked with the verbena only long enough to open up flavors without losing the raw beauty of the fruit. Use a mix of apricots, plums, nectarines, and peaches for a medley of yellows, oranges, and reds. This is beautiful as is, with a chilled glass of Moscato d'Asti, or with any of the suggestions opposite.

3 pounds (1.4 kg) mixed stone fruits, such as peaches, nectarines, plums, Pluots, and/or apricots

⅓ cup (65 g) sugar

⅓ cup (75 ml) water

6 large lemon verbena sprigs, 4 to 5 inches (10 to 13 cm) long, plus more for garnish

1 pint (about 280 g) berries, such as raspberries, blueberries, and/or blackberries

Use a vegetable peeler to peel the stone fruit. Don't worry if this gets a bit messy. Cut the fruit into 1- to 2-inch (2.5- to 5-cm) chunks and place in a wide pot or large skillet with a tight-fitting lid. Add the sugar and water. Crush or rub the lemon verbena leaves a bit with your fingers to release the oils, then add the sprigs to the pot, bending or breaking the stems as needed to fit.

Place the pot over medium-low heat and cook the fruit gently, stirring occasionally, until the mixture reaches a simmer, the sugar dissolves, the fruit is barely tender, and some of the juices have been released, 3 to 4 minutes. Cover the pot, remove from the heat, and let stand for 20 minutes. Stir in the berries and let stand 15 minutes.

Remove and discard the verbena sprigs and serve warm or at room temperature, garnished with additional verbena. Or, stone fruit can be cooked up to 1 day ahead and refrigerated. Serve the compote chilled, stirring in the berries 15 minutes before serving.

THIS COMPOTE IS GORGEOUS WITH

Cactus Pear and Raspberry Sorbet (page 286)

Granny's Citrus Sponge Cake (page 201)

Semolina and Walnut Oil Cake with Coffee Hawaij (page 243)

Thick plain whole-milk yogurt

MY GRANDMOTHER RACHEL'S APRICOT PRESERVES 2.0

MAKES ABOUT 5 PINT (500-ML) JARS

PAREVE

The years we lived in a house with a Blenheim apricot tree in the backyard were a golden moment in my childhood. That's when my *safta* Rachel introduced me to her apricot preserves, and I've been making some version of them almost ever since. Lush with large pieces of fruit that are especially appreciated come winter, these preserves are meant for more than just spreading on toast. Spoon them into Greek yogurt or over ice cream, or eat them by the spoonful. The more I've learned about jamming and canning, the braver I've become, revising the sugar ratio downward to better capture the honeyed flavors of the ripe apricots themselves. This version is noticeably lower in sugar than the one in *The Santa Monica Farmers' Market Cookbook*, and the cooking time is much shorter.

6 pounds (2.7 kg) small, ripe apricots
4 cups (800 g) sugar
1 lemon

Pit and halve the apricots, then cut about half of them into quarters to give textural variety. Transfer them to a nonreactive bowl. You should have about 5 pounds (2.3 kg) fruit after pitting. Pour the sugar over the apricots and give them a gentle stir. Don't worry if the fruit and sugar aren't completely blended. Let the fruit stand for at least 1 hour. You can do this step the night before you make the jam; cover the bowl and refrigerate. Bring to room temperature before cooking.

Have some tasting spoons close at hand. Scrape the apricot mixture into a wide pot. Place over medium-high heat and cook, stirring often with a heatproof spatula or wooden spoon and skimming off any foam that forms on the surface as needed. After about 15 minutes, the jam mixture will have reached a good boil, the foaming will

have subsided, and the juices will be shiny and starting to thicken. Reduce heat to medium-low as you get close to this point, to give you more control over the jam.

Dip a tasting spoon into the pot and let the mixture flow off. If some of the mixture clings to the spoon before it slips back into the pot, the jam is done. This usually occurs after about 5 more minutes of cooking. A second way to test for doneness is to spoon a bit of the mixture onto a small plate and put the plate into the freezer for a few minutes. Remove the plate from the freezer, run your finger through the mixture, and if it stays parted like the Red Sea, the preserves are done. Taste the preserves for sweet-acid balance and add lemon juice to taste.

Ladle the preserves into hot sterilized jars, leaving ½-inch (12-mm) headspace. Top with sterilized lids and rings and process in a boiling water bath according to USDA National Center for Home Food Preservation guidelines, http://nchfp.uga.edu/. Refrigerate any jars that do not seal properly and use those within 2 weeks or freeze up to 3 months. Properly sealed preserves can be stored in a cool cupboard up to 1 year. Alternatively, for refrigerator or freezer preserves, leave a 1-inch (2.5-cm) headspace when ladling the hot preserves into jars, cap tightly and store in the refrigerator for up to 2 weeks or in the freezer for up to 3 months (you can keep them longer than that, but they won't be as perky).

SHOPPING TIP: Apricots are more fragile than other stone fruit, and most commercial varieties are grown for their shipping and storage capabilities, or their suitability for machine harvesting, not their flavor. Unless you have a backyard tree, you must seek out varieties from passionate growers who are willing to let the fruit hang on the tree until fully ripe and harvest them by hand. Choose fruits that have a velvety, yellow-orange skin, a little give, and a hint of a sweet aroma.

MANGO AND PASSION FRUIT SORBET

MAKES 1 QUART (1 L), 8 TO 12 SERVINGS

PAREVE

Mango groves dot the Israeli agricultural landscape, tucked cheek by jowl among date, avocado, and other fruit orchards, and passion fruit vines weave through fences and climb walls. Not even the tiniest stretch of space is left unused. The silken texture of mango lends a creaminess to this refreshing summer sorbet, and passion fruit, with its edible dark seeds, adds tartness, texture, and eye appeal (see photo on page 288). This recipe is also delicious with ripe yellow nectarines. Both versions are lovely with Fresh Raspberry Sauce (page 289).

2 mangoes, about 1 pound (450 g) each

⅔ cup (135 g) sugar

⅓ cup (75 ml) fresh lime juice

¼ cup (60 ml) water

Pinch of salt

¼ pound (115 g) passion fruit (2 to 4), or ½ cup (120 ml) passion fruit puree

TO CUT AND PREPARE THE MANGOES: Stand a mango, stem end down, on a cutting board and use a serrated knife to cut from the top to the bottom, running the blade close to the pit. Turn the mango around and repeat on the opposite side. Use a spoon to scoop the flesh from the skin and transfer it to the jar of a blender. Cut away any usable flesh attached to the pit, peel it, and add to the jar. Squeeze the pit over the jar to extract the juices from any flesh clinging to the pit. Repeat with the second mango.

Add the sugar, lime juice, water, and salt to the blender and puree until smooth. Taste the puree, and if it is fibrous, strain it through a sieve into a bowl.

TO PREPARE THE PASSION FRUIT: If using fresh passion fruit, cut them in half crosswise and scoop the pulp and seeds into a small bowl. Mash the pulp with a fork to liquefy, then stir the pulp and the seeds into the mango mixture. If using prepared puree, stir it into the mango mixture. Cover and chill the mixture for several hours or up to overnight.

TO MAKE THE SORBET: Freeze in an ice cream maker according to manufacturer's instructions. Pack into a chilled container, cover tightly, and freeze, preferably for several hours, before serving. Remove from freezer about 10 minutes before serving to make scooping easier.

SHOPPING TIP: Look for Keitt or Valencia Pride varieties of mangoes that have a small "bone" (pit) and are less fibrous. They are available at some farmers' markets and at some Asian, Indian, and Latin groceries. Choose passion fruit that are heavy for their size and wrinkled (they wrinkle as they ripen). You should hear a sloshing sound when you shake a passion fruit, indicating that it contains plenty of pulp.

BROOKLYN BAR SUNDAES

SERVES 8

PAREVE OR DAIRY

When I was a little girl visiting Israel, my aunt Sigalit would take me to the Brooklyn Bar on Allenby Street in Tel Aviv, a popular café that served "banana splits." As I recall, they had neither bananas nor marshmallow crème and were not served in low-slung boats. What made the dessert memorable was the counterpoint of tart sorbets and vanilla and bitter chocolate ice creams. They were piled into tall glasses with a bit of fruit and toasted nuts and laced with raspberry and chocolate sauces. A mix of fruit and chocolate is de rigueur today, but to an American kid's palate back then, it was revolutionary.

Here are a delicious, no-cook raspberry sauce, a quick chocolate sauce, and a handful of building blocks to construct your own Brooklyn Bar sundaes. Mix and match as you like, or use good-quality store-bought ice creams and sorbets.

CHOOSE 2 OR 3 SORBET AND ICE CREAM FLAVORS

1 pint (500 ml) Cactus Pear and Raspberry Sorbet (page 286)

1 pint (500 ml) Tangelo Sorbet (page 196)

1 pint (500 ml) Mango (or Nectarine) and Passion Fruit Sorbet (page 287)

1 pint (500 ml) Carob Molasses Ice Cream (page 151)

CHOOSE 2 SAUCES

Fresh Raspberry Sauce (recipe follows)

Quick Dark Chocolate Sauce (recipe follows)

Silan (date syrup)

CHOOSE 1 OR 2 ADD-INS

1 cup Summer Fruit Compote with Lemon Verbena (page 283)

1 cup chopped fresh fruit

Chopped toasted pistachios, almonds, or pecans

FOR THE FRESH RASPBERRY SAUCE

1¼ cups (155 g) raspberries

¼ cup (50 g) sugar

1 tablespoon fresh lemon juice

3 tablespoons fresh orange juice

FOR THE QUICK DARK CHOCOLATE SAUCE

½ cup (120 ml) half-and-half

5 ounces (140 g) semisweet chocolate (62 percent cacao), coarsely chopped

1 teaspoon vanilla extract

Pinch of salt

1 tablespoon or more hot water, if needed

TO MAKE THE RASPBERRY SAUCE: Mash together raspberries and sugar with a spoon. Stir in lemon and orange juices and press through a sieve set over a bowl. Let sauce stand 30 to 60 minutes. The mixture will be opaque, but will turn clear as the sugar dissolves. The sauce can be made 1 day ahead and refrigerated.

TO MAKE THE CHOCOLATE SAUCE: In a small saucepan, bring half-and-half to a simmer over medium heat. Remove from the heat. Place chocolate in a heatproof bowl and stir in 6 tablespoons (90 ml) of the hot half-and-half until chocolate melts. Add remaining half-and-half as needed to achieve a good sauce consistency. Stir in vanilla and salt.

Use immediately or cover and let stand for up to a few hours. If the sauce becomes too thick, place the bowl in a pan of simmering water and stir 1 or more tablespoons hot water into the sauce to reconstitute. The sauce can be made 1 day ahead and refrigerated.

TO ASSEMBLE THE SUNDAES: Put a spoonful of Summer Fruit Compote or fresh fruit in each of 8 dessert glasses. Layer small scoops of the ice cream and sorbet, sauces, and nuts in each glass, ending with the sauces and nuts.

POPPY SEED SHORTBREAD COOKIES

MAKES ABOUT THIRTY-SIX 2½-INCH (6-CM) COOKIES

DAIRY

Poppy seeds are a traditional central and eastern European favorite in both sweet and savory dishes, and one of many round foods representing coins and wealth. Their nutlike flavor, with hints of eucalyptus, adds an earthy element to these beautiful slice-and-bake cookies. The dough keeps well in the fridge or freezer, at the ready when company drops in for a glass of tea, or when you want to make a wish for prosperity.

6 to 8 tablespoons (50 to 70 g) almonds
2 cups (250 g) all-purpose flour
1 teaspoon salt
1 cup (225 g) butter, at room temperature
1 cup (120 g) powdered sugar, sifted
½ cup (70 g) poppy seeds
Grated zest of 2 lemons
1 egg, lightly beaten

Grind enough almonds to yield ½ cup (50 g) packed (see directions on page 18). Sift together the flour and salt.

Using an electric mixer fitted with the paddle attachment, beat together the butter and sugar on high speed until blended and creamy, about 3 minutes. Add the ground almonds, 2 tablespoons of the poppy seeds, and the lemon zest and beat until well blended, 1 to 2 minutes longer. On low speed, beat in the flour mixture until a stiff, slightly sticky dough forms.

Have ready 2 pieces of parchment or waxed paper. Scrape the dough onto a work surface, divide it in half, and place each half on a sheet of the parchment. Shape each half into a log 6 inches (15 cm) long and 2 inches (5 cm) in diameter, using the paper to help you. Press each log firmly so there are no cracks in the dough. The heat of your hands will help bring the dough together.

Brush each log on all sides, but not the ends, with the egg. Lay out 3 sheets of plastic wrap, and sprinkle the remaining poppy seeds across middle of 1 sheet. Place a dough log on the poppy seeds and roll to coat evenly on all sides. Transfer the log to a clean sheet of plastic wrap and wrap well. Repeat with the second log. Chill the dough for at least 1 hour or up to 3 days. (The dough can be frozen for up to 1 month; thaw in the refrigerator to slice.)

Position oven racks in middle and upper third of oven. Preheat the oven to 350°F (180°C). Remove the dough from the refrigerator 5 to 10 minutes before slicing so it softens slightly. Cut into slices ¼ inch (6 mm) thick and place on ungreased sheet pans 1 inch (2.5 cm) apart.

Bake the cookies, switching the pans top to bottom and back to front halfway through the baking to ensure they bake evenly, until light golden and slightly puffed, about 12 minutes. Let the cookies cool on the pan on a wire rack for 5 minutes, then transfer to the rack to cool completely. Store the cookies in an airtight container; they will keep nicely up to 5 days at room temperature.

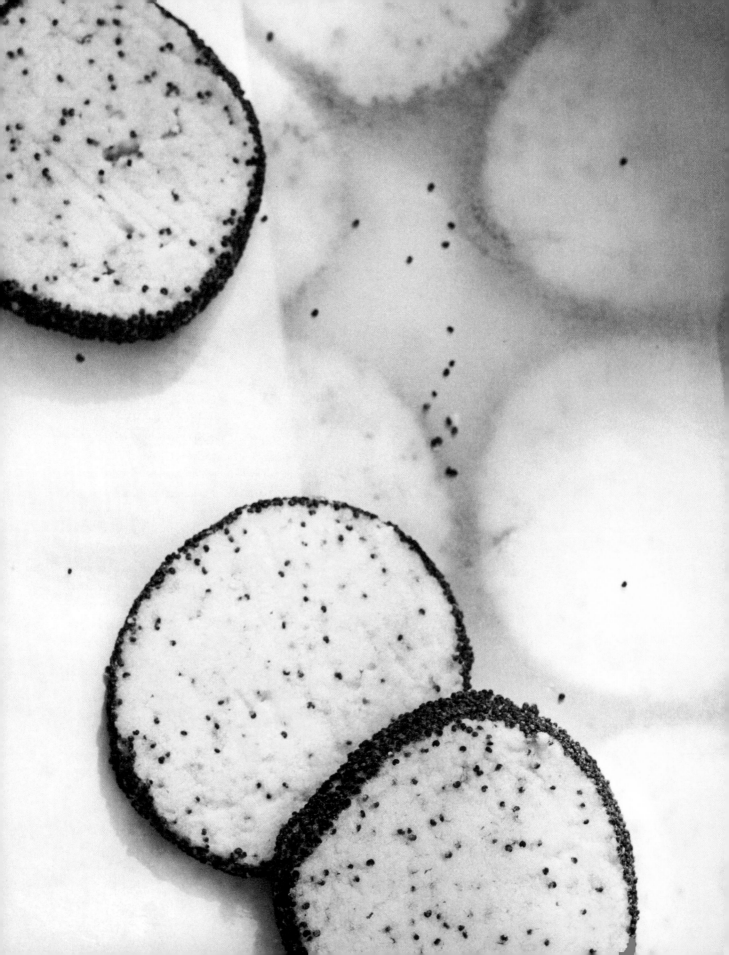

RECIPES BY COURSE

STARTERS AND CONDIMENTS

Bat-Sheva's Horseradish (174)

Bouikos: Bulgarian Cheese Puffs (214)

Fresh Grape Leaves Stuffed with Three Cheeses (209)

Green Fava Bean and English Pea "Hummus" with Pita Triangles with Za'atar (161)

Green Olives with Za'atar and Citrus (82)

Grilled Figs with Pomegranate Molasses and Aged Sheep's Milk Cheese (257)

Herring, Potatoes, and Eggs (38)

Israeli Eggplant Caviar Wraps (253)

Labneh (22)

Lemon Sauce (23)

"Manta Ray" Ceviche (212)

Matboucha (32)

Mom's Sort-of-Ashkenazic Charoset (170)

My Family's Gefilte Fish (172)

Parsley or Cilantro Pesto (90)

Pickled Green Tomatoes (249)

Pickled Okra (248)

Pita Triangles with Za'atar (161)

Quick Blood Orange Marmalade with Ras el Hanout (127)

Quick-Pickled Baby Turnips and Beets (125)

Quick-Preserved Kumquats (129)

Rustic Chopped Chicken or Duck Livers with Parsley and Celery Salad (35)

Safta Rachel's Iraqi Charoset (171)

Safta Rachel's Sesame Seed Bageleh (85)

Salata de Icre (83)

Salt-Grilled Fresh Chickpeas in Their Pods (254)

Savory Persian Herb and Cheese Hamantaschen (163)

Schmaltz and Gribenes (24)

Smoky Harissa (33)

Tahini Sauce (23)

Tunisian Lemon Rind Salad (31)

Vinegared Cabbage (22)

SALADS

Apple, Fennel, and Watermelon Radish Salad (130)

Arugula with Fresh Golden Barhi Dates, Dried Apricots, Nectarines, and Sumac (42)

Autumn Slaw with Beets, Carrots, and Kohlrabi (41)

Beets and Berries (217)

Blanched Amaranth with Olive Oil and Lemon (258)

Carrot, Date, and Preserved Kumquat Salad (129)

Citrus and Avocado Salad with Spicy Greens (132)

Creamy Lemon-Shallot Dressing (175)

Hearty Winter Slaw: Shaved Cabbage, Radicchio, and Celery with Bosc Pears (87)

Herb Salad with Feta Cheese, Halvah, and Green Almonds (176)

Israeli Salad (264)

Marinated Chickpea Salad with Tahini and Lemon Sauce (261)

Parsley and Celery Salad (36)

Spinach and Avocado Salad with a Lot of Lemon (215)

Spring Salad with Radishes, Peas, Avocado, Eggs, and Creamy Lemon-Shallot Dressing (175)

Tomatoes with Sardines and Rice (262)

SOUPS

A Basic Beef Stock (66)

Cabbage, Rice, and Green Garlic Porridge with Meatballs (135)

Chilled Sorrel and Cucumber Soup (269)

Golden Borscht with Buttermilk and Ginger (218)

Green Melon and Tomato Gazpacho (267)

Hand-Grated Chilled Tomato Soup with "Israeli Salad" Topping (266)

Homemade Vegetable Stock (92)

My Family's Matzah Ball Soup (178)

My Mother's Chicken Soup with Special Noodles (44)

Rapini and Rice Soup (179)

Simple Farro Soup with Chickpeas and Escarole (134)

Velvet Celery Root and Potato Soup with Spring Onions (180)

Yemenite Pumpkin and Carrot Soup (90)

SIDES

Barley Pilaf with Garlic Scapes, Fiddleheads, and Shiitake Mushrooms (220)

Basic White Rice, Sephardic Style (21)

Best Potato Latkes (94)

Buckwheat, Bow Ties, and Brussels Sprouts (137)

Cauliflower "Steaks" with Hawaij and Tahini (263)

Crisp Parsnip Latkes (94)

Crisped Artichokes with Gremolata (184)

Curried Roasted Cauliflower (142)

Freekeh with Kale, Butternut Squash, and Smoked Salt (88)

Fresh Black-Eyed Peas and Matboucha (51)

Grilled Corn with Za'atar (277)

Gvetch: Roasted Romanian Ratatouille (48)

Kigelach with Long-Cooked Leeks (181)

Raquel's Rice and Fideo (54)

Roasted Brussels Sprouts with Walnuts, Pomegranate Molasses, and Shanklish (101)

Roasted Carrot and Sweet Potato Tzimmes (47)

Roasted Fennel and Onions with Preserved Kumquats (139)

Roasted Smashed Apples and Pears (98)

Sarah's Steamed Potatoes (221)

Schmaltz-Roasted Potatoes (136)

Simcha's Rice with Almonds and Raisins (188)

Snap Bean and Red Quinoa Tabbouleh (270)

Spring Greens Sauté (182)

Summer Squash Latkes with Labneh, Sumac, and Thyme (50)

Sweet Potato and Butternut Squash Mini-Latkes with Labneh and Smoky Harissa (96)

Vinegared Potatoes with Bay Laurel, Garlic, and Aleppo Pepper (259)

Winter Greens Sauté (102)

MAINS

A Pashtida: Baked Pasta with Spinach, Ricotta, and Brown Butter (230)

Blistered Chicories with Tuna and Salsa Verde (144)

Braised Beef with Semolina Dumplings (107)

Braised Lamb Shanks with Crisped Artichokes and Gremolata (192)

Buckwheat, Bow Ties, and Brussels Sprouts (137)

Cheese Blintz Soufflé (233)

Duck with White Beans and Gribenes (146)

Freekeh, English Peas, and Smoked Fish (227)

Fresh Black-Eyed Peas and Matboucha (51)

Green Garlic and Leek Matzah Brei with Smoked Salmon and Horseradish Cream (187)

Grilled Fish Three Ways (272)

Grilled Spatchcocked Rock Cornish Game Hens (279)

Hamut: Syrian Chicken Fricassee (53)

Israeli Omelet (62)

Kitchri: Red Lentils and Rice with Golden Garlic Puree (143)

Ktzitzot: Chicken Patties (226)

Lamb, Butternut Squash, and Quince Tagine (67)

Lamb Kebabs with Parsley, Mint, and Tahini Sauce (278)

Late Spring Chicken-in-a-Pot (225)

Mamaliga (235)

Meat-and Rice-Stuffed Summer Squash (57)

One-Pan Striped Bass with Fennel, Potatoes, and Cream (190)

Oven-Braised Romanian Chicken (189)

Penne with Zucchini Sauce (271)

Pure and Simple Brisket (65)

Roast Chicken with Tangerines, Green Olives, and Silan (111)

Roasted Roots and Their Greens with Wheat Berries and Horseradish Cream (141)

Salmon, Green Tomatoes, and Sorrel with Taglierini (228)

Shakshuka (62)

Steak "Dak Dak" (281)

Toasted Israeli Couscous in Winter Squash Cases (104)

Tomato-Braised Romano Beans and Salt Cod (61)

SWEETS

Apple, Pear, and Concord Grape Galette in Rye Pastry with Ginger Cream (75)

Apples in Nightgowns (115)

Aunt Sarah's Honey and Apple Cake (77)

Blood Orange and Olive Oil Polenta Upside-Down Cake (154)

Braised Cherries (234)

Brooklyn Bar Sundaes (289)

Cactus Pear and Raspberry Sorbet (286)

Carob Molasses Ice Cream (151)

Cheese and Honey Filo Pie (237)

Cheese Blintz Soufflé (233)

Cherry and Goat Cheese Tart (239)

Chocolate Pavlovas with Tangelo Sorbet and Seville Orange Sauce (195)

Cozonac: A Simple Sweet Yeast Cake (113)

European Plum Meringue Torte (72)

Granny's Citrus Sponge Cake (201)

Mango and Passion Fruit Sorbet (287)

Meyer Lemon Poppy Seed Tart with Roasted Rhubarb and Strawberries (198)

My Grandmother Rachel's Apricot Preserves 2.0 (284)

Peppered Red Wine Fruit Compote (112)

Pomegranate-Orange Gelée with a Citrus Side Salad (70)

Poppy Seed Shortbread Cookies (290)

Quark Cheesecake (240)

Roasted Autumn Fruit (68)

Roasted Rhubarb and Strawberries (200)

Rustic Almond-Orange Macaroons (152)

Salted Almond and Chocolate Meringues with Matzah Shards (197)

Semolina and Walnut Oil Cake with Coffee Hawaij (243)

Silan and Tahini Ice Cream Sundaes (116)

Spiced Date and Walnut Oatmeal Cake (153)

Strawberries and Roses (242)

Summer Fruit Compote with Lemon Verbena (283)

Tahini Butter Cookies (149)

Tangelo Sorbet (196)

Zengoula with Lemon Syrup: Iraqi Funnel Cakes (117)

RECIPES BY KOSHER CATEGORY

DAIRY

A Pashtida: Baked Pasta with Spinach, Ricotta, and Brown Butter (230)

Apple, Pear, and Concord Grape Galette in Rye Pastry with Ginger Cream (75)

Apples in Nightgowns (115)

Best Potato Latkes (94)

Bouikos: Bulgarian Cheese Puffs (214)

Buckwheat, Bow Ties, and Brussels Sprouts (with variation) (137)

Carob Molasses Ice Cream (151)

Cheese and Honey Filo Pie (237)

Cheese Blintz Soufflé (233)

Cherry and Goat Cheese Tart (239)

Chilled Sorrel and Cucumber Soup (269)

Cozonac: A Simple Sweet Yeast Cake (113)

Curried Roasted Cauliflower (142)

European Plum Meringue Torte (72)

Fresh Grape Leaves Stuffed with Three Cheeses (209)

Golden Borscht with Buttermilk and Ginger (218)

Grilled Figs with Pomegranate Molasses and Aged Sheep's Milk Cheese (257)

Herb Salad with Feta Cheese, Halvah, and Green Almonds (176)

Israeli Eggplant Caviar Wraps (253)

Kigelach with Long-Cooked Leeks (181)

Kitchri: Red Lentils and Rice with Golden Garlic Puree (143)

Labneh (22)

Mamaliga (235)

Meat-and-Rice-Stuffed Summer Squash (variation) (57)

Meyer Lemon Poppy Seed Tart with Roasted Rhubarb and Strawberries (198)

Penne with Zucchini Sauce (271)

Poppy Seed Shortbread Cookies (290)

Quark Cheesecake (240)

Quick Dark Chocolate Sauce (289)

Roasted Brussels Sprouts with Walnuts, Pomegranate Molasses, and Shanklish (101)

Roasted Roots and Their Greens with Wheat Berries and Horseradish Cream (141)

Safta Rachel's Sesame Seed Bageleh (85)

Salted Almond and Chocolate Meringues with Matzah Shards (197)

Sarah's Steamed Potatoes (221)

Savory Persian Herb and Cheese Hamantashen (163)

Silan and Tahini Ice Cream Sundaes (116)

Spiced Date and Walnut Oatmeal Cake (153)

Strawberries and Roses (with variation) (242)

Summer Squash Latkes with Labneh, Sumac, and Thyme (50)

Sweet Potato and Butternut Squash Mini-Latkes with Labneh and Smoky Harissa (96)

Tahini Butter Cookies (149)

Velvet Celery Root and Potato Soup with Spring Onions (180)

PAREVE

Aunt Sarah's Honey and Apple Cake (77)

Autumn Slaw with Beets, Carrot, and Kohlrabi (41)

Best Potato Latkes (94)

Braised Cherries (234)

Buckwheat, Bow Ties, and Brussels Sprouts (137)

Cactus Pear and Raspberry Sorbet (286)

Chocolate Pavlovas with Tangelo Sorbet and Seville Orange Sauce (195)

Crisp Parsnip Latkes (94)

Fresh Raspberry Sauce (289)

Granny's Citrus Sponge Cake (201)

Israeli Omelet (62)

Kigelach with Long-Cooked Leeks (181)

Mango and Passion Fruit Sorbet (287)

Mom's Sort-of-Ashkenazic Charoset (170)

My Grandmother Rachel's Apricot Preserves 2.0 (284)

Peppered Red Wine Fruit Compote (112)

Pickled Green Tomatoes (249)

Quick Blood Orange Marmalade with Ras el Hanout (127)

Raquel's Rice and Fideo (54)

Roasted Autumn Fruit (68)

Roasted Rhubarb and Strawberries (200)

Roasted Smashed Apples and Pears (98)

Rustic Almond-Orange Macaroons (152)

Salted Almond and Chocolate Meringues with Matzah Shards (197)

Semolina and Walnut Oil Cake with Coffee Hawaij (243)

Shakshuka (62)

Spinach and Avocado Salad with a Lot of Lemon (215)

Spring Salad with Radishes, Peas, Avocado, Eggs, and Creamy Lemon-Shallot Dressing (175)

Strawberries and Roses (242)

Summer Fruit Compote with Lemon Verbena (283)

Summer Squash Latkes with Labneh, Sumac, and Thyme (50)

Tangelo Sorbet (196)

Toasted Israeli Couscous in Winter Squash Cases (104)

Zengoula with Lemon Syrup: Iraqi Funnel Cakes (117)

SELECTED BIBLIOGRAPHY

Cohen, Jayne. "The Well-Traveled Chicken." *JW Magazine* (Spring 2014): http://www.jwmag.org/page.aspx?pid=3860#sthash.Spa5If2V.YgXua8iP.dpbs.

Facciola, Stephen. *Cornucopia II: A Source Book of Edible Plants.* Vista, CA: Kampong, 1998.

Goldstein, Joyce. *Cucina Ebraica: Flavors of the Italian Jewish Kitchen.* San Francisco: Chronicle Books, 1998.

Jenkins, Steven. *Cheese Primer.* New York: Workman, 1996.

Jewish Encyclopedia Online (unedited full text of 1906 edition). "Agricultural Colonies in the United States": http://www.jewishencyclopedia.com/articles/909-agricultural-colonies-in-the-united%20states.

Jewish Farm School. *Jewish Food Justice: Service-Learning Curriculum.* N.p., n.d.

Jewish Publication Society, eds. *Tanakh: The Holy Scriptures—The New JPS Translation According to the Traditional Hebrew.* Philadelphia: Jewish Publication Society, 1985.

Kander, Mrs. Simon. *The Settlement Cook Book: Treasured Recipes of Six Decades.* New York: Simon & Schuster, 1965.

Kann, Kenneth L. *Comrades and Chicken Ranchers.* Ithaca, NY: Cornell University Press, 1993.

Kasdan, Sara. *Love and Knishes: An Irrepressible Guide to Jewish Cooking.* New York: Vanguard, 1957.

Machlin, Edda Servi. *The Classic Cuisine of the Italian Jews: Traditional Recipes and Menus and a Memoir of a Vanished Way of Life.* New York: Dodd, Mead, 1981.

Madison, Deborah. *Vegetable Literacy: Cooking and Gardening with Twelve Families from the Edible Plant Kingdom, with over 300 Deliciously Simple Recipes.* Berkeley: Ten Speed Press, 2013.

Marks, Gil. *Encyclopedia of Jewish Food.* New York: John Wiley & Sons, 2010.

McGee, Harold. *On Food and Cooking: The Science and Lore of the Kitchen.* New York: Scribner, 2004.

Nathan, Joan. *Jewish Cooking in America.* New York: Alfred A. Knopf, 1995.

———. *The Foods of Israel Today.* New York: Alfred A. Knopf, 2001.

Ray, Richard, and Lance Walheim. *Citrus: How to Select, Grow and Enjoy.* Tucson: Horticultural Publishing, 1980.

Roden, Claudia. *The Book of Jewish Food: An Odyssey from Samarkand to New York.* New York: Alfred A. Knopf, 1996.

Savage, Nigel, and Anna Stevenson. *Food for Thought: Hazon's Curriculum on Jews, Food & Contemporary Life.* New York: Hazon, n.d.

Schneider, Elizabeth. *Vegetables from Amaranth to Zucchini: The Essential Reference.* New York: William Morrow, 2001.

Shalev, Meir. *My Russian Grandmother and Her American Vacuum Cleaner: A Family Memoir.* New York: Schocken Books, 2011.

Sortun, Ana. *Spice: Flavors of the Eastern Mediterranean.* New York: Regan Books, 2006.

Thomas, Cathy. *Melissa's 50 Best Plants on the Planet: The Most Nutrient-Dense Fruits and Vegetables, in 150 Delicious Recipes.* San Francisco: Chronicle Books, 2013.

Walheim, Lance. *Citrus: Complete Guide to Selecting & Growing More Than 100 Varieties for California, Arizona, Texas, The Gulf Coast and Florida.* Tucson: Ironwood, 1966.

Waskow, Arthur. *Seasons of Our Joy: A Modern Guide to the Jewish Holidays.* Boston: Beacon, 1991.

THE WANDERING HOLIDAYS OF THE JEWISH CALENDAR

The Jewish calendar is lunar. Each of its twelve months represents one 28-day cycle, from new moon through dark. A lunar year is eleven days shorter than the solar, Gregorian year, and although the Jewish holidays fall on the same lunar dates each year, they shift around on the solar calendar. If this discrepancy were left unchecked, eventually Passover would slide into summer, Rosh Hashanah into winter, and so on. To keep Jewish holidays in their appropriate two-month seasonal windows (so the spring harvest falls in the spring and the fall harvest in the fall), a system was devised to add a second month of Adar (the twelfth, and last, month of the year) in leap years, which occur seven times in a nineteen-year cycle. Here are the most celebrated Jewish holidays with their Hebrew dates and Gregorian timeframes. The Jewish day begins at sunset; like Shabbat, holidays begin at sundown of the day preceding.

HOLIDAY	HEBREW MONTH AND DAY	GREGORIAN TIMEFRAME
Rosh Hashanah (*Jewish New Year*)	Tishrei 1 and 2 (seventh month of the year)	September/October
Yom Kippur (*Day of Atonement*)	Tishrei 10	September/October
Sukkot (*Feast of Tabernacles/Autumn Harvest*)	Tishrei 15-21	September/October
Simchat Torah (*Celebration of the Torah*)	Tishrei 23	September/October
Hanukkah (*Festival of Lights*)	Kislev 25	November/December
Tu b'Shvat (*Arbor Day/New Year of Trees*)	Shvat 15	January/February
Purim (*Festival of Lots*)	Adar or Adar II 14 or 15	February/March
Pesach (*Passover*)	Nissan 15–21 or 22 (first month of the year; seven days in Israel, eight elsewhere)	March/April
Shavuot (*Giving of the Ten Commandments/ Spring Harvest*)	Sivan 6	May/June

RESOURCE GUIDE

Here are some of my favorite brands, stores, and online resources for the ingredients used in this book, as well as a sampling of Jewish farm movement groups. But before you click that button to order online, do check your local farmers' markets, groceries, and specialty stores. You may just be surprised at what's available close to home. I've included some regional brick-and-mortar stores to get you thinking. Please let me know your favorite resources.

BRICK-AND-MORTAR SAMPLER

ANN ARBOR
Zingerman's

ATLANTA
Buford Highway Farmers Market
DeKalb Farmers Market (more global food meccas than local truck-farm resources)

AUSTIN
Central Market
Sarah's Mediterranean Grill and Market
Phoenicia Bakery and Deli

BOSTON AREA
The Butcherie
Formaggio Kitchen
Sevan Bakery
Sofra Bakery & Café
Wegmans

LOS ANGELES
Jon's Markets
The Rabbi's Daughter: A Kosher Butcher Shop
Spice Station
Tehran Market

NEW YORK
Citarella
Fairway Market
Kalustyan's
Zabar's

TWIN CITIES
Holy Land
Surdyk's Liquor & Cheese Shop
The Wedge Co-op

FOR THE KITCHEN

GRAINS
Anson Mills
(803) 467-4122
www.ansonmills.com

Bob's Red Mill
(800) 349-2173
www.bobsredmill.com

SPICES
Penzeys
(800) 741-7787
www.penzeys.com

The Spice House
(847) 328-3711
www.thespicehouse.com

Whole Spice
(707) 778-1750
www.wholespice.com

World Spice Merchants
(206) 283-9796
www.worldspice.com

MEDITERRANEAN, MIDDLE EASTERN, AND OTHER SPECIALTY FOODS
Al Wadi
(*Lebanese brand of canned goods and condiments*)
www.alwadi-alakhdar.com

Ancient Organics
(*excellent ghee*)
www.ancientorganics.com

Flying Disc Ranch
(*Citrus and dates, including yellow/golden Barhi*)
(760) 399-5313
www.flyingdiscranch.com

Formaggio Kitchen
(888) 212-3224
www.formaggiokitchen.com

G.I.T. USA (for Al Arz tahini)
(856) 795-1519
www.gitfood.com

Kalustyan's (almost everything!)
(800) 352-3451
www.kalustyans.com

The Kitchen Clique (Kinneret Farm *silan*)
(800) 282-6141
www.kitchenclique.com

ParthenonFoods.com (tarama, semolina)
(877) 301-5522
www.parthenonfoods.com

Sesame Story (Israel-direct artisanal products)
www.sesamestoryshop.com

Zingerman's (almost everything!)
(888) 636-8162
www.zingermans.com

KOSHER FOOD

AviGlatt.Com)
(718) 947-1000
www.aviglatt.com

Kolatin Kosher Gelatin
(732) 364-8700
www.koshergelatin.com

Pomegranate
(718) 951-7112
www.thepompeople.com

SMOKED FISH

ACME Smoked Fish
(718) 383-8585
www.acmesmokedfish.com

Russ & Daughters
(800) RUSS-229
www.russanddaughters.com

Vital Choice Wild Seafood & Organics
(800) 608-4825
www.vitalchoice.com

FARM, HUNGER, AND SUSTAINABLE PRACTICES ORGANIZATIONS

Food Forward
North Hollywood, California
(818) 530-4125
www.foodforward.org

The Garden Gleaning Project
Twin Cities, Minnesota
(651) 645-6159
www.mnproject.org/food-GardenGleaningProject.html

Hazon
(212) 644-2332
www.hazon.org

Jewish Farm School
Philadelphia, Pennsylvania
(877)-537-6286
www.jewishfarmschool.org

Kayam Farm at Pearlstone Conference & Retreat Center
Reisterstown (near Baltimore), Maryland
(410) 500-5417
www.pearlstonecenter.org/welcome-to-the-new-pearlstone/

Netiya
Los Angeles, California
(213) 500-1973
www.netiya.org

Rachel's Table
Worcester, Massachusetts
(508) 799-7600
www.rachelstable.org

Rotary First Harvest
(206) 236-0408
www.firstharvest.org

7Seeds Project
"Envisioning Sabbatical Culture: A Shmita Manifesto"
by Yigal Deutscher
www.7seedsproject.org/manifesto/

TreePeople
Los Angeles, California
(818) 753-4600
www.treepeople.org

Urban Adamah
Berkeley, California
(510) 649-1595
www.urbanadamah.org

ACKNOWLEDGMENTS

The seasonal life, and this book, would not be possible without the farmers who grow for flavor and sustainability. In particular, I thank the unstintingly generous California growers at the Santa Monica Farmers' Market, whose farms and produce you mostly see in this book: Cirone Farms; Coastal Farms; Coleman Family Farms; John de Rosier; Fat Uncle Farm; Fitz Kelly; Flying Disc Ranch; Garcia Organic Farm; J.J.'s Lone Daughter Ranch; Lily's Eggs; Maggie's Farm; McGrath Family Farms; Murray Family Farms; Peacock Farms; Polito Family Farms; Rinconada Dairy; Rutiz Family Farm; Schaner Family Farm; Thao Farm; Tenerelli Orchards; Weiser Family Farms; and Windrose Farm. Thanks also to Robert Schueller (Melissa's Produce), Karen Beverlin (Freshpoint), and Rich Collins (California Endive) for their generous help.

To my editor Jennifer Williams at Sterling Epicure, I'm grateful you saw I had something "fresh" to offer. Thanks to you, Executive Vice-President Theresa Thompson and Editorial and Subrights Director Marilyn Kretzer, for boundless faith in "our" book. To Project Editor Hannah Reich, it was an absolute joy to work with you. Many thanks to designers Christine Heun, Elisabeth Mihaltse Lindy, and Barbara Balch for translating my work into a beautiful, user-friendly book, and for their collaborative spirit. To my agent Lisa Ekus, for her longtime support and for connecting me with Jennifer to bring this book to life. Profound thanks, as always, to copyeditor Sharon Silva, whose quest for perfection exceeds my own.

Deepest appreciation to my talented photography team: the exceptional and generous photographer Staci Valentine and noble Ilan Davidyan; food stylist Karen Gillingham (your still life arrangements!) and crew, Kristen Deweber and Kayla Jacobs; and the always tasteful Kim Wong, prop stylist. Thanks to all who graciously loaned their gorgeous wares for the book: Chehoma, Alison Evans (through Table Art Los Angeles), Humble Ceramics, Joan Platt Pottery, Sierra Pecheur, Mark Strayer Pottery, Denise Young Linens, Zodax, and the late, lamented Luna Garcia Pottery Studio, and to Ralph Meyer, Sandy Garber, and Sara Jane Boyers for their contributions. Very special thanks to Patricia Williams for my lovely author photo.

Many contributed their invaluable expertise and time: food pioneer Alice Waters, Tori Avey, Inbal Baum (DeliciousIsrael.com), Nicole Bruno, Mehira Cheer, Susan Dietrich, Nealey Dozier, Sam Fromartz, Sara Kate Gillingham, Suzanne Goin, Harvey Guss, Robin Holding, David Karp, Lisa Lucas, Sydny Miner, Gaby Mlynarczyk, Nati Passow, Greg Patent, Alex Prud'homme, Jessica Ritz, Ana Sortun and Chris Kurth, Jeannine Stein, Barbara Streicker, Ari Weinzweig, and Robert Wemischner. The multitalented Alison Ashton (Content Kitchen) arrived in my hour of need and has been supportive ever since. I'm grateful to Gillian Ferguson and Evan Kleiman for the opportunity to share my food with the KCRW audience.

To my deep readers, advisors, testers, shoppers, scouts, and lifesavers—I hold you in my heart: Libbie Agran, Laura Avery, Jane Bard, Jennifer Ferro, Barbara Haber, Deborah Madison, Alice Medrich, Constance Pollock, Angela Rinaldi, Lisa See, Jill and John Walsh, Anne Willan, and Tomi-Jean Yaghmai.

The Ben-Aziz, Brayer, Cohen, Garonzik, Gabai, Laks, Schneider, and Volpert families root me in tradition. Thank you for your recipes, stories, and loving help, especially Hanna, Ruthie, Elan, Eyal, and Michal. And to the memory of my familial culinary mentors: Mina Haimer, Rachel Ben-Aziz, Sigalit Fingerhood, Sarah Feiles, and Dorit Schneider.

To my parents Serilla and Benjamin Ben-Aziz, who taught me to dare; my daughter Jessica Buonocore, for endless recipe testing and beautiful baking for some of the book's photos; daughter Rebecca Saltsman, my naturally gluten- and dairy-free guide; my son Adam Saltsman, writing compatriot still, and his lovely wife Stephanie Khoury; son-in-law Rodolfo Buonocore, forever my grill master; granddaughter Delfina, for her discerning palate; grandson Eliseo, who is working his way to a varied menu; and to my husband Ralph Saltsman, who makes everything possible. You are why I cook.

ABOUT THE AUTHOR

AMELIA SALTSMAN is the daughter of a Romanian mother and an Iraqi father who met in the Israeli army and immigrated to Los Angeles, where she was born and raised. Her cooking reflects her eclectic background, with the diverse flavors and cultural touchstones that have made her first book, *The Santa Monica Farmers' Market Cookbook*, a beloved classic. Amelia's name is synonymous with intuitive, seasonal cooking. She is regularly sought out for her expertise by publications such as *Bon Appétit, Cooking Light, Vegetarian Times, U.S. Airways, Fit Pregnancy, The Jewish Journal*, and *Los Angeles Times*. Amelia is a frequent guest on KCRW's "Good Food with Evan Kleiman" and appears at Rancho La Puerta, Los Angeles County Arboretum, and restaurants, farmers' markets, cooking schools, culinary history groups, Jewish community centers, and synagogues around the country. She has served on state committees to advocate for California farmers' markets and is a contributor to the *Sage Encyclopedia of Food Issues*. Amelia lives with her family in Santa Monica. Visit her at www.ameliasaltsman.com.

INDEX

Note: Page numbers in *italics* indicate photos on pages separate from recipes.

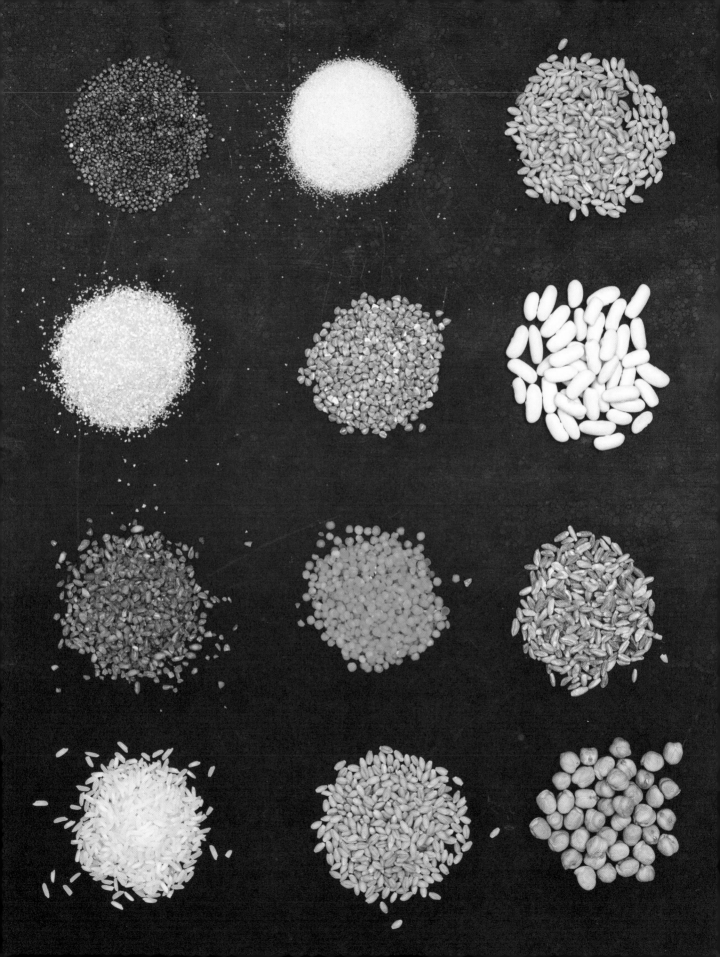